Politics, Society
and Secondary Education
in England

Politics, Society and Secondary Education in England

by *Andreas M. Kazamias*

PHILADELPHIA

UNIVERSITY of PENNSYLVANIA PRESS

© 1966 by the Trustees of the University of Pennsylvania
Published in Great Britain, India, and Pakistan by the
Oxford University Press
London, Bombay, and Karachi

Library of Congress Catalogue Card Number: 65-22383

7499
Printed in the United States of America

To Valerie

Acknowledgments

It would be difficult to enumerate all those to whom I owe a sense of gratitude for what is included in this book. I was introduced into English education in Cyprus, more than twenty years ago, first as a pupil in an English secondary school and then as a teacher and government civil servant. My interest in the subject has continued unabated since. To the many dedicated overseas English teachers and colleagues, wherever they may be now, I am most thankful for the beginning. Subsequently, in English and American universities I was exposed to a more systematic study of English history, society and politics. For this I am indebted to my former professors and friends at the University of Bristol and at Harvard University. Professors Robert Ulich and Bernard Bailyn, in particular, encouraged me to embark upon the present study, guided me in its many stages, and they were kind enough to read and comment on an earlier version of it. While I profited from the counsel and criticisms of many individuals, they are in no way responsible for the outcome.

From start to finish, nobody has been as helpful, patient and understanding as my wife, Valerie, to whom this book is dedicated.

INTRODUCTION   15

I THE BRYCE COMMISSION AND THE
    EXISTING EDUCATIONAL SYSTEM   26
  The Members of the Commission   27
  Terms of Reference and Method of Investigation   34
  Existing Educational Institutions   36
  Existing Educational Opportunities   46

II CONTEMPORARY EDUCATIONAL IDEAS
    AND THE VIEWS OF THE COMMISSION   54
  Contemporary Educational Opinion   55
  The Views of the Commission and
    Its Recommendations   60

III THE BRYCE REPORT, THE BILL OF
    1896 AND SECONDARY EDUCATION   73
  Reaction to the Report   74
  Politics and Education:
    The Education Bill of 1896   77
  Assessment of the Abortive Bill   90
  The Nature and Scope of Secondary Education   94

IV CONSERVATISM AND EDUCATIONAL
    REFORM: THE FOUNDATIONS OF A
    NATIONAL SYSTEM OF SECONDARY
    EDUCATION   100
  The Evolution of Ideas and Social Change   102
  The Challenge of Germany   107
  The Boer War   111
  Educational Politics and Reform   114

9

V THE NATURE AND FUNCTION OF
SECONDARY EDUCATION, 1902–1906   130
A Scientific Bias in the Curriculum   131
The 1904 Regulations   135
Meaning and Scope of Secondary Education   140
The Role of the Secondary School in
Contemporary Society   142

VI HIGHER ELEMENTARY EDUCATION   148
Reaction to Higher Elementary Schools   153

VII THE NEW LIBERALISM AND EDUCATION   162
Politics and Educational Reform   163
Toward the Extension of Educational
Opportunity: The Free-Place System   170

VIII THE PRACTICAL, THE VOCATIONAL
AND THE LIBERAL IN THE
CURRICULUM   182
Curriculum Change and a New Rationale   183
The Views of Educators   194
The Effects on the Schools   201
Central Schools: A Successful Experiment   205

IX THE FIRST WORLD WAR AND THE
FERMENT FOR REFORM   210
Dislocation and Adjustment   210
Ferment for Reform: Who Shall be Educated?   215

X THE FUNCTIONS OF SECONDARY
EDUCATION AND THE CONFLICT
OF STUDIES   230
Liberal Education   233

XI POST-WAR DEVELOPMENTS AND
OUTLOOKS   244

Education and Political Tendencies   244
Education and Socio-Economic Tendencies   258
Education and New Outlooks in Psychology   261

XII TOWARD A NEW PROSPECT IN
        EDUCATION: THE HADOW REPORT   271
The Members of the Committee and Their
        Terms of Reference   272
Secondary Education for All   274
Selection at Eleven-Plus   278
A Differentiated Institutional Pattern   283
Aims and Content of Education: The General,
        the Practical and the Vocational in the
        Curriculum   289
The Aftermath of the Hadow Report   295

XIII HADOWISM AND THE "RE-FORMATION"
        OF THE FORTIES   298
The Spens Report   298
The Reform Movement and the Education Act
        of 1944   302
The Debate on Selection and Tripartitism   311

XIV GENERAL CONCLUSIONS   320

    NOTES   331

    INDEX   373

Politics, Society
and Secondary Education
in England

Introduction

In 1894 a Royal Commission under the chairmanship of James Bryce was appointed to investigate existing education deficiencies, and to suggest "the best methods of establishing a well-organized system of Secondary Education."[1] In retrospect, neither we nor the contemporary observers would have to search long in order to find adequate reasons to justify such an enterprise. For at that time there was not only administrative chaos at this level of education; it was also difficult to understand what the term "secondary education" meant. Although the previous decades were marked by major social and political changes, and a comprehensive Elementary Education Act was passed in 1870, secondary education continued to function on an uncoordinated basis, and to be latched onto the doctrine of laissez-faire with all its class associations and its by then dubious philosophical underpinnings.

It is always dangerous to generalize on a historical epoch, and more so to attempt to do so with respect to the Victorian Age, "a very elastic term to denote an extremely dynamic society."[2] We might agree with Lytton Strachey's assertion that "the history of the Victorian Age will never be written," but not, as he believed, because "we know too

much about it.''[3] Certainly, if one judged by the immense
volume of printed material that has appeared and continues to appear on the Victorians and the society in which
they lived, one would readily refute Strachey's explanation. As one historian who dared write a history of the Age
put it, no longer can we afford "to laugh at the foibles of
the 'Eminent Victorians.' " For behind the puritanical and
priggish façade and the stuffy complacency, a not uncommon stereotype picture, lay a people who, in Thomson's
words, "engaged in a tremendously exciting adventure—
the daring experiment of fitting industrial man into a
democratic society."[4]

When Queen Victoria acceded to the throne in 1837,
there were already faint but noticeable signs that the
foundations of the existing social order were being cor-
roded by new inexorable forces created by the industrial
revolution. The entrenched landed aristocracy still maintained their political and economic supremacy, and continued to live an extravagant but "genteel" life. But with
the new industrial changes there began to emerge par-
venus and a powerful middle class which in the course of
the century not only attained political and economic
power, hitherto the prerogative of the landed gentry, but
also introduced new ways of thinking and behaving. By
the nineties, when the Bryce Commission issued its report,
there were significant social, economic, and political
changes. The cause of political democracy was advanced
by the extension of the franchise to include not only the
emergent middle classes, but also the urban and rural
artisans and unskilled laborers, and by reforms in the
system of parliamentary representation and local government. Individual effort, self-help, and unlimited competition, the hallmarks of laissez-faire, were gradually giving

place to "collectivism and municipal and State managed business." The working classes, who as late as the sixties were characterized by Bagehot as "content to be voteless," and by Cobden as "politically inert," by the nineties had organized themselves into the Reform League, an efficient instrument in bringing about the Reform Act of 1867, and into Trade Unions. In 1886, ten working men were elected to Parliament, and one of them, Henry Broadhurst, was appointed by Gladstone as Under-Secretary of State.

In addition to these changes, the Victorian Age was characterized by an intellectual ferment and output unparalleled in the history of England. The prolific pen of the well-known Victorian literati left no aspect of life untouched and at times poured venom on existing injustices.

These conditions, and the inexorable advance of industrialism, contributed to the decline of the laissez-faire philosophy and its bourgeois liberal associations which were so prevalent in the eighteenth and the first half of the nineteenth centuries. Adam Smith's negative doctrine that "no contrivance of statesmanship could achieve such beneficent results as might be trusted to emerge from a witch's brew of conflicting egotisms,"[5] which was later buttressed by Jeremy Bentham's utilitarian theory and Herbert Spencer's law of social evolution, was countered by the more positive views of T. H. Green and his Oxford colleagues. Moreover, the social injustices that developed out of the laissez-faire negative concept of government, and the associated liberal doctrines of individual freedom and unrestricted competition, were exposed in their stark nakedness by such men as Carlyle, Ruskin, Matthew Arnold and Charles Dickens. Finally, an extreme theory of laissez-faire ran counter to the developing tendencies in the political, economic and social spheres.[6]

Yet, in spite of the many advances and the tangible results of the Victorian social experiment, Victorian England had by no means attained its aim of "fitting industrial man into a democratic society." The liberal temper of the period, especially during the early phase of the Victorian era, called for the extension of the franchise, and the reform of local government, as well as for the abolition of certain Church privileges, patronages in the civil service, and certain remaining disabilities of the Roman Catholics and the Nonconformists. In this, as students of English history well know, considerable progress was made. But, as R. H. Tawney has pointed out, there was more concern with the elimination of legal privileges and the assertion of equal rights before the law, rather than with the elimination of economic and social inequalities based on wealth and birth.[7]

The liberal negative conception of freedom, the emphasis on unrestricted competition, and the exclusive concern for legal and political equality, left unbridled the forces released by the industrial revolution, and implicitly sanctioned a sort of economic natural selection analogous to the theory of biological natural selection whereby the road was left open for the amassing of large fortunes and the creation of what Disraeli had appropriately called the two nations. Hence, although theoretically an individual was by law unhampered in his personal advancement and opportunities were open to him, in practice the mechanisms created by the industrial revolution created conditions which favored certain groups for wealth, position and education, and relegated others to poverty, limited education and a life of inferior social status. Theoretically the principle of *la carrière aux talents,* the epitome of what Michael Young has called "meritocracy"[8] was there, but in fact there was lack of the necessary condition of "practical equality,"[9] or equality of circumstances, to make this principle a reality.

In the area of education, opportunities were to a large extent based on the economic and social position of the parents. Thus, a child born to a family of wealth or position had decidedly more advantages and indeed received more education than his poorer counterpart. The social composition of the student bodies of the endowed grammar schools as investigated by the Schools Inquiry Commission of the eighteen sixties bears testimony to the class orientation of secondary education. For example, in reporting on the endowed grammar schools of the counties of Devon and Somerset, C. H. Stanton, an assistant commissioner, classified these schools as "upper schools," and characterized them as "schools intended for, and to some extent used by, the first or upper stratum of society . . . They are generally situated near or in large towns . . . They prepare to some limited extent for the Universities, but their *spécialité* is, perhaps, rather to send boys into the civil and military and East Indian services. . . ." Stanton added that "the school [endowed grammar] is popularly regarded as the gentleman's school."[10] H. A. Giffard, the Assistant Commissioner for Surrey and Essex, wrote: "At Reigate Grammar School only 4 out of 31 are farmers' sons, and there is not a farmer's son amongst the boys in the grammar school either at Lewes or at Guildford."[11] And finally, D. R. Fearon reporting on the Metropolitan District concluded: "Viewed educationally, all these boys whose general education is now prolonged beyond their 14th year, but not quite to the close of their 19th are of the middle class."[12]

The endowed grammar schools constituted by far the

largest number of what might be called secondary schools.
The class character of the school system in general is further revealed by looking at the Public schools and the
elementary schools. In some of the former, entry was
limited to "the sons of gentlemen"; and, in general, by
the middle of the nineteenth century children attending
most of these schools belonged to the aristocratic or
wealthier middle classes.[13] The elementary schools were
for children of the laboring poor, or, as Robert Lowe put
it, "for children of persons who are not able to pay for
their teaching."[14]

This class conception of education, which in part developed out of the class structure of the society, was justified on several grounds. In a society which placed heavy
emphasis on unrestricted individual freedom, and minimum interference on the part of the State, the divisions of
society into the powerful, the wealthy and the privileged,
on the one hand, and the poor on the other, and hence
the differences in the education of each group, were regarded as natural. Walter Bagehot, for example, considered the English as a "deferential people," and he viewed
"the unequal development of human race" as natural. In
a similar vein, Robert Lowe felt that the lower classes
should be educated "in a very different manner" from the
high classes, so that "they may appreciate . . . bow down
. . . and defer to a higher cultivation when they meet it."[15]

The "deferential" characteristic of the English people
was indeed the secret of the stability of their political institutions. According to Bagehot, there were the "educated ten thousand," whose responsibility was to rule, and
the masses, who were "narrow-minded, unintelligent and
curious," as well as "confused and erroneous."[16] But the
"educated ten thousand" were also the wealthiest and the

powerful, hence the implication was that this social class possessed characteristics which were absent in the lower classes. Ability and education were thus assumed to be closely related to social class.

The correlation between social class and the educational system was reflected in the recommendations of both the Taunton Commission of 1868 and the Bryce Commission of 1895. Neither of these Commissions envisaged secondary education as a logical sequel to elementary and as one which everybody, in some form or other, should get. The Taunton Report felt that only 10 per thousand of the population ought to be provided with secondary education, and its successor frankly admitted that under the circumstances "social exclusiveness" was justified. Although the Education Acts of 1870 and 1891 extended and made elementary education free and compulsory, they did not rid it of its low social class status. When the Bryce Commission embarked upon its investigation, elementary and secondary education continued to be envisaged as different and unrelated types, befitting different types of individuals in the social hierarchy.[17] The desire for any legislation to make secondary education free for all was, in the words of the Bryce Commission, "still comparatively small," and the witnesses, who were called to give evidence, thought that "it is scarcely within the horizon of practical politics."[18]

Within education itself, the post-primary level presented a confusing and in many respects sorry picture. The term "secondary" officially denoted a variety of schools (endowed grammar schools, Public schools, private and proprietary schools). The great majority of these schools still adhered to the traditional classical conception of education, which rested on the assumption that classical learning was the most important tool for disciplining the mind and educating the English "gentleman." Many small grammar schools were quite impoverished and continued to exist because of original endowments and because they were on the statutes. Administratively, the State continued to hold a "hands-off" policy, and thus the "system lacked coordination. This laissez-faire attitude, at a time when there were even whisperings of a welfare state, resulted in overlapping with new types of post-primary schools which had sprung up after the 1870 Act. Called "higher grade," "higher elementary," or "higher standard," these schools grew out of an increasing demand for a type of education extending beyond the bare essentials, a demand created by the need for better educated and better trained artisans, and by the importance placed upon scientific and technological education. They, therefore, offered a type of education that was essentially scientific and practical. But administratively as well as educationally, the emergence and rapid growth of higher grade schools created an embarrassing situation. Although their educational work went beyond the primary stage prescribed by the 1870 Act, they were officially treated as "elementary" schools, and thus drew grants from the Education Department and the Science and Art Department. As "elementary" schools they were also controlled by the School Boards which were set up after 1870. But under the provisions of the 1870 Act, the School Boards were authorized to support only that primary stage of education which did not extend beyond instruction in the three R's. Thus, one observed the paradoxical situation whereby schools offering post-primary education drew public funds for which there was no legal provision, and were controlled by bodies which were not empowered to do so. Moreover, they offered a type of education which unofficially was considered secondary, but officially elementary.

It was against such a background that the Bryce Commission embarked upon its undertaking. The Commissioners were asked to tackle problems which, in their own words, "have been approached from different sides, at different times, and with different points of view."[19] In this task their work was monumental. The Report which appeared in 1895 was a comprehensive examination of the contemporary education scene, and the culminating stage of an inquiry into education stretching back into the eighteen sixties. It was also epoch-making. It not only defined "secondary education" in terms which had impact upon the subsequent development of educational thought; it also suggested lines of action and laid the basis for administrative reform in English secondary education.

Yet the Report of the Bryce Commission was only a beginning in the evolution and consolidation of new educational ideas. It was not until about thirty years later that such ideas were crystallized and the ideological framework of the educational reforms of the forties emerged. The Education Act of 1944, and the changes following it, were to a large extent based upon the conception of secondary education embodied in the Report of the Consultative Committee of the Board of Education in 1926, commonly referred to as the Hadow Report,[20] and not upon those of the Bryce Commission as has often been contended. The Hadow Report, therefore, occupies a pivotal position in the evolution of English secondary education. It represented the consummation of the educational ideas and tendencies of the period separating it from the Bryce Commission, and it laid the foundation of what ensued. Within the confines of the period from 1895 to

1926 lies a significant shift in English educational ideology, the careful examination of which would furnish an indispensable background to the understanding of subsequent reforms and the situation today. This book is an attempt to describe and illuminate this shift, and as such it will focus on two major areas: (a) the nature and scope of secondary education, i.e., what its meaning, aims and content were envisaged to be, and (b) the social role of education, i.e., what its functions were conceived to be in relation to the society.

Although a great deal has been written on English secondary education, which, in some form or another, includes aspects of the areas that will be considered here, no adequate historical study is known to the writer. The histories that touch upon this period treat education as an autonomous area, and for the most part no attempt is made to place it in its proper historical context. Where attempts *are* made to examine education in its contextual framework, they are inadequate and often incorrect. For example, references have been made to the importance of the rise and consolidation of the Labour movement as a factor in the expansion of educational opportunity, and as a contribution to the doctrine of secondary education for all. But when and how this happened have been superficially and erroneously treated. Similarly, the impact of the First World War on educational thinking and policy, though believed to have been great, has not received adequate attention. Moreover, where attempts have been made to illuminate or explain educational events of the past, this has been done in terms of *current*, i.e., today's problems, rather than in terms of *contemporary* conditions. Historians of English education have fallen victims to what H. C. Butterfield has appropriately called "The

Whig Interpretation of History." To take but one example: In seeking explanations of the Board's educational policy after the passing of the Education Act of 1902, educational historians, influenced by problems of today, and without examining the various forces at work at the time, have censured Robert Morant, the permanent secretary of the Board of Education, as being solely responsible for foisting upon the nation an "illiberal" conception of secondary education. In other instances, as for example in the case of the Bryce Commission's Report of 1895 and the Hadow Report of 1926, the historical treatment of the material has been rather perfunctory. This has led to hasty generalizations and "whig" historical judgments.

This study will seek to interpret educational events in their *historical* context. It is not within its purview to find answers to present questions or to assess past events in terms of current problems. Rather, it purports to recapture the complex character and the spirit of a historical epoch, and to depict a changing period in English educational history by seizing upon the central strands and selecting from the infinite number of objects those that will illuminate and answer the compound question: What were the ideological changes in English secondary education, especially from the Bryce Commission to the Hadow Report, and how can they be explained?

The scope of this study does not include Public, private, or denominational schools. It covers only public secondary education. Moreover, it is limited essentially to the examination of the official conception of education, although such a conception will be treated against the mainstream of English social, political and intellectual history, and the contemporary climate of opinion.

I

The Bryce Commission and the Existing Educational System

Although the nine-volume report of the Bryce Commission is considered a landmark in the history of English education, no careful historical analysis of the data and ideas embodied in it has been written. Historians have frequently alluded to it and have been all too eager to pass historical judgments, but these have been made on the basis of isolated statements in the main volume of the report. The massive evidence on contemporary ideas and practices gathered by the Commissioners has for the most part been ignored. In this and the following two chapters an attempt will be made to analyze this important document. In line with the two main foci of this study, the emphasis here will be on the nature and function of secondary education and its social role in contemporary England.

THE MEMBERS OF THE COMMISSION

Few of his contemporaries possessed James Bryce's background or exhibited his unusual combination of scholarly erudition and knowledge in the more practical affairs of life. Brought up in a family of educators and schoolmasters—one of his uncles advocated the establishment of Chairs of Education in every university—the young and precocious James was imbued early in his life with a zeal for the study of the dynamics of education at a time when few people were eager to pursue such a "dull and technical subject," as he himself later called it. Educated in the academic and rigorously classical tradition of Glasgow College and Oxford, Bryce developed a depth, sensitivity and affection for classical education which he maintained throughout his life. His Scotch Presbyterianism, however, coupled with a liberal social and intellectual outlook, was too strong to allow him to sign the Thirty-nine Articles, required of Oxford scholars. At that ancient citadel of Anglicanism, the obscure Scottish student carried out a vigorous dispute with the venerable Oxford dons, and in the end he "carried his point." H. A. L. Fisher, his biographer, wrote that later, when the battle of the Tests was engaged, Bryce "was one of those who fought hardest for the liberation of his University from these ancient fetters on religious and intellectual freedom."[1]

His Nonconformist, liberal outlook continued throughout his life.[2] Bryce's appetite for knowledge was whetted by intensive study in a wide variety of areas besides Greek, in all of which he attained a position of eminence both at home and abroad.[3] While at Oxford, he had joined a small undergraduate society called the Essay Society, which was noted for the brilliant achievement of its members; and when it was his turn to read select passages in English prose or an original essay, Bryce chose as his subjects "History, scenery, Greek letters, and education."[4] His catholicity of intellectual interests, his wide travels in many parts of the world, his searching inquiries into and analyses of the workings of political and social institutions with his passion for accuracy, detail and fairness, and his long career of twenty-six years as a member of Parliament representing different segments of the population, could not but be regarded as suitable qualifications for the kind of investigation he was called upon to head.

But perhaps the most salient qualification he possessed for such an undertaking was that he had already served as Assistant Commissioner for a similar body about thirty years earlier. As an assistant commissioner of the Schools Inquiry Commission of the sixties, Bryce acquired a firsthand knowledge of education in the rapidly changing English industrial society. His reports on individual secondary schools in such industrial regions as Lancashire and Birkenhead are, in Fisher's words, "models of the way in which such work should be accomplished, clear, precise, and practical, placing each school in its proper national and social setting with more of life and colour and with a more frequent recourse to generalities than are usually found in official documents."[5]

No less significant for our purposes than Bryce were the other members of the Commission. One of these, who at the age of thirty-three had already made his mark as an ardent devotee of the cause of education, was Michael Sadler. Like Bryce, Sadler had a distinguished academic career, having won high honors at Rugby and Trinity College, Oxford. He was nurtured in the classical tradition of both of these institutions, and the humanistic literary imprint of this type of education remained quite vivid throughout his long and distinguished life (1861–1943).[6] As early as 1884, however, Sadler left Oxford and immediately carried out a successful campaign for the development of adult education through University Extension, which also won him public acclaim as an educational reformer.[7] While he was engaged in the promotion of University Extension, Sadler was unavoidably drawn to the inadequate and chaotic state of affairs that existed in the field of secondary education. In 1893 he took the initiative to write resident members of the University of Oxford to petition the Hebdomadal Council for the convening of a conference where secondary education could be discussed. The move, though quite unprecedented, was effective, and a conference representing many organizations was convened. This conference stirred up interest and on November 14, 1893, in a memorial addressed to Mr. Gladstone, the Prime Minister, the University Convocation begged the government to appoint a commission to "inquire into the present state of secondary education within the kingdom, the further needs of Her Majesty's subjects in this respect and the best means whereby those needs may be met."[8] The appeal was heeded and the Royal Commission on Secondary Education was appointed early in 1894, with Michael Sadler as a member. Not only did Sadler serve as one of the Commission's most active members, but, as Grier has observed, "many people look on him as the chief author of its report."[9]

Through an examination of biographical data in the *Dictionary of National Biography* and the *Who Was Who*, it was possible to secure information on fourteen of the remaining fifteen Commissioners.[10] In some respects the group was quite heterogeneous. Richard C. Jebb was a world famous Greek scholar and at the time Regius Professor of Greek at the University of Cambridge and a Conservative M.P.; James Henry Yoxall, the son of a manufacturer, was general secretary of the National Union of Teachers, the only member of the Commission who was a certified elementary school teacher, and the first certified teacher who later won a seat in the House of Commons;[11] Henry Hobhouse, described as a "public-spirited country gentleman," was a country squire with an inherited estate of 2,500 acres, and a Unionist M.P.; Charles Fenwick, M.P., was an ex-miner who had served as a delegate to the Trades Union Congress and as Secretary to the Parliamentary Committee on Trade Unions; Andrew M. Fairbairn, the son of a miller, was a "Congregational divine," and Edward C. Maclure was Dean of the Cathedral Church of Manchester; Sir Henry E. Roscoe, son of a banker, was a distinguished chemist, Fellow of the Royal Society, and at the time held the chair of Chemistry at Owens College, Manchester; Richard Wormwell and Sophie Bryant were mathematicians; Sir John T. Hibbert, described as a "business-like administrator," was a Liberal M.P. and a lawyer; Hubert L. Smith, the son of a grocer, was a civil servant and an economist; and George J. Cockburn, was an East India merchant who took an active part in the development of the Higher Grade School system. Finally, there were two public-spirited ladies: Lucy C. Cavendish, maid of honor to the Queen, second daughter of G. W. Lyttelton, the fourth baron of Lyttelton, who had been a good classical scholar and a member of the Schools Inquiry Commission; and Eleanor M. Sidgwick, wife of Henry Sidgwick, the distinguished professor of moral philosophy.

On the other hand, there were certain noteworthy similarities in the educational background and occupations of many members of the Commission. Seven of the Commissioners, i.e., only slightly less than half, were educated in Public or endowed grammar schools and the two ancient Universities,[12] where classical humanistic learning constituted a very important element of the curriculum. Of these seven, four (Bryce, Sadler, Hobhouse and Jebb) held degrees in the classics, three had distinguished themselves in those fields, and five were graduates of Oxford. Of the other nine, two were clergymen and three were scientists and mathematicians. Two of the ladies were wives of distinguished classicists. Of the total number of Commissioners, six were members of Parliament at the time and two became M.P.'s later (James Yoxall was elected in 1895). Lucy C. Cavendish was the widow of Lord Frederick C. Cavendish, a Liberal statesman, and she had many family connections with political circles. Three of the six M.P.'s were Liberals and one a Liberal-Unionist; and before the report appeared, Yoxall joined as another Liberal M.P.

Twelve of the Commissioners had been active at some time or another in matters affecting education. Excluding Bryce and Sadler, to whom reference was made earlier, one observes the following interests and participation in educational matters by the Commissioners. Richard Jebb, aside from the role he played in the revitalization of classical studies in the latter part of the nineteenth century, had taken active part in the debates over the 1870 Education Act, he sat on several other educational commissions, and in 1900 he was appointed as member of the Consultative Committee of the Board of Education; Edward Maclure served as chairman of the Burnley School Board, the Manchester School Board, and the School Board Association of

England and Wales, he was Governor of Owens College and Manchester Grammar School, and in 1899 he was one of the first members of the newly formed Consultative Committee of the Board of Education; Sophie Bryant was mathematics mistress and later became headmistress at North London College School for Girls, she served on the Senate of the University of London and as president of the Headmistresses' Association, wrote several articles and books on education, and from 1900–1911 she was a member of the Consultative Committee; Richard Wormwell was Fellow and President of the College of Preceptors and served as mathematics master in a Middle Class School, as instructor in the Royal Naval College, Greenwich, as headmaster of the Central Foundation School of London, and as president of the Headmasters' Association; Henry Roscoe served as a professor at Owens College, Manchester, as Vice-Chancellor of the University of Leeds, and as a member of the Royal Commission on Technical Instruction; George Cockburn was for twenty-one years leader and chairman of the Leeds School Board, was a member of the West Riding Education Committee, and a pioneer of the Higher Grade School system; and James Yoxall, the only ex-pupil teacher of the group, served as headmaster of the Sharrow Lane Board School and in 1909 took over the editorship of the *Schoolmaster*, a weekly magazine and official organ of the National Union of Teachers. Even Henry Hobhouse, the "public-spirited Country gentleman," took active part in the debate on the establishment of county councils in 1888 and on the Education Bill of 1902.

In order to get a better understanding of the composition of this Commission and of how educational policy was initiated in England, it might be helpful to contrast briefly the Bryce Commission with the Committee of Ten in the United States, a body appointed two years earlier (1892) by the National Education Association.[13] Both bodies addressed themselves to questions pertaining to secondary education; and both have been regarded as historical landmarks in the development of that level of education in the two countries. Yet the Bryce Commission was appointed by the Government and included quite a few political figures, mostly members of the party in power. On the other hand, the Committee of Ten was appointed by a professional, though national, organization. Half of its members were presidents of colleges and universities,[14] two were headmasters of academic secondary schools, one was a principal of a high school, and one was a professor, and later president of Oberlin College. The only member who had any government connections was William T. Harris, the U.S. Commissioner of Education.

There is no comparable preponderance of university people in the Bryce Commission (of the sixteen Commissioners, about seven had had some connection with universities at some time or another, but at the time only two were directly connected with universities). There was a conspicuous absence of teachers or headmasters from the prestigious Public schools or the better known grammar schools, although, as stated previously, many of the Commissioners had received their secondary education in such schools. Also, unlike the Committee of Ten, there were representatives from School Boards, there were two clergymen whose major work was other than purely educational, there was a representative of the Trades Union Congress, an ex-barrister country squire, the General Secretary of the National Union of Teachers, and two public-spirited ladies.

One of the reasons for these differences was the fact that the Bryce Commission was appointed primarily in order to investigate the administrative and organizational aspects of secondary education, while the Committee of Ten examined the curriculum of the secondary schools. In England questions of administration and organization were essentially political questions requiring a representation of persons from various groups and organizations. Nevertheless, the Bryce Commission also looked into questions on the nature and scope of secondary education, as well as access to education, and in these respects it was more similar to the Committee of Ten.

TERMS OF REFERENCE AND METHOD OF INVESTIGATION

The full question referred to the Commission in 1894 was phrased as follows:

> . . . to consider what are the best methods of establishing a well organized system of Secondary Education in England taking into account existing deficiencies, and having regard to such local sources of revenue from endowment or otherwise as are available or may be made available for this purpose, and to make recommendations accordingly.[15]

The Commission understood the terms of reference to apply to the *organization* of secondary education; questions of the type and method of instruction given in schools it considered important but incidental to its purpose. Accordingly it inquired into the existing administrative features of secondary and technical schools, their government, their sources of support, their relationships with each other, and the degree to which they met the needs of different classes of the community.

In order to gather full and reliable information, the Commissioners adopted several methods. They called a number of witnesses, "possessing special competence," and through oral questioning obtained statements of fact and opinion concerning the existing situation and methods of improving it. All in all they examined eighty-one witnesses. A breakdown of this group of witnesses shows a wide representation of professional, governmental and private groups. There were representatives from the three departments (the Charity Commission, the Education Department and the Science and Art Department) which, in some form or another, were involved in the supervision or support of secondary education; there were nine professional organizations represented, ranging from the prestigious Headmasters' Association and the Private School Association to the National Union of Teachers (almost exclusively an elementary school teachers' association) and the Teachers Guild of Great Britain and Ireland; there were several headmasters and headmistresses of endowed schools, Her Majesty's and other inspectors, representatives from School Boards, training colleges, technical committees and boards of county councils, the Municipal Corporations Association, the Lancashire Local Trades Council, the Educational Committee of the Cooperative Union, and the College of Preceptors.

In addition to the evidence gathered from these witnesses, the Commissioners solicited information through circulars sent to members of the universities of Oxford, Cambridge, Durham and Victoria, and to a number of persons and bodies "specially competent to supply inforfation and materials on the matters to which they relate." They also invited memoranda on particular topics, including foreign systems of education, from a number of other persons whom they believed "capable of furnishing valuable data or views." Finally, they appointed a number of assistant commissioners, who conducted investigations and reported on selected districts of England, which in their opinion were "sufficiently typical of the country as a whole."

EXISTING EDUCATIONAL INSTITUTIONS

Three Grades of "Secondary Schools"

First grade: The voluminous evidence gathered from the various sources showed that the term "secondary" was used to describe a variety of establishments. The Commission classified secondary schools into three "grades" (first, second and third), a terminology which it borrowed from the Schools Inquiry Commission. First grade schools included the seven great Public schools, and endowed grammar, proprietary and private schools which provided an advanced type of instruction. The school leaving age in such schools was usually eighteen or nineteen; they prepared students mostly for the universities; and their main function was "the formation of a learned or a literary and a professional or cultured class."[16] The curriculum of these schools varied, but in many of them there was a distinct emphasis on classical education. The universities for which they prepared required Greek, for example, in the entrance examinations, and many of the scholarships for which students competed were still in the classical languages. However, it is difficult to make any valid generalizations that would apply to all types of schools under the category of "first grade." There *were* variations within each group (endowed, proprietary and private) in terms of curriculum, social composition of student bodies, and vocational destinations of students. Thus, for example, the older proprietary schools of Liverpool varied in their relative emphasis on literary and scientific subjects. In reporting on the schools for girls, often called high schools, in the hundreds of Salford and West Derby in the County Palatine of Lancaster, Mrs. Kitchener noted that these institutions were expensive, rather socially exclusive and academic in their curriculum.[17] On the other hand, in another high school belonging to the same company, the Girls' Public Day School Company, Mrs. Kitchener observed some differences in the social background of students. In still another girls' school in Liverpool, she found more "practical" subjects as well as a new chemical laboratory.[18]

A good example of an endowed grammar school of the first grade was the Manchester Grammar School, described by Mr. F. E. Kitchener, an assistant commissioner, as standing far ahead of any other secondary school in the district in terms of the "advanced character of education given" and the "extraordinary number of boys which it sends up annually to the universities." The school curriculum was differentiated into (a) classical, with emphasis on Latin and Greek, (b) modern, with emphasis on French and German, and (c) special, with three departments for specialists in mathematics, natural science, and for "those who are about to matriculate at London or Victoria."[19] Another example of a first grade grammar school was King Edwards' School, Birmingham. According to Rev. A. W. Vardy, its headmaster, a substantial proportion of the students came from public elementary schools, which was certainly not the case with the seven great Public schools.[20] Many of these children's parents were artisans and public elementary school teachers. However, in the Grammar School of Bedford, another first grade endowed school, the majority of the boys' parents were retired military men and civil servants.[21]

Second grade: Second grade schools included endowed grammar, and proprietary or private schools, some day schools and technical institutes, and the highest departments of some higher grade elementary schools. The school-leaving age was usually sixteen or seventeen and, although their special function did not exclude "an ideal of culture," they, nevertheless, focused on a type of education aimed at "some form of commercial or industrial life."[22] But here again, more than in the case of the first grade schools, generalizations must be used with major qualifications. Some of these schools placed heavier emphasis on scientific subjects; others on literary. Some were more "technical" in their orientation; still others sought to ape the first grade schools. There were also variations in terms of the social composition of student bodies, the financial status, and the vocational destinations of students.

Thus, for example, in the second grade endowed grammar schools of the hundreds of Salford and West Derby in Lancashire, the Hulme Grammar School of Manchester devoted 43.7 per cent of its weekly school time to "literary" subjects, 45.8 per cent to "scientific," and 10.5 per cent to "artistic" subjects, whereas the Hindley and Abram Endowed School devoted 52.8 per cent of its weekly time to literary, 28.2 per cent to scientific, 11.4 per cent to technical and 7.6 per cent to artistic subjects.[23] Or take the example of seven grammar schools in Birmingham, which were classified as second grade because education terminated at about the age of sixteen. In testifying before the Commissioners, Miss Cooper, headmistress of Edgbaston High School for Girls, described the curriculum as essentially literary and scientific, with no emphasis on technical education and very little on commercial and practical subjects. Miss Cooper stressed the fact that physical education and sports were emphasized in an attempt, as she put it, "to develop a certain public school spirit."[24] It is clear that these second grade grammar schools in Birmingham sought to give a "general type of education" which for the most part included literary and scientific subjects.

Another varying characteristic of the second grade schools was the number of students whom they recruited from the public elementary schools. In this respect there were significant variations in individual schools, as well as in total number of students in the several counties. In the Hindley and Abram School, 93 per cent of the students enrolled in the years 1892–94 were admitted from public elementary schools, but in the Leigh Grammar School of the same county only 20 per cent were registered as students admitted from public elementary schools.[25] Similarly, in the County of Bedfordshire, whereas the Dunstable Crew's Foundation admitted all of its students from the elementary schools, the Bedford Modern School admitted only 12 per cent.[26] The statistical evidence gathered by the Commissioners for selected counties shows that in the case of boys registered in endowed schools there was a range from 43.97 per cent in West Riding, York, to 8.14 per cent in the case of Bedfordshire. More marked variations are to be seen in the endowed girls schools classified as second grade;[27] and in all the second grade endowed grammar schools of Birmingham, as many as 62.6 per cent of the students enrolled came directly from the elementary schools.[28]

In certain counties, e.g., Devonshire, there were marked social distinctions attached to the different schools. H. T. Gerrans, an assistant commissioner for this county, reported that parents preferred the socially "selective" character of private schools to the endowed or proprietary schools in the county. These latter types of institutions admitted scholarship holders who came from public elementary schools, thus introducing a socially mixed element. Some parents did not favor this and preferred the exclusiveness of the private school for their sons rather than "run the risk of exposing them to 'contamination.' "[29] In some cases, private schools for girls were what may be called fashionable finishing schools, without any explicit purpose of preparing the girls for a career. For example, Mrs. Kitchener reported that in some of the expensive private schools of Lancashire a usual reply from headmistresses was: "My pupils will never need to do anything"; the best preparation for every sort of life was a "good all round education."[30]

In matters of curriculum the higher grade elementary schools placed heavier emphasis upon scientific and technical subjects than the other types of second grade schools.[31] The distinction in curriculum emphasis between a grammar and a higher grade school was brought out by Dr. D. Forsyth, principal of the Higher Grade School of Leeds. Forsyth believed that the emphasis on classical education should be left to the grammar school. Although in his own school he had "a small classical side," he placed more emphasis on the "modern and science" sides.[32] The Higher Grade School of Leeds received high commendation from A. P. Laurie, an assistant commissioner, who reported on education in the West Riding of Yorkshire. To Laurie this school was of the same caliber as the ordinary grammar schools. He was particularly impressed by the "perfect discipline" among the students, as well as their brightness, alertness and intelligence. In his opinion, schools of this nature represented a new development in secondary education, for they provided a type of secondary education to satisfy the demands of the "large masses of the population." Although both Latin and Greek were taught, as Dr. Forsyth had testified, the school relied heavily on grants from the Science and Art Department, which resulted in an "undue bias to science."[33]

Third grade. Under the category of "third grade schools," three types of institutions were identified: endowed schools, private schools in which the ordinary standard was that of the third-class certificate in the College of Preceptors' examinations, and higher grade elementary schools. According to the Commissioners, third grade schools were those "whose special function is the training of boys and girls for the higher handicrafts, or the commerce of the shop and town." Education in these schools usually terminated at the age of fourteen or fifteen.

An example of a third grade endowed school was the Prescott Grammar School in Lancashire. Its enrollment at the time was forty-four boys, and the only member of the teaching staff was the headmaster. Mr. Kitchener reported that on the day he visited the school the headmaster was teaching "five small sets of arithmetic at the same time." Kitchener's recommendation was that the school would fare better if the endowment were turned into a co-educational school or into a higher grade elementary school.[34]

Other evidence on the third grade endowed and private schools is rather scanty. In general, their condition and status were not good. Sir George Young, a Charity Commissioner, stated that such schools had been "crowded out" between the elementary school on the one hand, and the ordinary second grade school on the other. According to him, the Charity Commission had not been able to establish third grade schools, although they desired to do so, because (a) there was a social stigma attached to them, which caused people to prefer a school of a higher grade, and (b) the growing higher grade elementary schools were taking the place of the type of education offered in third grade schools. Any attempts to set up other schools would face the competition of the higher grade elementary schools, which were rather successful.[35]

The most noteworthy type of a third grade school was the higher grade elementary school. This, it should be remembered, was a type of institution which started in a rather haphazard manner after the Education Act of 1870. By 1895 the higher grade elementary school had become so important that the Bryce Commission devoted a substantial portion of its efforts to an examination of its character and role in the educational system of the country. A noteworthy aspect of this institution was the fact that, although legally considered as part of the elementary school system, it was generally regarded as giving an education beyond the elementary stage.

The higher grade schools of the third category placed a distinct emphasis on scientific and technical subjects in their curriculum compared to other types of secondary schools. However, here again the amount of time spent on such subjects varied from region to region and from school to school. In Lancashire, out of 18 such schools investigated by Kitchener, 14 assigned over 50 per cent of their weekly school time to "scientific" subjects, 10 over 60 per cent, and at least 3 over 75 per cent. In addition, all these schools included "technical" and "artistic" instruction, yet in the same group there were at least two schools which devoted more of their time to "literary" subjects.[36] In Bedfordshire, Mr. Mitcheson found that the school at Bedford devoted less time to literary subjects than the School at Luton, and consequently "fell below" it "mainly in the absence of French and Latin."[37] There was also some variation in Yorkshire. The Sheffield Higher Grade School was divided into a commercial department, where French, German and English were taught in addition to such subjects as shorthand and bookkeeping, and an organized science school, where no languages were taught. In the five higher grade schools at Bradford, on the other hand, most of the instruction was in scientific and technical subjects.[38]

Higher grade elementary schools were, as the name implies, more directly related to elementary schools, which was not the case with the other types of secondary schools. Of the 39 of these schools examined in seven selected counties and in London, 14 were free and 25 charged a weekly fee, varying from one penny to one shilling per student.[39] Most of the higher grade elementary schools drew grants from the Science and Art Department for science and art subjects. Indeed, their financial status and consequently their very existence depended on such grants, a situation which, according to many observers, resulted in an undue emphasis on non-literary subjects and a lopsided trend in secondary education. The views of Sidney Webb, chairman of the Technical Education Board of the London County Council, was widely shared among witnesses and assistant commissioners.

With certain modifications there are these dangers in higher grade schools, that the schools are so largely dependent upon the Science and Art Department that there is a temptation to induce the children to study too many science subjects, and to study them superficially at the sacrifice of thoroughness and depth in their scientific training, and the almost total sacrifice of literary culture.[40]

The higher grade schools of the third category recruited most of their students from the artisan and trading classes or, to use Laurie's terms,[41] from the "better working class" and the "poorer middle class"; they were located largely in cities, and they were regarded as schools for "the masses of the people," although the poor, unskilled laborers were not represented. In the main, they prepared students for employment in commercial establishments or to become skilled artisans. Some students entered the technical schools at the age of fifteen, few competed for entrance examinations into the local "secondary" schools, and in comparatively rare cases, after further schooling, they matriculated at the local university college, or at London University.[42]

Comparison of three grades: The three grades of secondary schools were often differentiated in terms of certain areas of the curriculum, the social composition of the student bodies, the vocational destinations of the students, and in terms of prestige. Subject to the qualifications mentioned previously, it would, nevertheless, be true to say that the higher the grade, the greater the emphasis on literary-humanistic studies. This was in part due to the entrance requirements of the universities and the careers open to students who followed the secondary-university course, to the number of scholarships in the classical subjects, and to the value attached to such a type of education.[43] As will be shown later, a strong emphasis on literary-humanistic studies was still regarded as a very important ingredient of secondary education.

The very fact that second and first grade schools charged higher fees than the third grade schools, restricted recruitment to segments of the population that could afford such fees. Even where there was a liberal provision of scholarships, the financial obstacle was present because scholarships did not cover all expenses.[44] Mrs. Armitage, reporting on secondary education for girls in Devonshire, noted that there was almost a "caste system" in that county: the "high caste" included county families, naval and military officers, and high ranking professionals; the "half caste" included shopkeepers, farmers, and small employers of labor; and the "low caste" included the working classes. The three grades of education corresponded with the three "castes" and, according to her, "the mixture of classes in a public school is regarded with horror."[45]

It should be noted, however, that there were also some variations in certain schools and regions. There were cases in which different social classes were represented in schools of the same grade. For example, in Lancashire Mrs. Kitchener reported that there was a mixture of social classes in the cheaper day schools "whether endowed, proprietary, or private;"[46] and, whereas in Devonshire public elementary schools recruited their students solely from the poor, working classes, in Birmingham many parents who could afford to send their children to private schools preferred the public elementary schools.[47] Although many children from the lower classes could not take advantage of the scholarships offered, there were others who did; hence, it was not uncommon to find some children of porters, messengers or doorkeepers in second grade schools, and some children of artisans and tradespeople in some first grade schools. Nevertheless, such numbers were small and the ladder from the elementary school to the university was difficult to ascend.

The three grades of schools were envisaged by both the Commissioners and those who reported as preparing for different occupations: the first grade school for the universities and the professions, the second grade for "middle" occupations, and the third grade for "lower" occupations. In his memorandum to the Commissioners, J. G. Fitch stated that the third grade higher elementary schools prepared students "to take better positions in the ranks of skilled industry."[48] According to D. Forsyth, of the Association of the Headmasters of Higher Grade and Organized Science Schools, the purpose of the schools his association represented was to train boys and girls "for future usefulness in life," an aim which, unfortunately, subordinated the important aim of "culture."[49]

In answer to a query in a "circular letter" sent to various people, Miss Buss, of the North London Collegiate School for Girls, drew a distinction between first grade and second grade schools. The girls who left the former type of institution "either go home or proceed to places of higher education," and the girls who left the latter, "either go home, or go out into the Civil Service, or similar employment." The schools were, accordingly, "adapted respectively to these different ends."[50]

In view of the career opportunities to which each of the three grades of schools led, it is not surprising to observe that the schools were ranked in terms of social prestige. But it would not be quite accurate to view the prestige differential solely in terms of career opportunities. Schools were also ranked in terms of their curriculum emphasis. The presence or absence of Latin, for example, was a factor in the school's ranking. So was the relative emphasis on the broader literary and scientific, or general and practical areas. The more practical the curriculum, the lower the school's ranking; and the more literary-humanistic, the higher the ranking.

EXISTING EDUCATIONAL OPPORTUNITIES

It is clear from what has been said thus far that access to secondary schools was dependent in part upon the social and economic background of the parents. The fees charged in almost all secondary schools, except some higher grade elementary, were a definite barrier to access into such schools. The grades of schools, subject to the variations mentioned above, corresponded to social gradations in the society. There was, to be sure, an unusually liberal system of scholarships; but this system did not seem to work in all cases as many hoped it would. In some cases the system of competitive examinations for the award of scholarships restricted such awards to only the very brightest poor children, in spite of the fact that the scholarships were intended for a wider section of this student population. This system resulted in the award of scholarships to children of well-to-do parents who could afford to pay for their sons' or daughters' schooling. In answer to the question, "Is the system of competitive entrance scholarships satisfactory?" the Rev. M. G. Glazebrook of Clifton College wrote that the worst abuses of scholarship awards took place in boarding schools. Although the object was "to enable poor and promising boys to obtain a good education," the funds were used "quite cynically as a means of buying clever boys for their own purposes." Whether these clever boys' parents were rich or poor did not seem to matter.[51] Sir George Young testified that a similar situation existed in all first grade schools.[52]

The fact that scholarships did not always carry the full cost of secondary education prevented poor children from making use of them. This was true in London, which restricted competition for junior county scholarships to parents whose income did not exceed £50 per annum.

However, access into secondary schools was also hampered by certain curriculum provisions. Schools of the first and the second grade required some previous knowledge of Latin. This placed elementary school pupils at a disadvantage compared to the pupils who went to preparatory schools. Also, in many places it was found that the general preparation in the public elementary schools was inferior to that in the preparatory schools for purposes of admission and maintainance of a satisfactory standard in the secondary schools other than the higher grade elementary. This placed ex-elementary school children at a disadvantage, and, if they secured a place in a secondary school, they were given a lower place.[53] In answer to the General Circular sent to selected persons and groups, the Yorkshire Ladies' Council on Education reported: "It is found in secondary schools, that scholarship-holders from elementary schools are at a disadvantage on account of their ignorance of history, geography etc."[54] Referring specifically to boarding schools of the first grade, the Rev. M. G. Glazebrook said: "The standard of the entrance examinations is such that few boys stand a chance of success who have not been trained at an expensive preparatory school."[55]

It is noteworthy to observe that in secondary schools in which fees were relatively high the number of pupils who had prepared in the public elementary schools was significantly small. This is clearly borne out in the memorandum presented by Mrs. Henry Sidgwick, a member of the Commission. Mrs. Sidgwick analyzed the enrollments of nine cities ranging from Thetford, with a population of 4,247, to Greater Birmingham, with a population of 530,000. In all these cities the grammar schools for boys and the high schools for girls recruited the least number of their students from public elementary schools. At least three schools had no students who had been in an elementary school. All schools except one charged fees higher than £10. On the other hand, the higher grade elementary schools, some of which were free, and the technical schools recruited most of their students from public elementary schools.[56]

In its efforts to assess the provision of secondary education, the Commission sought to find out the number of pupils per 1,000 of the population. The data gathered did not cover the whole of England, but only selected counties. There were also several other references to this question in special memoranda, in reports, and in the evidence given by witnesses. Nevertheless, it is very difficult to get a reliable picture of the existing situation. In some estimates, only the endowed schools were included; in others, all schools. Often it was difficult to give accurate statistics because of differences in what should be included as secondary education. All available data, therefore, are rough approximations and should be interpreted as such.

According to the Commission's estimates, the total number of scholars in the endowed schools of six selected counties, representing roughly 30 per cent of England's total population, were 21,878, or 2.5 per thousand of the population. When the scholars in the proprietary schools were added, the number rose to 30,588, or 3.6 per thousand of the population.[57] Mrs. Sidgwick's survey of educational provision for boys in the nine cities, which covered all types of secondary schools including the higher grade elementary, shows a range of 7.0 per thousand of the population in the case of Birmingham to 11.8 in the case of Thetford. The reason, of course, for such an increase was the inclusion of higher grade elementary and other schools.[58]

There were, however, wide variations in different counties and in different districts of the same county. For example, according to the estimates of Mr. John Massie, an assistant commissioner, in Leamington, Warwickshire, a place where there were "tolerably well-to-do residents," the proportion of children in all types of secondary schools was as high as 16 per thousand of the population. In Birmingham, on the other hand, where the population was "overwhelmingly artisan," the proportion was found to be 10 per thousand.[59] (Note here the disparity between Mrs. Sidgwick's and Mr. Massie's calculations). Mrs. Kitchener examined the number of students in all grades of secondary schools in certain places of Lancashire and reported that the proportions varied from 1 per 1,000 boys and girls in the case of Oldham, to 4.5 per 1,000 boys in the case of Wigan. In Liverpool the proportion in such schools was 5 per 1,000 of the population of the district.[60]

It is difficult to make valid generalizations on the basis of these data. We do not in all cases know what the numbers of children of secondary school age were, or what proportion of these children went to secondary schools. However, it would be justifiable to conclude that only a small percentage of children of secondary school age, as the case of Lancashire shows, were enrolled in secondary schools. It should also be mentioned that the demand for secondary education varied and there were places where the supply was adequate for the existing demand. For example, it was found that in rural districts of Devonshire the farmers did not particularly want an education beyond the three R's,[61] and in many areas provision of first grade schools was considered sufficient. On the other hand, several of the assistant commissioners, witnesses and others who reported attested to the fact that the supply in many cases was quite inadequate relative to the demand.[62]

One final question needs to be examined here: that is the degree to which children from the lower classes were

able to climb the educational ladder. Some writers have
pointed out that the statistics gathered by the Bryce Commission show sizable percentages of ex-elementary school
pupils enrolled in endowed grammar schools. This has
been interpreted as indicating that such schools were not
"socially exclusive,"[63] since presumably most of the children who attended elementary schools belonged to the
lower classes of society. It is quite true, as stated earlier,
that in West Riding, Yorkshire, for example, as many as
43.97 per cent of students enrolled in endowed schools
were admitted from elementary schools. Taking all selected seven counties (Bedford, Devon, Lancaster, Norfolk, Surrey, Warwick, and York, West Riding),
representing roughly 30 per cent of the total population
of England, the Commission estimated that 26 per cent of
the students in endowed schools came from public elementary schools. Combining enrollments in endowed and
proprietary schools the percentage was given as 24.82.[64]
These statistics, assuming they are reliable, would make a
strong *prima facie* case to discredit the allegations that
secondary and elementary education were rigidly separated
at that time, and that opportunities for the lower classes
were non-existent. However, in order to assess the degree
to which secondary schools were socially accessible to the
lower classes, one needs more information than the gross
percentages given by the Commission. It has already been
shown that the number of students enrolled in secondary
schools of all types and grades was small relative to the
population. It has also been shown that fees and the curriculum were a definite barrier for entry into second and
first grade schools. Even if one considers the percentages
of ex-elementary pupils in the endowed schools, it does
not follow that the poorer classes had many opportunities.

For in many cases the social composition of the student body in the elementary schools themselves was diverse. The assumption that the elementary schools recruited their pupils *solely* from the working and lower classes is not quite valid. The evidence given by the Rev. A. W. Vardy, headmaster of the King Edward School, Birmingham, clearly refutes this assumption, at least in so far as Birmingham schools were concerned.

I am bound to say that most of those who have been previously in public elementary schools are to some extent picked boys. Many of them, for instance, are the sons of public elementary schoolmasters; others, one or two, the sons of men who are connected with public elementary education, sub-inspectors or assistant examiners. There are a few who are the sons of artisans, but I think most of them come from homes where education is more thought of, and where there has been from the first a good deal of thought expended and judgment brought to bear upon the training of the boys.[65]

Without supplementary data on the social and economic background of the ex-elementary school children in the secondary schools, it is difficult to estimate the extent to which the lower classes were represented. Furthermore, taking the percentage enrollment of such pupils in all types and grades of secondary schools obscures the disparities that existed among such schools. The chances for a working-class child to enter a first grade school, especially an endowed grammar, were almost negligible, although as indicated previously not completely non-existent.[66] Speaking about Manchester Grammar School, a first grade school, Kitchener wrote: "It is impossible to resist the conclusion that the number of Manchester boys making use of the 'ladder' is very small."[67]

A tabulation of schools classified as endowed secondary in the seven counties shows that at least 14 schools admitted no students at all from the elementary schools, 8 admitted from 1 to 4 per cent, and 27 from 5 to 15 per cent. Many of those which admitted none were in Surrey, whereas high percentages were recorded in Lancashire.[68]

In conclusion, therefore, it may be stated that, although children from the working classes were able to enter secondary schools and even the universities, their numbers varied considerably depending on type and grade of school and on geographical locality. The higher the grade, the more restricted the social base of recruitment.

II

Contemporary
Educational Ideas
and the Views
of the Commission

The Bryce Commission's views on the nature and scope of secondary education have often been singled out by historians and other writers as exemplifying a radical departure from traditional ideology. Statements have been made that, whereas the Commission advocated a new and progressive idea of what secondary education meant, subsequent policy, especially that of the Board of Education under Sir Robert Morant, completely ignored it, with results little short of disastrous for English education. What such writers have focused their attention on, and have frequently quoted, is the Commission's definition of secondary education and its relation to technical education. Whereas, according to them, the Commission urged that secondary education be viewed as inclusive of technical, subsequent formulations and policies sidetracked the Commission's recommendations, and, after the Act of 1902, established a system that was based completely on the grammar school tradition. The synthesis of technical and secondary education was not accomplished until the Act of 1944.[1]

Allegations of this nature, however, have often been based on isolated statements taken from the main report of the Commission. There has been no attempt to analyze carefully the Commission's views or to examine them in relation to the other evidence in the report. In this chapter, the ideas embodied in the entire document will be examined, and an assessment of the Commission's views will be made.

CONTEMPORARY EDUCATIONAL OPINION

Although the various people who submitted reports and memoranda, or gave evidence, referred to the types and grades of institutions examined above as being secondary, when they were called upon to give a more comprehensive definition of what they understood secondary education to be, there was quite a variety of viewpoints. To quote from the Commission's main report, definitions and descriptions were of "a rough and ready kind, occasioned for the most part by the experience of the witness or the need of enforcing some special point."[2] Some envisaged secondary education in terms of the age at which pupils finished the elementary school (13 or 14) and continued their schooling in another institution for three, four or five more years; some conceived it in terms of the curriculum and an emphasis on "general culture;" others, in terms of the stage at which schools became eligible for grants from the Science and Art Department; still others defined it circularly as that given in secondary schools; and there were some who fell upon the ambiguous description that secondary education was the education which lay between the elementary school and the university. In some cases there was a blending of these views.

Thus, for example, the Rev. T. W. Sharpe, Her Majesty's Senior Chief Inspector of Schools, testified that education after the age of fourteen, the normal leaving age of elementary schools, was, properly speaking, secondary. But he was quick to point out that secondary education included more subjects, and that the purpose was "general culture" rather than a specific trade.[3] J. G. Fitch differentiated between primary and secondary schools as follows: primary schools gave instruction up to the age of fourteen to "those scholars who will as a rule enter on the business of life at that age"; secondary schools carried the instruction forward "to the seventeenth year or beyond it." Such schools might be of two distinct types: (a) they might receive students at the age of seven or eight and give them in addition a "larger Programme" than that of the elementary school, and (b) they might begin their work after the age of fourteen, i.e., after the student had completed his primary education, and continue it further "on the same general lines."[4] G. W. Kekewich, the Secretary of the Committee of Council on Education, was quite vague in his statements. At first he drew the line between primary and secondary education at the point in the curriculum where, in his own words, "elementary education passes into Secondary Education." Pressed on to be more specific, Kekewich envisaged secondary education as beginning at the stage when children received grants from the Science and Art Department for certain specific subjects.[5] On another occasion he defined secondary education as "the opposite of the definition of an elementary school" and a secondary school as "a school in which the greater part of the education is in secondary subjects."[6] From his evidence it may be inferred that Kekewich interpreted secondary education in terms of subjects more advanced in scope than the 3 R's, and that could mean subjects already taught in the organized science schools and the higher grade elementary schools. The Lord Bishop of London separated elementary and secondary education in terms of "the length of time that the parents can afford to give to education."[7] On the other hand, D. R. Fearon, who had previously served as assistant commissioner to the Schools Inquiry Commission, as inspector of schools, as assistant commissioner to the Endowed Schools Commission, and who at the time was secretary of the Charity Commission, defined secondary education as any kind of education beyond primary education, by which he meant "very good reading, very good writing and very good arithmetic." He also pointed out that secondary education was not correlative with secondary schools.[8]

One of the clearest statements on the nature and scope of secondary education was expressed in a memorandum submitted to the Commission and signed by fifty representatives of Trades and Labour Councils, Co-operative and Industrial Societies. There secondary education was defined as "the education which follows and continues primary or elementary education." According to the memorandum, secondary education should be related to primary in its curriculum and the distinction between the two should be "strictly and solely *educational*," marking two successive stages in the curriculum, rather than *social*, "marking merely different grades of social rank." If secondary education were conceived in these terms, then the children of the poorer classes could pass easily from one stage to another. Since working-class children would probably leave school at fourteen in order to work, then secondary evening schools should be provided for them, in which not only the intellectual, but also the physical, social and emotional elements of education should be cared for. Finally, in view of what will be found to be a different case later in this study, it is of interest to note that these representatives of the working classes urged that the type of secondary education best suited for such classes should "to a large extent be technical and manual."[9]

The question of the relation between secondary and technical education received a great deal of attention from the Commission. The evidence shows that there was no general consensus on it. For example, Sidney Webb, in almost the same terms as those used by the Commission in its final report, stated: "I should be sorry to define technical education as exclusive of Secondary Education, or Secondary Education as exclusive of technical." C. H. Bothamley, the Director of Technical Instruction in the County of Somerset, was not very clear on this point: some parts of what was commonly called technical education, e.g., scientific principles, could be regarded as secondary education; others, e.g., the *application* of such principles to manufactures, could not. Also, he felt that technical education, especially at the higher levels, could not be successful without a solid foundation in a "good Secondary Education."[10] Answers to a question in a circular sent to twenty-one persons and to the Yorkshire Ladies Council on Education show that the respondents were quite definite in distinguishing between technical and secondary education and in keeping them apart in separate schools.[11] The Yorkshire Ladies Council on Education stated that technical instruction could be given in upper secondary schools, but it should be taught for its "purely educational value."[12] And a certain Miss E. E. M. Creak favored the teaching of needlework, cooking, domestic economy and hygiene as part of a girl's regular school course, but she believed that other technical subjects should be taught in separate technical schools.[13]

The evidence presented above, although limited, shows that there were diverse views on the nature and scope of secondary education. Although generalizations should be made with a great deal of caution, it would be justifiable to say that secondary education was not envisaged as the logical sequel to elementary. The only exception to this was the statement by the representatives of the various laboring organizations. Yet even there one notices that, in the case of existing endowed grammar and other secondary schools, the laboring groups called for the opening of "exhibitions" to the poor children "who have shown conspicuous ability" in the elementary schools, and the increase in scholarship grants to include maintenance as well. Another conclusion that may be drawn is the fact that in the majority of cases a distinction was made between secondary and technical education: the secondary school was envisaged as essentially an institution whose main province was the provision of a general education. Where the word "technical" was mentioned, there was a clear distinction drawn between knowledge of basic scientific facts and principles, which to some were legitimate areas to be included in secondary education, and *application* of such facts and principles, which was not. It is also interesting to notice the distinction drawn between "education" and "instruction," the latter definitely not belonging to secondary schools. Further, where scientific facts and principles were accepted as areas worthy of inclusion in the secondary school curriculum, there was, as indi-

cated earlier, a definite objection to their undue emphasis. Finally, secondary education was not envisaged in
terms of the pupil to be educated, but rather in terms of
subjects, future occupations, ability of parents to keep the
child at school, leaving age, etc.

THE VIEWS OF THE COMMISSION AND ITS RECOMMENDATIONS

The Meaning of "Secondary Education"

In attempting to answer the question "what is secondary education?" the Commission was confronted with a
very complex problem. A workable definition was rendered difficult not only by the lack of consensus among
witnesses and others who reported, but also by considerations of the *actual*, or, in the Commission's words, "what
we must for the purposes of our inquiry conceive and
hold it to be," and the *ideal*, or what it "ought to be."[14]

The Commission rejected the view that secondary education was that which lay between the elementary school
and the university, since only a few secondary schools prepared for the university. It also found the views of its
predecessor, the Schools Inquiry Commission, inadequate
because in the intervening years significant changes (social, political and educational) had taken place. In the
earlier Commission secondary schools were graded into
first, second and third grade schools, according to school-
leaving age, and according to "gradations in the society";
the three grades were considered as separate entities; language was regarded to be "distinctively the most educative"; and all schools were to emphasize general education
rather than preparation for any special employment in
later life.

At least four conditions were identified as necessitating
a modification of the idea of secondary education: (1) the

increased age of pupils attending schools with the concomitant expansion of the curriculum; (2) the changes in the social composition of the student bodies and the growth of urban schools; (3) the growth of special and technical subjects; and (4) the pressing need, arising out of the previous conditions and the changing educational climate, to re-examine the relation between general, or liberal, and specialized education. It was found, for example, that the system of scholarships forced early specialization, it turned the "old humane studies" into "bread and butter sciences,"[15] and, to borrow C. P. Snow's terminology, it widened the gap between the "two cultures."

Taking all these factors into consideration, the Commission rejected the view that instruction in the practical arts and sciences, by means of which "a man becomes a craftsman or a breadwinner," could not legitimately be termed "education." It accordingly described "education" as follows:

All education is development and discipline of faculty by the communication of knowledge, and whether the faculty be the eye and hand, or the reason and imagination, and whether the knowledge be of nature or art, of science or literature, if the knowledge be so communicated as to evoke and exercise and discipline faculty, the process is rightly termed education.[16]

Modifying this general idea, the Commission defined secondary education in these terms:

It is the education of the boy or girl not simply as a human being who needs to be instructed in the mere rudiments of knowledge, but it is a process of intellectual training and personal discipline conducted with special regard to the profession or trade to be followed.[17]

Secondary education thus conceived, according to the Commissioners, must "comprehend" technical instruction. Although the two (secondary and technical) were not "identical," they, nevertheless, differed from each other as "genus and species or as general term and particular name," rather than as "genus and genus or as opposed terms." It was not possible to define technical instruction outside secondary education, nor was it possible to define secondary education "absolutely to exclude from it the idea of technical instruction." The Commission then formulated what has often been interpreted as a synthesizing definition of secondary and technical education.

Technical instruction is secondary, i.e. it comes after the education which has awakened the mind by teaching the child the rudiments, or as it were, the alphabet, of all knowledge, and the better the whole of this alphabet has been mastered the better and the easier will the later learning be. And Secondary instruction is technical, i.e., it teaches the boy so to apply the principles he is learning, and so to learn the principles by applying them . . . as to perform or produce something. . . . Secondary education, therefore, as inclusive of technical may be described as education conducted in view of the special life that has to be lived with an express purpose of forming a person fit to live it.[18]

These statements appeared in the Commission's main report. According to H. C. Dent, the Commission's definition was "the fullest and the most precise definition . . . which has ever appeared in an official document in this country."[19] John Graves has called it "so powerful, so lucid and so convincing."[20] And, according to David V. Glass, in defining secondary education, the Bryce Commission "took the revolutionary view that 'secondary' and 'technical' education were in large measure interchangeable concepts."[21]

Now, even if one limited oneself, as these writers have done, to the Commission's views in the main body of the report, one is befuddled, to say the least, by ambiguities and generalities. First of all, one might say that a quite novel idea was expressed when the Commission stated that different kinds of knowledge (of nature or art, of science or literature) may contribute to the "development and discipline" of various faculties, e.g., eye, hand, reason, imagination. That is, the *method* of communication of such knowledge becomes the crucial criterion of mental discipline, and, as such, practical arts and sciences may perform as disciplinary a function as the "more humane or generous studies." Alternately, "humane or generous studies" may be quite "illiberal" and "technical." But clearly the introduction of the term "technical" here obscures the argument. One might infer that what the Commissioners meant was that literary or scientific instruction may be both "liberal" and "illiberal" or "technical," depending on how it is taught, and, conversely, technical instruction may be "liberal." However, the lines of demarcation are not clearly drawn. The Commission fell upon such general and ambiguous terms as "evoke and exercise and discipline" the faculties, or "intellectual training and personal discipline." Furthermore, in one instance the Commission described secondary education as instruction in the "mere rudiments of knowledge" and as "a process of intellectual and personal discipline. . . ." In another instance it described technical instruction as one that comes *after* the acquisition of such "rudiments of knowledge." Then again the Commission referred to secondary and technical education as differing not "as genus and genus" but as "genus and species." This clearly does not mean, as Glass has maintained, that the Commission used the terms "interchangeably."

The ambiguities of the Commission's definition are more sharply evident when other statements and recommendations in the report are taken into account. Indeed, in reading the entire document, one is frequently led to believe that different portions were written by different people, without any synthesis of the various viewpoints. Very often the Commission distinguished between "education" and "instruction." Pupils in secondary schools, according to it, should not only "be instructed but educated."[22] The Commission's views on the nature and scope of secondary education become more confusing when one examines them in connection with its views and recommendations about the various types and grades of institutions. Here the Commission leaned heavily backwards and in many respects was very similar to the Schools Inquiry Commission, whose views it had found inadequate. Although not quite satisfied with the terminology, it nevertheless recommended the tripartite classification of schools discussed previously, according to age, function, character of instruction, and vocational destinations of students. There was little in the recommendations to obviate the separate entity of each grade, or indeed the ranking in prestige. And, although in its attempts to *define* secondary education it averred that secondary and technical instruction were not different as "genus and genus," yet there was little in the three grades of schools that would lead one to believe otherwise. There were no "technical" schools in the first grade, which prepared for universities and whose ideal was "general culture," mostly of the literary-humanistic kind. Indeed the more "humane and generous" the curriculum was, the higher the grade, and the higher the prestige. The linking of the different grades of schools with specific careers, already differentiated in terms of status and prestige, did little to obviate social distinctions attached to "humane and generous studies" on the one hand, and "scientific and practical arts" on the other.

Turning now to the *historical* judgments of many writers, it is difficult to agree with the criticism that subsequent policy completely ignored the Commission's definition which, in Graves' view, was "so powerful, so lucid and so convincing." For, assuming for a moment that the Commission's views were precisely what they have been made out to be, public and educational opinion was not entirely in agreement with them. The evidence in the rest of the Commission's reports shows that most of those who testified or submitted reports, memoranda, and answers to circulars, clearly distinguished between secondary and technical education. Secondary schools were one thing to them, technical schools another, and if they had a choice they would prefer the former for their children.

It is true that many members of the laboring classes sent their children to the third grade schools which had a scientific and technical bias. But they had no other choice, for the social, economic and educational reasons discussed in the previous chapter. If they did, it was more likely that they would send them to the other types of schools. In a special memorandum appended to the "minutes of evidence," Sidney Webb and W. Garnett wrote that in the case of London the great majority of the children who were awarded junior county scholarships "elected to attend secondary schools," by which they meant other than technical schools.[23] Also, it should not be forgotten that many workers, especially from the rural areas, were quite apathetic to the whole thing. A Devonshire farmer put it in plain but poignant language:

A man consists of three parts—back, belly and brains—and what we have to do is to fill the belly. Now this technical education may work the brains, but it won't fill the belly, and so I say it is of no practical use; but if you work the back then you can fill the belly, and so get on. My boys want to go in for bicycling and athletics and these 'ologies, but I say to them: 'They won't fill your belly, and how are you to get on if your belly is not filled?' And so I say you must always recollect that a man consists of three parts—back, belly and brains.[24]

An assessment, therefore, of the views of the Commission and subsequent developments must not ignore the contemporary historical events and the degree to which there was a correspondence between what the Commissioners said and what the rest of the people wanted. For, as R. L. Archer rightly pointed out, "besides the individual initiator and the State organiser, there must exist a public to welcome and to demand."[25]

Educational Opportunities

In a previous section it was concluded that secondary schools of all types and grades recruited a small percentage of the total population, and in one survey, at least, it was found that only a small percentage of children of post-elementary age found themselves in secondary schools. In discussing the question of adequate educational provision, the Commission stated that "endowed schools, whether good or bad, afford very inadequate provision for the Secondary Education of the whole country." The same was true of other schools, including the higher grade Board schools.[26] The Commission, accordingly, recommended that a more liberal system of scholarships be provided in order to enable selected children of the poorer classes "to climb the educational ladder." It specifically stated that such a selection would apply to boys and girls of "exceptional ability." Scholarships would be given either by the newly recommended local authority or by individual schools from their own funds. In order to eliminate abuses, it proposed that local authorities see that their own scholarships went to the children for whom they were intended. Scholarships could cover only tuition or tuition and maintenance, depending on the financial resources of the parent. On the other hand, in the case of scholarships in schools belonging to foundations, the Commission, although deprecating the practice whereby poorer children did not receive their due share, felt that the system should continue, for "we do not think it would be either fair or wise to exclude altogether the children of well-to-do, or even of wealthy, parents from the laudable ambition of winning the distinction conferred by a scholarship."[27]

The Commission rejected the idea of free secondary education, although some of the witnesses testified that they favored it. "None of the witnesses," it averred, "who came before us as representative of associations appeared to have received any mandate in favour of free Secondary Education." In what seems to this writer to be a fairly true reflection of public and educational opinion at the time, the Commission discussed the advantages and disadvantages of free secondary education. On the one hand, it was argued that it would make it possible for more children to get into secondary schools, and that somehow it was more equitable; but, on the other, it is clear that the majority of those who testified or submitted reports and memoranda raised several objections to a system of complete public support. It was argued that such a policy would place a check upon "private munificence," it would not necessarily "improve" quality, and it would widen the gap between free secondary schools and the Public schools. Moreover, the argument in favor of it was partly based on the erroneous assumption that "the number of children who can make good use of such education is greater than it really is." Faced with a diversity of viewpoints, the Commissioners sided with the opponents of free secondary education. They felt that the arguments against "still exercise a potent influence," and, in any case, free secondary education was "scarcely within the horizon of practical politics."[28]

It may, therefore, be concluded that, ideologically, at the time of the Bryce Commission Report, secondary education was regarded as the education of the few. The concept of "secondary education for all" was not seriously entertained either by official circles or by educational and public opinion. In so far as the poorer sections of the population were concerned, the general view was that there should be opportunities for the *brightest* among them to enter the types of secondary schools already in existence.

However, the obstacles even for the brilliant poor child were quite formidable. More likely than not, such a child would follow a different educational path from his wealthier counterpart. He was decidedly at a disadvantage in the secondary school, and, if he aspired to get into the University, he had to stay at school until the age of eighteen or nineteen, something which was rendered difficult by the economic position of his parents. Secondary education was not envisaged as the logical sequel of, or as organically connected with, elementary education. An exception to this was the higher grade elementary school; but even there the transition was not automatic, as there were different kinds of higher grade schools. All other secondary schools were separate, requiring specialized preparation and the payment of high fees.

The Commissioners deprecated social distinctions

among schools, and indeed called for "parity of esteem"; but realistically all other conditions and the classification of schools made this impossible. And they acquiescingly remarked that there were cases in which "social exclusiveness" was justified.[29]

Organization and Administration of Secondary Education

Although the major concern here has been the investigation of educational ideologies and practices concerning the nature, scope, and function of secondary education, it would be necessary also to look into the Commission's views on the organization and administration of secondary education. This, after all, was the area to which it devoted most of its energies and which was specifically referred to it; and, as will be shown later, the Commission's views furnished the groundwork for subsequent debates and the Acts of 1899 and 1902.

Of great historical importance was the Commission's notion that the progress of secondary education could no longer depend exclusively on voluntary efforts, and that public authorities must intervene. In its own words:

> While trusting that the other measures we recommend may stimulate private enterprise, . . . we conceive experience to have conclusively shown that private enterprise cannot be entirely relied on, and that the duty of seeing that an adequate supply of secondary instruction is provided must be thrown on a public authority.[30]

This was a clear repudiation of the ideology of extreme "laissez-faire" in secondary education. In seminal form the idea was contained in the Schools Inquiry Commission; but in the Bryce Commission its sphere of application was widened and more clearly defined. Moreover, by 1895 the laissez-faire doctrine was weakened and, as a result of changing conditions, an anti-laissez-faire ideology was more widely accepted. The evidence before the Commissioners was overwhelmingly in favor of the State assuming more responsibility in secondary education.

In addition to the changing climate of opinion, the Commission noted that in the intervening years (1868–1895) the State had indirectly been aiding secondary schools (higher grade elementary, technical, modern sides of grammar schools) through grants by the Education Department and the Science and Art Department. Accordingly it recommended: (a) the establishment of a central authority whose function would be the *supervision* of the "interests of Secondary Education in England as a whole," and (b) the setting up of local authorities "which shall be responsible for all Secondary (including Technical) Education within their respective areas." According to the Commission, the central authority should consist of a "Department of the Executive Government, presided over by a Minister responsible to Parliament." Local authorities should be created in every county and in every county borough (boroughs with a population of over 50,000). In the case of the counties, the local authority would have the majority of its members appointed by the already existing and "democratically elected" county councils. In the case of county boroughs, it was recommended that the borough council and the school board each appoint one-third of the education authority; that the central authority appoint one-sixth after consultation with a university or a university college; and that the remaining one-sixth "be co-opted by those previously chosen."[31]

Clearly the Commission's recommendations relative to the organization and administration of secondary education were a departure from existing practice. However, it should be carefully pointed out that the Commission did not view the role of the State as one of direct control and as superseding local control and initiative. The role of the central authority was explicitly stated as one of *supervision* rather than of control. Such a body would "stimulate" and "advise" local authorities in the provision of secondary education, and "coordinate" and "harmonize" their efforts. The Commission carefully pointed out that "freedom, variety and elasticity" which had characterized English education "must at all hazards be preserved."[32] Local education authorities were to examine carefully the existing provision of secondary education and devise plans for its improvement along the lines discussed earlier. They were to see, for example, that there was no overlapping of the different grades of schools; that monies from the central government and the rates were judiciously allocated; that a liberal provision of scholarships was available; that endowed schools were remodelled where necessary; that private and proprietary schools were maintained, but that they complied with certain prescribed conditions in order to be recognized as "efficient"; and, in general, that a "due provision of secondary instruction" was secured. The Commission refrained from making any specific recommendations on the numbers per thousand of the population that should receive secondary education. This was left up to "an enlightened public opinion working both within and from without upon the local authorities to abide by the statutory provision."[33]

Thus, although there was a clear shift against the laissez-faire ideology, the transition was to be a gradual one. The Commissioners wished that the policy of the government be shifted from one of indirect *assistance* to one of direct *supervision*, but not of control. There was as yet no desire to apply the same policy to the field of secondary, as it was applied to the field of elementary education. However, in so far as the role of the State was concerned, the Bryce Commission provided the basis for subsequent discussion on the subject, and particularly for the Education Bill of 1896, and for the Acts of 1899 and 1902.

III

The Bryce Report,
The Bill of 1896, and
Secondary Education

The Commission's views and recommendations evoked considerable comment. They were discussed in the pubilc press, in literary and popular magazines, in professional journals, at professional gatherings, and on the floor of the House of Commons. There was literally no segment of the British public that did not, in some form or other, comment on them or marshal its forces to positive lines of action; and the Government hastened to introduce a Bill to give statutory sanction to some of the Commission's recommendations. Educational issues were once again thrust upon the public stage.

A look at what was said, written and done in response to the Report is necessary, not only because it will help us assess the impact of the Commission's views on English educational thought and practice, but also because it constitutes the necessary background to an understanding of

73

the Acts of 1899 and 1902. Furthermore, it sheds more light on contemporary views about education and in this way adds to our interpretation of the ideas and recommendations of the Commission.

The bulk of the commentaries in the immediate year following the appearance of the Report revolved around the organization and administration of education, which was not unexpected considering the Commission's terms of reference. In this regard, major attention was focused on the functions of the proposed central and local authorities, and on the coordination of the entire system.

In general, the reception was favorable insofar as the broad principles of the proposed organization were concerned. Laudatory comments appeared in the public press, in professional and non-professional journals, and at professional and public gatherings. For example, *The Times* of London thought that the proposed framework was a "distinct, coherent and intelligible policy"; *The Daily News* singled out the appointment of a Minister of Education for special commendation; *The Star* hailed the document as "a statesmanlike and complete proposal"; Whitaker's *Almanack* of 1896 used the terms "businesslike thoroughness" and "admirable work" in its description of the Report as a whole;[1] an article in *The Athenaeum* praised the Commissioners for "statesmanlike breadth of conception";[2] and an editorial comment in *The Educational Times* felt that the Report would "certainly be found to be an epoch-making Report."[3] Other statements in professional journals emphasized its comprehensiveness, moderation and spirit of compromise.[4] Similarly, the main features of the Report's recommendations were praised at the many con-

ferences specially convened by the several educational
organizations, such as the National Union of Teachers, the
Headmasters' Conference, the Incorporated Association of
Head Masters, the Assistant Masters' Association, the
Teachers' Guild, the Association of Teachers in the Secondary Schools, and others. For example, at its meeting at
Eton in December, 1895, the Headmasters' Association
passed the following resolution: "That this Conference
welcomes the Report of the Royal Commission on Secondary Education, as promising in its main features a satisfactory solution of the problem of secondary education in
England";[5] and at its meeting the following month,
January, 1896, the Incorporated Association of Head
Masters thought that the Report was "at once judicious
and impartial," and that it offered "a statesmanlike
solution of the difficulties attending the organisation of
secondary education in England."[6]

Interest in the Report reached a climax in April, 1896,
when a conference was held at Cambridge University at
which at least thirty-nine bodies were represented. It was
one of the most diverse gatherings ever assembled to discuss matters concerning education. It included teachers,
inspectors and examiners, parents, administrators, businessmen and representatives of local government. Focusing
their attention on the Report's proposed scheme, or what
they called "a scheme propounded to them by practical
politicians," they passed eight resolutions in connection
with it. The interesting thing about these resolutions is
that they were not only a mere echo of the Commission's
recommendation; they also indicated an amazing educa-
tional-political-social consensus about the organizational
pattern that people thought education should take. They
endorsed the Commission's proposed organization at the

central and local levels, and, at the same time, reiterated its views that "freedom, variety and elasticity," the hallmarks of the English system, should be carefully preserved in any plans for educational change.[7]

The consensus so manifestly apparent at the Cambridge Conference and elsewhere on the proposed general organizational framework should not obscure the fact that questions were also raised. These, for the most part, pertained to details in the proposed scheme. For example, *The Daily News* felt that the duties of the Educational Council were too limited, and it was critical of the restrictions placed upon the local authorities in the amount of rates to be raised; the *Pall Mall Gazette* and the *School Guardian* had serious reservations about the powers of the central authority and were apprehensive lest it should lead to too much centralization;[8] and, in the columns of educational journals, criticisms were directed against certain omissions in the Report, such as the failure to take into account the religious question.[9]

Such voices of discontent, however, were drowned, as it were, in the sea of applause that characterized the immediate months following the appearance of the Report. Although there were some grumblings that the Commissioners did not go far enough,[10] the consensus that was so manifest was yet another indication of the congruence of the Commission's views with contemporary educational opinion. Like the Commissioners, those who spoke and wrote on the subject approached the problem of educational change at the structural-administrative level, in pragmatic terms, not in terms of some well-defined theory of change or government. As such, they sought to give shape and structure, as well as some direction, to the system, which would constitute the basis for development, but without at the same time sacrificing traditional values such as freedom, variety and elasticity. In this sense the Commission's Report may be viewed as a crystallization of contemporary opinion about education, as a projection of contemporary thoughts on the subject. Like so many other English plans or proposals for reform, it was neither revolutionary, nor obstructionist. It was a middle-of-the-road attempt to satisfy the various interests of the public.

Under such circumstances, one would have thought that any concrete measure which aimed at the practical application of all or some of the Commission's broad recommendations would have weathered any storm that might have arisen on matters of detail. Such, however, was not the case, as shown by the failure of a Bill which was introduced only four months after the publication of the Report, and which was purportedly based on it.

POLITICS AND EDUCATION: THE EDUCATION BILL OF 1896

We would not have to search long to find connecting links between the Report and the Education Bill of 1896 which followed it so closely. They were evident in many of the arguments adduced both in the support of the Bill, and in its rejection. Thus, for example, Sir John Gorst, the Vice-President of the Privy Council on Education, who was known to have endorsed rather strongly the Commission's recommendations,[11] and the man who introduced the Bill, thanked the Commission for their "admirable suggestion"; and, more explicitly, when the Bill went into Committee, Gorst hoped that "the Committee would support the Government in giving effect to the views of the Royal Commission on Secondary Education."[12] Likewise, R. C. Jebb, who had served as a member of the Commission, concurred that the Bill's central provision regarding local organization was "in harmony with the intentions of the Commission."[13]

On the other hand, several members of the Liberal Opposition, including James Bryce, the chairman of the Commission, rejected the Bill, either because it embodied the recommendations of the Bryce Commission in what Asquith termed "crude and imperfect form,"[14] or, to use F. A. Channing's words, because it "was not the Bill of the Royal Commission."[15] Bryce put it this way: "The Bill purported to follow in the main the Report of the Secondary Education Commission, but it diverged in many points from that Report, and where it differed . . . it differed for the worse."[16]

What then were the features of the Bill which seemed to arouse so much controversy, and which in the end caused it to be withdrawn by the Conservative Government? In his introductory speech to the first reading, Gorst laid down the basic principle of the measure as "the establishment in every county and county borough of a paramount education authority . . . to be one channel through which public money is to reach the schools; it is to supplement and not to supersede, existing educational effort."[17] According to the provisions of the Bill, it was made mandatory that the education authority for the county should be the county council, which should "act" by an education committee appointed by every county. The education authority was empowered to administer all the government grants to the schools which fell under its jurisdiction, and the funds from the Local Taxation (Customs and Excise) Act of 1890.[18] The county council, in turn, could levy a rate of 1d in the £ for the support of education within the county. Local authorities were instructed to "supplement and not to supplant such existing organizations for educational purposes as for the time being supply efficient instruction." Clause 27 of the Bill allowed, under certain circumstances, religious denominational teaching in Board schools,[19] and other provisions, e.g., the abolition of the 17s.6d limit, aimed at the assistance of voluntary schools.

A corollary to the shifting of responsibility in the disbursement of government grants was the provision that the Education Department, one of the existing central authorities, should transfer to the proposed local education authorities, any school or department of a school which provided an education "other than elementary" and was maintained by a School Board. The local authorities would then seek to promote such a type of education by (a) aiding existing schools, (b) establishing new secondary ones, (c) setting up and maintaining scholarships and exhibitions, (d) supplying or aiding in the supply of teachers, and (e) inquiring into the educational efficiency and sufficiency of any county school except those of non-local character.[20]

Thus, the Government sought to approach the problem of the reorganization of education by focusing on the local level of administration. Administrative change at this level had been recommended by the Bryce Commissioners and endorsed by several segments of public and educational opinion. But, by confining itself to local reorganization, the Bill aroused the antagonism of those who wanted to see a reorganization at the central level as well,[21] a point also recommended by the Commission. Furthermore, and this is what created pandemonium which finally wrecked the Bill, by concentrating on the local level, politically the most touchy and contentious area of English government, the Conservatives opened a Pandora's box of religious antagonisms, vested interests, and jealously guarded political gains. The debate, at times characterized by brilliant oratory on both sides of the House, covered all aspects of the proposed measure, including those that pertained to education "other than elementary." But, while due respects were often paid to the high educational principles and lofty aims of the Commission's Report and of those who allegedly patterned the Bill after it, the discussion seldom deviated from what were perceived to be the effects of the Bill on denominational and Board schools, on religious teaching in them, and on the role of the central authority in education. These questions, although relevant in the case of secondary education, applied more to elementary education.

Early in the debate, Yoxall, a Bryce Commissioner, a Liberal, and a representative of the interests of teachers, raised the main points of contention, which characterized the subsequent course of the debate. He first regretted the Bill's omission of a central authority.[22] Reorganization at the central level was felt to be absolutely necessary in the case of secondary education by the Bryce Commissioners, by the Liberal Opposition,[23] and by several groups outside Parliament. At the Cambridge Conference, referred to earlier, the Bill received as much attention as the Report of the Bryce Commission which had precipitated the meeting. In the case of "reorganization at the top," the Conference openly criticized the omission of the central authority in the Bill.[24] So did the Teachers' Guild of Great Britain and Ireland, whose president was R. C. Jebb, a Bryce Commissioner, but a Conservative M. P., i.e., a member of the party in power.[25]

Nevertheless, it was Yoxall's comments and criticisms on the implications of the Bill regarding the religious question and the School Boards that foreshadowed the future course of political controversy. According to him, the Bill, especially in its financial provisions, was "tinged with a desire" to strengthen voluntary schools and make them a permanent element "in the mosaic of education in the country." It was also a veiled attempt to restrict the powers of the School Boards and to introduce denominational teaching in the Board schools. School Boards, set up as *ad hoc* authorities, had grown since 1870 and many people believed in them. They provided schools which educated a large number of children and were free from the denominational influence of the Church schools. Hence, Yoxall concluded, in spite of its majority, the Government could never carry through the House a measure designed to curtail their growth and the religious freedom they enjoyed.[26]

In the debate on the first reading, the Liberal Opposition continued its attack on these elements in the Bill, amplifying what Yoxall had said, and adding new criticisms. Bryce enumerated five objections: the lack of organization through a central authority, and its corollary, the complete localization of elementary education; the placing of secondary and elementary education under one authority, which would infuse secondary education with the same denominational partisanship that characterized elementary education; the transfer of grants to local authorities for distribution without the necessary provision for vigilance; and the fear of sidetracking the Cowper-Temple Clause.[27] F. A. Channing, one of the strongest opponents of the measure, let the cat out of the bag when he said that the Bill "promised to alter completely the educational system of the country in favour of the sectarian party and their reactionary classes."[28]

The Bill passed the first reading, but the comfortable majority belied the strong feeling of discontent that it

engendered among the Liberals and the feeling of dis-
enchantment that it fostered among the Conservatives and
their allies, the Liberal Unionists. Outside Parliament,
while the Bill was being prepared for its second reading,
the various coalitions and groupings (political, professional, and religious) were consolidating their positions
and were becoming more vociferous against the Bill.

The Dissenting or Nonconformist groups (Congregational, Unitarian, Wesleyan and Baptist) of England
and Wales held conferences and passed resolutions against
the Bill. They condemned its religious and financial provisions, as well as its alleged emphasis on "decentrali-
zation," on similar grounds as the Liberals. One Nonconformist group called the Government's proposals "mis-
chievous" and "reactionary"; another, "injurious to the
interests of education, hostile to the principles of popular
government and religious equality." At a meeting of the
London Baptist Association, the eminent Dr. Clifford
stated that, "If passed, the Bill would seriously impair the
efficiency of education and would arrest the development
of Board schools."[29]

Among professional groups, the National Union of
Teachers (N. U. T.) was particularly active. At its annual
conference at Brighton, amidst a stormy debate on the
Bill, it passed three resolutions. In one resolution, it approved the proposed creation of education authorities for
the control of both primary and secondary education, but
it rejected the Bill's provision that these be the county
councils. Instead, according to the N. U. T., education
authorities "should be directly elected by the parochial
electors *ad hoc*." In another resolution, the N. U. T. objected to the proposal that the local authorities could use
funds obtained under the Local Taxation (Customs and

Excise) Act of 1890 for purposes other than those stipulated by that Act. They did not want to see funds which
were allotted for technical and similar schools used for
other types of post-elementary education.[30]

Liberal associations among political pressure groups, and
Liberal M.P.'s, either by themselves as speakers, or at
meetings with Dissenters, carried the Liberal case against
the Bill to the voter and sought to marshal public opinion
against it.[31]

The National Education Emergency Committee, which
included, among others, Dr. Clifford and Mr. Mundella,
Liberal M.P., passed a resolution condemning the Bill as
"essentially bad in principle."[32] On the other hand, the
Church (Anglican), the National Society and the Catholics in general approved the board principles of the Bill.
But they were also cautious in their commendation, critical
of certain of the Bill's provisions, and they wanted it to be
amended.

The most authoritative statement from the Church
group emerged at the Convocation of Canterbury, at
which, all in all, eleven resolutions were passed. The Convocation thanked the Government for its attempts to help
decentralize education. But it also made it known that
the Church considered the stipulated grants "insufficient
for voluntary schools" and, while it approved Clause 27,
it laid down the proviso "that Church of England teach-
ings [should] not be restricted under . . . the Cowper-
Temple Clause when giving instruction to schools other
than those of the Church of England."[33] The National
Society, which represented the interests of the Church
schools, approved the "principle of the Bill" but criticized
the permissive elements regarding the powers of the county
councils; and they felt that the special aid grants to volun-

tary schools were inadequate.[34] What is of further importance, however, as regards the position of the Church, is
that within its own ranks there were strong dissident
elements against the Bill altogether.[35]

The Catholic position was, in the main, similar to the
Anglican. In a declaration signed by Cardinal Archbishop
Herbert Vaughan and fifteen bishops, the "religious principle" of the Bill was approved, but the Bill was also found
to contain two defects: it did not provide for the establishment of new denominational schools in places considered
"unnecessary" by others but "necessary" by the Catholics;
and, in matters of "maintenance," it still left denominational schools "at a great disadvantage as compared with
Board schools." The Catholic clergymen suggested that the
Bill be amended accordingly.[36] Earlier, the Catholic feeling
concerning the inadequacy of the aid for voluntary schools
provided by the Bill had been expressed at the meeting of
the National Union of Catholic Teachers. At this meeting,
however, the Catholic teachers endorsed the other provisions of the Bill, especially those that pertained to the
local authorities and the training of teachers.[37]

Within the ranks of the Liberal Unionists, the allies of
the Conservatives, there was neither any strong solidarity,
nor any overflowing enthusiasm for the Bill. Some Liberal
Unionists found themselves in an uneasy and difficult
position. Prior to the Liberal Party's split over non-
educational questions (imperialism and Irish Home
Rule), and the resulting coalition with the Conservatives
in 1895, they were known to be the champions of the educational interests of Dissent. In 1870, for example, some of
the most radical of the group, e.g., George Dixon and
Joseph Chamberlain, had taken an extreme position
against public support of voluntary schools,[38] and, since
then, they were known to be in favor of the School Boards.

Chamberlain's position in 1896 was not only difficult, but also embarrassing to the Government of which he was a member. For, since 1870, he had been a strong supporter of the School Boards, and he was against the intrusion of the Church into publicly supported schools.[39] Now, as a member of the party in power, he was called upon to defend a measure that ran contrary to his previous pronouncements. Although, as the *Annual Register* recorded, he tried to "avoid the net which had been spread for him" and did it with "considerable skill," he admitted that there were many points in the Bill which "deserved careful discussion and might require modification."[40] Other members of the Unionist Party held conferences and openly criticized the Bill.[41]

Among the press, the most consistent supporter of the Bill was *The Times* of London which, in the interval between the two readings, gave extensive coverage of the measure and devoted several lengthy editorials to it. In a leader on April 11, *The Times* gave the Bill its wholehearted blessing and termed it "a fair and practical attempt to deal with elementary education under the conditions of the time." To be sure, the Bill favored the voluntary schools and the maintenance of religious education, but this, *The Times* averred, reflected "the real wishes of the people."[42] Later, *The Times* mellowed its overwhelming support, and, while it still thought the Bill was sound "in principle," admitted that it contained some objectionable features.[43]

The reaction to the Bill in the columns of the educational press was at first mixed, and rather calm and restrained.[44] Later, after the second reading, and after the Bill was withdrawn, criticisms appeared more often, although the spirit of restraint was still evident.

The attacks of the Liberals and the Nonconformists, the

ambivalence of Liberal Unionists, and the lukewarm feelings of the Church and the Catholics, were bad omens for the success of the Bill. Moreover, it became quite apparent that the Bill was to be fought on religious and political grounds, as well as, strictly speaking, educational. Sir John Gorst and the others were fully aware of this, and, in his address before moving the second reading of the Bill, Gorst went beyond high-sounding educational principles in justifying the measure. Instead, he took the bull by the horns and addressed himself to the issues to which the Bill gave rise. In a speech marked by constant interruptions of "hear, hear," "no, no" and "oh, oh," Gorst explicitly stated that one of the purposes of the Bill was to strengthen the voluntary schools. This, he claimed, was based on the assumption that such schools performed an indispensable educational function, and, more significantly, that there was general agreement as to the need for their continued existence. He then took up four main issues raised by the Bill, argued in favor of the Government's position on them, and tried to prove that counter-arguments were "obstacles to progress." Two of these issues were the provisions affecting secondary education, and the central authority. Gorst spent very little time on these because, according to him, there was not much opposition to what the Bill intended to do for the former, except in matters of minor details that could easily be ironed out, and a central authority did exist in the case of the latter, in the Committee of Council on Education.[45]

The third, "the most contentious portion of the Bill," was the financial one giving special aid to voluntary and Board schools. Gorst argued that the aim of this part of the Bill was to eliminate the great range of variation that existed in the financial support of schools, in terms of both

Imperial grants and local rates, subscriptions, endowments and school fees. Glaring variations were found to exist, not only between voluntary schools and Board schools, but also within each of the two types, especially between schools in the country districts and those in the cities. In order to make sure that funds were more equitably distributed, and that voluntary schools were made as efficient as Board schools, it was necessary to have a paramount authority with powers to disburse the allocated funds. No authority could do this better than the existing county councils with the help of an education committee. Turning to the implications of this provision for the School Boards, Gorst tried to show that such an arrangement would in no way jeopardize their existence or growth. It would merely bring them into closer administrative relationship with the locally elected bodies which represented the rate-payers.[46] Finally, Gorst dwelt on Clause 27 of the Bill, the so-called religious clause, which allowed for denominational teaching in the Board schools. According to him, the basic principle underlying this stipulation was the generally recognized right of the parent to "have his child brought up in the religion which he selects," a statement which was accompanied by "cheers" from the House. As things stood at the time, this right was not respected either in the Board schools or in the voluntary schools. In the case of the Board schools the parents "had no choice," for, subject to the Cowper-Temple Clause, "either they have what is called undenominational religious teaching, or they have no religious teaching at all"; in the case of the voluntary schools, "they must either accept the religious dogmas of the managers of the schools, or they have no religious teaching."[47] Gorst went to great length to assure his audience and the critics of the Bill that Clause 27 did not "abolish the Cowper-Temple Clause," although he admitted he never liked it. It merely declared "the parental right" and forbade the school managers "to throw obstacles in the way." Yet, his argument about the clause was unclear, and he did concede that, in the sense that denominational teaching would be allowed in Board Schools, the Bill did indeed imply abolition of the controversial Cowper-Temple Clause.[48]

Gorst's defence was eloquent and in the main lucid; but to the Liberal Opposition it was hardly convincing. In the interval between the first and the second readings, the Liberals had a chance to study and discuss the Bill, and the more they did that, the stronger their objections grew.[49] Although they were overwhelmingly in the minority, they presented a solid front. And their spokesmen in Parliament proved as eloquent and as lucid as their opponents.

The cudgels for the Opposition, immediately after Gorst moved the second reading, were taken up by H. H. Asquith.

Asquith rebutted most of the points made by Gorst, who, according to him, enumerated a number of "unproved assumptions" and drew a series of "illegitimate inferences." He amplified and pressed even harder than Yoxall and Bryce the Liberal opposition to certain features of the Bill, while at the same time he acknowledged some of its values. He felt, for example, that those provisions dealing with secondary education, although "of a more disputable character," would be "in a Parliamentary sense" regarded as non-contentious; and, although they embodied the recommendations of the Royal Commission on Secondary Education "in a crude and imperfect form," if submitted as an independent measure, both sides of the House would co-operate in supplementing any omissions and "in strengthening their efficacy." But the Bill went beyond that and, therefore, it was unacceptable. It sought to decentralize all levels of education and throw all responsibility in the hands of local authorities, an arrangement which, without the necessary supervision from the central authority, would create "administrative chaos," and would place education at the mercy of local rivalries and jealousies; it would pave the way for the elimination by means of "capture" of the School Boards, an avowed aim of the Conservatives, but one which ran contrary to the wishes of the ratepayers; and Clause 27 would make the "conscience clause" and the "Cowper-Temple Clause" dead letters.[50]

The debate on the second reading continued, and more people participated in it; but by then the points of dispute had already become clearly delineated. Among the chief political groupings, what followed was a mere extension of the previous positions: more support by the Conservatives, stronger opposition by the Liberals, and greater ambivalence by Liberal Unionists.[51] In addition, Lord Edmund Talbot, expressing the interests of the English Catholics, "welcomed the main principle of the Bill," but he admitted that it was "absolutely inadequate in its financial clauses."[52] And the Irish contingent, much to the chagrin of the Nonconformists, who expected some gratitude from those whom they supported over Irish Home Rule, indicated that, although they were not very happy with various provisions of the Bill, they would vote for the second reading.[53]

Although the Bill passed its second reading by a sizable majority including the Liberal Unionists and the Irish Catholics, its subsequent future on the floor of the House, in Committee, and outside Parliament, was not a happy one. Rumors had spread that the Government was out to destroy the School Boards, in spite of Balfour's assurances to the contrary, and that it was planning to adopt the method of closure to pass the Bill, which to some was evidence of "the most cynical political inconsistency." Some of the Bill's staunchest supporters, e.g., L. H. Court-ney, even suggested that the Government withdraw the measure for that session. In summarizing the political climate of the day, the *Annual Register* recorded: "This [Courtney's] suggestion was at first met by a torrent of objections, but it showed that in impartial minds doubt already had sprung up as to the value of the bill, and of the time required to surmount the objections which might be taken to its numerous and complicated clauses."[54]

But the Bill was not withdrawn, not just then. It was dragged into discussion again, but its doom was sealed. The Government was beset by more conflicting views from friends and foes; countless amendments were made (not fewer than 1,238) until "every line of each section seemed smothered by friends who desired to improve or opponents who sought to shelve the Education Bill."[55] The Bill foundered in Committee, and finally, on June 18, Mr. Balfour announced that, under the circumstances, "it was obviously impossible for the Government to adhere to their scheme."[56] With this acknowledged impasse the Bill of 1896 was abandoned.

ASSESSMENT OF THE ABORTIVE BILL

The year 1896 upon closer examination has turned out to be a most fascinating stage in English educational de-velopment, and its Education Bill an intriguing episode in the growth of a system where religion, politics and edu-cation have been inextricably interwined. To say that the demise of the Bill of 1896 was due to political and religious rather than educational factors is to express a mere half-truth concerning English education. For it is impossible to divorce English education from its twin cohabitants, namely, religion and politics, especially when one examines education from the standpoint of administrative structure. Educational questions in this respect are also political and religious questions. It is, therefore, with this basic consideration in mind that any assessment of the Education Bill of 1896 must be made.

The Report of the Bryce Commission created considerable commotion in political and educational circles, and, together with comments about what the Commission had said and recommended, there were frequent references to anticipated legislation based on the Report. The reaction to the Report, during the year following its publication, centered in the organization and administration of education, and not in its ideology. There was a conspicuous paucity of statements on what the Commission had said about the nature and function of education. The pressing question seemed to be action regarding the structure of education, and it was only after the abandonment of the Bill that questions of ideology acquired more prominence.

The Bill of 1896 was an outgrowth of a climate of opinion favoring some sort of change in the administrative structure of education, and one which was strengthened by the Report of the Bryce Commission. Our analysis of the debate on the Bill has shown that the Commission's Report was constantly invoked by both the supporters and the opponents of the Bill in justifying their respective positions. So great in fact was the authority of the Commission, that it weathered the storm engendered by the Bill and emerged unscathed after the Bill was withdrawn. Indeed it continued to be a motivating force in subsequent discussions and in the reforms of 1899 and 1902. In an editorial after the abandonment of the Bill, *The Educational Times* put it as follows:

Once again the Report of the Royal Commission holds the field. We fall back upon that statesmanlike document as our text, and take the draft of Sir John Gorst's Bill . . . as a footnote useful for future guidance.[57]

Our examination of the debates on the Bill has also shown that most of the controversies revolved around those features of the Bill which affected "elementary" education more than "secondary." Thus, at first sight, there seems to be a paradox insofar as the impact of the Report on the Bill was concerned, for the Report was essentially concerned with secondary education. Yet, the perplexity that this creates becomes clearer when one considers the following aspects of the problem: first, that the School Boards which were affected by the Bill's proposals were in many instances providing a type of education that went beyond the limits prescribed by the 1870 Act. This was in the form of "higher elementary classes" or of "higher grade schools" which were regarded by some as providing secondary education. Hence, any discussion of the functions of the School Boards raised questions that affected a type of secondary education as well. Secondly, in the proposed scheme of reorganization, elementary and secondary education were placed under the jurisdiction of the same authority, the local authority. The Bryce Commission had recommended reorganization both at the local and at the central levels for secondary education; but by tacking the reform of secondary education on to that of elementary, and by doing this only at the local level, those aspects of the Bill which affected secondary education became eclipsed, so to speak, by those which essentially affected elementary education. The Bill, therefore, did not, strictly

speaking, embody the recommendations of the Commission, in spite of the fact that its supporters based many
of their arguments on it. The controversies to which it gave
rise, and the conflicts created, clearly showed what would
happen if secondary reorganization was confounded with
elementary. As one professional journal put it, the proposed scheme of secondary organization was "tacked upon
a voluntary school relief Bill," something which the profession rejected and found quite impossible.[58] The controversies further showed that the religious problem could
not be ignored—something to which the Bryce Commission
paid little attention—when the governmental aspects of
education were being involved. To be sure the politico-
religious aspect of education had been a persistent source
of conflict since 1870; but it was with the 1896 Bill that
it was put to the test in the case of secondary education.
And, more important than this, was the fact that by then
the political power structure had changed, different coalitions had emerged, and the School Boards had become
an important feature of the system and an important
political force that could not be ignored.

Since their establishment in 1870, the School Boards had
been providing a non-denominational type of education
to an increasing number of children, and were thus becoming more formidable competitors to the Church, and to its
Conservative allies in Parliament. The Church, anxious to
maintain its influence over popular education, was becoming hostile to the School Boards; and so were its Conservative allies. However, the School Boards were very
successful in the urban districts, and they were backed by
the Liberals and the working classes, and all those who
were suspicious of the proselytizing tendencies of the
Church. Lord Salisbury and Balfour were quite aware of
this. Soon after becoming Prime Minister, Salisbury urged

the members of the National Society "to capture" the Board schools under the present law and then put them under a better law, "which would place the church people under no religious disadvantage."[59] Apparently, however, when "the better law" was introduced in the Bill of 1896, Salisbury underestimated the political power that had gathered around these *ad hoc* bodies.

But the failure of the Bill of 1896 cannot be explained solely in terms of the strength of the Liberal Opposition, which championed non-denominational education and the School Boards. Nor did the added ambivalence of the Liberal Unionists create sufficient grounds for the withdrawal of the Bill, although both were necessary conditions. The Church supporters of the measure, and the Catholics, were themselves divided, and wanted too many changes. There were even dissident voices within the Conservative ranks, and the Government itself did not follow a resolute action.

The failure of the Bill was a clear warning to all parties concerned. The Liberals and the supporters of the School Boards knew that their political opponents were anxious to see their power over education curtailed. To the Conservatives, the Bill was an indication that they must henceforth change both the substance of educational reform and their strategy. Herein, therefore, lay the significance of the Bill, not in what it achieved, but in what contributed to its failure. It was truly, as an educationalist put it, "a footnote useful for future guidance."[60]

THE NATURE AND SCOPE OF SECONDARY EDUCATION

Interest in the Report and in reform continued. Together with considerations about the reorganization of education, a matter which will be taken up in Chapter V,

there was also some discussion about the ideological
questions raised in the Report, that is, about the nature
of secondary education and its relation to technical, and
about the role of the secondary school in the society.
Whether, in fact, the ideological climate of the years following the Report was directly an outgrowth of it is difficult
to establish. But that the Report articulated certain principles of secondary education, which gave added impetus
to the need for clarification of the meaning of secondary
education, cannot be questioned. Clearly also it was evident
that reorganization of the structure of the educational
system entailed a clearer understanding of the scope of the
various levels of education and their relationship to each
other.

As in the evidence gathered by the Commissioners, the
views expressed on these and similar questions varied.
There were arguments in favor of the view that technical
education is secondary, but also that such a type of education must be built on a solid foundation of general
liberal culture, which was regarded as solely the purview
of the secondary school; there were arguments in favor of
scientific and practical subjects, but also that the humanities "are the best foundation of an all round education";
there were advocates of higher elementary schools (the
third grade schools in the Commission's Report), but also
that such schools must be clearly differentiated from
secondary schools in terms of content, leaving age, and
vocational destinations of students; and there were arguments in favor of expansion of opportunities, but also that
the selective character of the secondary school must be
preserved. In several instances the positions taken were
bolstered by the authority of the Bryce Commission; in
most others there were striking similarities. Equally sig-

nificant, however, was the fact that similar arguments were adduced by divergent political and educational groups.

Thus, on the question of the relationship between secondary and technical education, one finds Balfour (a leading Conservative), E. Lyulph Stanley (a Liberal and a leading member of the London Technical Education Board), Professor Jebb, the Director of Technical Instruction for Manchester, and the editor of *The Educational Times,* all agreeing that technical education should be grounded in a solid secondary education.[61] It was generally agreed that the educational function of the secondary school was the development of the intellectual faculties and the cultivation of a humane general culture, and not specialization, or any kind of "technical" or vocational orientation. Its educational scope was clearly differentiated from that of a technical or a higher grade school. The latter types of schools were not envisaged to be strictly speaking "vocational" or "trade" schools, but they were supposed to have a certain direction or "bias" towards some vocational or practical pursuits.[62]

At the same time that these pronouncements were made, the Education Department, through its Office of Special Inquiries and Reports created in 1895 by A. H. D. Acland, the then Vice-President of the Committee of Education, issued a series of reports on foreign systems of education by its director, Michael Sadler, and its assistant director, Robert Morant. Sadler was a key member of the Bryce Commission, an acknowledged educational authority, and the educational consultant of prominent statesmen; Morant was relatively unknown at the time, but he was soon destined to dominate the educational arena for about a decade. Although in these reports both men were chiefly concerned with the administrative aspects of education, they also discussed the nature of secondary education, and its relation to technical. In this respect their positions were very much in accord with contemporary opinion. They both viewed technical education as built upon a solid foundation of general secondary education, and not co-extensive with it, and they advocated a clearly different-iated pattern of post-primary schools.[63]

There was also a surprising consensus concerning the social functions of secondary or post-primary education. In the broadest meaning of the term, secondary education was envisaged to be a selective type of education; it was not the logical sequel of elementary, nor a stage in a continuous process. The selective character of this level of education was even more apparent when different types of schools within the broad category of "secondary" were being discussed. There was a clear differentiation of such institutions in terms of intellectual, educational, and social criteria. Thus, for example, secondary schools, in the contemporary meaning of the term, were thought to be academic institutions for students who were able to con-tinue their education up to the age of seventeen or nine-teen, and who planned to enter professional, scientific, and high mercantile or public careers.[64] In many instances, there was mention of merit or intellectual competence as a criterion for selection and attendance in these schools. But it is interesting to note that, more often than not, this criterion was applied to the more intelligent children of the elementary schools rather than to all the students attending secondary schools. And, as things were, these two types of schools were already socially differentiated, the elementary drawing their students mostly from the lower classes, and the secondary from the middle and upper classes. In the collection of essays written on behalf of the

Incorporated Association of Head Masters, one writer summed up the selective function of secondary education as follows: "Primary and Secondary Education cannot be compared respectively to the lower and upper storeys of a single tenement. They are rather to be figured as two adjacent tenements, with an easy passage from near the top of the lower to the mezzanine floor of the higher of the two houses."[65]

As in the case of the relationship between secondary and technical education, the principle of selection for secondary education was entertained by diverse groups. For example, the President of the N. U. T., which represented the interests of elementary schools, openly stated that the needs of "the artisans and foremen and leaders of labour were not within the boundaries of secondary education."[66]

In contrast to the secondary academic schools, the higher grade schools were envisaged as schools which drew their students from the elementary schools and from the lower classes; the school-leaving age in them was fourteen or fifteen; they prepared students "for livelihood"; and they imparted knowledge of immediate utility. In short, they were schools of "bread winning," rather than of "brain-forming" studies, as one writer put it.[67]

Our examination of the ideological climate of the immediate years following the Bryce Report has revealed strong similarities between the views of the Report and the witnesses that testified before the Commission, on the one hand, and those who followed them, on the other. Although those who spoke and wrote on the nature and function of secondary education did not classify schools systematically, as the Bryce Commissioners had done, nevertheless, the basic principles were there. One finds the same ideas about selection, curriculum emphasis, and institutional differentiation as in the Bryce Report.

These were indeed important questions, for the ideological element justified the existing and the proposed institutional framework and educational practices. Ideologies lubricate, so to speak, the workings of a system. But, at the time, since there was no "system" in the strict meaning of the term, the ideological element was discussed in conjunction with the administrative-structural element, and was often overshadowed by it. The people wanted action so that a more coordinated educational system could be established. In this connection, what happened after 1896 was at once a continuation of the ferment which reached a climax in the Education Bill of that year, and a prelude to subsequent legislation which constitutes another chapter in the evolution of English education.

IV

Conservatism and Educational Reform: The Foundations of a National System of Secondary Education

There was hardly any mourning over the demise of the 1896 Education Bill. In fact, those who were anxious to see a reorganization of secondary education along the lines suggested by the Bryce Commission heard of the abandonment of the Bill "with something like a sigh of relief."[1] They continued to discuss the main ideas of the Commission's Report and, as before, paid glowing encomia to it. Interest both in the Report and in reform gathered fresh momentum. There was hardly an issue of the educational journals of the time, especially of the years 1897 and 1898, that did not have something to say about the need for comprehensive legislation, and about the impatience and disappointment of the educational world at the Government's

100

slow-moving pace. An encouraging statement by the Duke of Devonshire, the President of the Council on Education, was construed and acclaimed as signalling the introduction of a new Bill; a more restrained word was received with disappointment and frustration.

The question of reform was again discussed at professional meetings, resolutions were passed, committees were appointed to enlighten public opinion and the Government, and draft proposals for a new Bill were formulated. One remarkable feature of these pronouncements was that the impact of the Bryce Report was stamped on almost all of them. It was felt, for example, that no reorganization of secondary education could possibly be effective without the coordination of the existing central authorities under one central department; that organization at the top must be accompanied by organization at the local level; and that the profession must have a voice in both cases. *The Journal of Education,* expressing the views of the teachers, exclaimed: "The Report, the whole Report and nothing but the Report."[2]

The ferment for reform was also evident among political groups, and in the Houses of Parliament. In the House of Lords, Lord Norton talked about the possible introduction of a secondary education bill which would create a central department, and local authorities whose powers would be wider than those of the School Boards;[3] and members of the House of Commons pressed for an answer as to when the Government would recommend the Bryce Commission's proposals.[4] Early in 1898, the Duke of Devonshire hinted at how the Conservatives would approach the reorganization of secondary education: they would organize in a better way "that which already exists, and possibly supplement it to a great extent."[5]

Our analysis of the climate of opinion in the 1890's and the persistent concern for the reform of secondary education raises the important historical question of why reform had become so pressing a problem in the last decade of the nineteenth century. For we know that reform of secondary education was in some form or another advocated since the eighteen sixties. It had been recommended by the Schools Inquiry Commission, and in the person of Matthew Arnold, with his oft-quoted slogan "organize your secondary education," it had found a powerful spokesman. Yet, except for sporadic attempts like the Endowed Schools Act of 1869[6] and the Local Taxation (Customs and Excise) Act of 1890, nothing in the way of comprehensive state legislation affecting secondary education had been made. The laissez-faire doctrine continued to hold the field.

Since the sixties, however, several conditions, both internal and external, had undermined the social philosophy of laissez-faire; new currents of thought had emerged, and new problems had arisen, for which the old doctrine had no satisfactory answers. The educational reform movement of the nineties, and such expressions of it as the Bryce Commission Report, the Education Bill of 1896, and the Education Acts of 1899 and 1902, form an integral part of a broader social and political change. The illumination of all these educational events would consequently be quite incomplete without some understanding of the broader matrix of forces at work.

THE EVOLUTION OF IDEAS AND SOCIAL CHANGE

"Sharply defined periods," André Maurois has said, "are only historians' concepts."[7] Bearing this qualification in mind, we notice that in the second half of the nineteenth century there was a current of ideas which deviated from the orthodox laissez-faire views. Matthew Arnold, the most caustic critic of laissez-faire liberalism, called it the creed of the Philistines, the "afyeis," or the people who did not possess "sweetness and light" or "culture." Liberalism, according to him, connoted "democratic equality" or "social liberty," rather than the cult of individualism or the rule of one class. Culture, his favorite word, and the object of education, could not be achieved without the intervention of the State, especially in the education of the middle classes.[8]

Like Arnold, Thomas Carlyle and John Ruskin protested against Benthamism and the material progress that was ascribed to Benthamite liberty. Ruskin demanded that public authorities step in to remedy the evils that had resulted from private enterprise, and advocated that schools and factories should be established under State control;[9] and according to Carlyle, "a government of the under classes by the upper on a principle of *let-alone* is no longer possible in England in these days."[10]

Among the more systematic thinkers of the time were the Oxford philosophers, and notably T. H. Green, who was accounted the most influential teacher at Oxford since Newman. Green, an active participant in educational, civic, and political affairs,[11] approached problems from the ordinary citizen's standpoint, rather than from the high level of the Utilitarians, and sought to furnish a more realistic rationale for democratic theory. Like the Utilitarians, he conceived the aims of the State to be the securing of a "good life," but, unlike them, he held that the State had a positive function to perform in the attainment of this goal. It should create the conditions whereby all individuals may be capable, as free men, to live a good life.

To Green, freedom did not connote absence of restraint, but "a positive power of doing or enjoying something worth doing or enjoying."[12]

The latter part of the nineteenth century was also characterized by a growth of the spirit of science, and especially as it was sought to be applied to human affairs. Some, like Herbert Spencer, used the scientific doctrine as developed by Darwin to arrive at a laissez-faire theory of government, yet others, like T. H. Huxley, used it to denounce the idea that the State was a worse bungler than any other "joint-stock company." Huxley distinguished between natural and moral rights, and maintained that in order to guarantee the latter, which are characteristic of "rational man," the State must intervene, even compel, especially in the case of education.[13]

Apart from these "external forces", there was an "inner" development of laissez-faire individualism itself, best exemplified in John Stuart Mill, who was often associated with it. In the successive editions of his classic work on State non-interference, Mill was adding more and more exceptions to a laissez-faire policy, one of these exceptions being education.[14] In his hands there was an ideological transformation of the philosophy of utilitarianism. Having distinguished between higher and lower pleasures, and having identified happiness with the former, he went as far as to abandon self-interest, and to adopt the principle of self-sacrifice, by advocating that happiness is attained by those who seek the happiness of others, or the improvement of mankind.[15] And in his *Autobiography*, he looked forward to the time when " the division of the produce of labour, instead of depending, in so great a degree, as it now does, on the accident of birth, will be made by concert on an acknowledged principle of justice."[16]

Finally, in the evolving anti-laissez-faire ideology, one must mention the various brands of socialist thought that appeared in the last two decades of the nineteenth century, especially Fabianism. Under the vigorous leadership of middle class intellectuals and social investigators like Sidney and Beatrice Webb, G. B. Shaw, Graham Wallas, and H. G. Wells, Fabianism called for the establishment of conditions which would promote "the utmost possible development of faculty in all human beings." It advocated more State responsibility in matters of education, a more efficient representative central government, the gradual extension of the franchise, and the transfer of rent and interest to the state.[17] The Fabians constantly sought to enlighten public opinion, and, through their strategy of "permeation," to influence politicians of both parties in programs of reform. This, as will be shown later, was particularly evident in the Education Act of 1902.

To what extent this changing ideological climate impregnated educational thought is difficult to determine, but we do know that some of the critics of extreme laissez-faire policies were actively engaged in the reform of education. We also know that, because of fast-moving social, economic and political changes, voluntarism in education could not cope with the new demands created. Whether the emerging ideologies preceded social change, or merely furnished a new rationale of what was already happening, is again difficult to establish. It might not, however, be particularly illuminating for our purposes. The fact is that, together with the changing views of the role of the State in matters of social policy, there were other significant changes which hastened the need for a better organization of the educational system at the secondary level.

Passing reference has already been made to some well-known events in late nineteenth century English history. There was first a political awakening of the laboring class, which culminated in 1899 in the setting up of the "Labour Representation Committee." From this grew the Labour Party whose aim was to promote legislation "in the direct interest of labour."[18] Thus, by the end of the century, labor emerges as a political force in British politics, having won in the meantime the right to combine, picket and strike in any trade dispute that would arise between employers and employees. These gains in themselves implied the negation of the conviction that the individual knew what his own interest was, and the acceptance of the belief that "associations," or "combinations," as organisms would guarantee better the workers' interests. Since the State was conceived to be such an organism, it was its responsibility to guarantee the interests of the individual, not by permissive legislation, but by compulsive action.

In the area of popular government there was a series of Acts by which the central and local governments were set on a more democratic basis. The Reform Acts of 1867 and 1884 broke down the middle class monopoly of political power by extending the franchise, and by altering parliamentary representation. In Ensor's words: "the historic *communitates* (counties and boroughs) ceased to be, as such, the basis of the House of Commons. The individual for the first time became a unit, and numerical equality (one's vote one value) the master principle."[19] Furthermore, the County Councils Act of 1888, the Local Government Act of 1894, and the London Government Act of 1899 altered local government by placing administration into the hands of elected county councils and metropolitan borough councils.[20]

Finally, there were changes in commerce and industry. Collectivism (companies with limited or unlimited liability) and municipal and State-managed business were gradually replacing the individual "captains of industry." Joint-stock companies emerged, with larger aggregates of capital demanded by the growing technology.[21] The growth and organization of industry and commerce created a greater need for scientific, technical, and high managerial training.[22]

In addition, however, to these "internal" conditions, there were at least two "external" factors which are relevant for an understanding of the reform movement of the nineties. These were the increasing threat of foreign competition, and a resurgence of imperialism which found ready followers among the ranks of the Liberals, the working classes, and intellectual groups.

Foreign competition and imperialism, which reached a climax in the South African War, highlighted the need for a re-examination of British institutions, especially those concerned with the function of education. Of the external factors, none seemed to arouse the nation to positive action in secondary education more than Germany, England's chief European competitor.

THE CHALLENGE OF GERMANY

In the heyday of laissez-faire liberalism, England was, as Knowles put it, "the forge of the world, the world's carrier, and the world's entrepôt."[23] In the eyes of their European rivals, Englishmen had discovered the secrets of political stability and economic prosperity, as well as the "philosophy of happiness." But, by the end of the century, all this had undergone major transformations. Germany and the United States had not only outgrown Britain numerically; they had also challenged her indus-

trial and commercial supremacy. Britain's exports of manufactured articles (cotton goods, woolen and worsted,
linen), which constituted the largest portion of her foreign trade in the mid-Victorian period, declined because
of tariffs in other countries. Her exports of machinery,
ships, and coal had increased, but this made the consumer
countries less dependent on British manufactures and
shipping. By the last decade of the nineteenth century, the
United States surpassed England in coal production, and
both Germany and the United States were producing more
and better steel. In 1885–6, Gottfried Daimler, a German,
patented the high-speed internal combustion engine, and,
in 1897, Germany took away from Britain the Atlantic
"blue ribbon."[24]

Similarly, by that time England's "philosophy of happiness" had ceased to occupy the intellectual position it
had hitherto occupied, or to furnish the rationale for social, political and educational reforms. Instead, the eyes
of British thinkers, statesmen, social reformers and educators, had turned to Europe, and especially to Germany,
which at the time was dominated by the spirit of Kant and
Hegel.

T. H. Green had inaugurated in the British universities a tradition which went by the names of "Neo-Kantism," "Neo-Hegelianism," "Idealism," or "Neo-Idealism,"
and which, in addition to Green, included such figures as
F. H. Bradley, Bernard Bosanquet, J. M. E. McTaggart,
James Seth and Edward Caird. From the historical standpoint, the essence of the thinking of these men was similar. Drawing their inspiration from Plato and Aristotle,
as well as from Kant and Hegel,[25] the "idealists," unlike
the "individualists," conceived of freedom, not in abstract
negative terms, but in concrete positive terms, and of the
State as a necessary basis for society.[26]

The influence of the German spirit was so great, that R. B. Haldane, a leading Liberal, wrote: "The name of the little territory which encloses Weimar and Jena stirs the imagination of thousands of our youth of both sexes, even as the name of Jerusalem moved the hearts of men in the centuries behind us."[27] Haldane, himself a student of German life and thought, constantly warned his countrymen of the "peril of German rivalry if they continued to neglect Science and Education."[28]

The phenomenal commercial and industrial expansion of Germany, as well as her intellectual ascendancy, were attributed to the efficient organization and administration of her system of education, as well as to the nature of the instruction given in her schools.

The alarm at the threat of foreign competition had been sounded earlier by two Royal Commissions. In the seventies, the Royal Commission on Scientific Instruction (the Devonshire Commission) stressed the need for more scientific instruction in the schools, and its importance to industry;[29] in the eighties, the Royal Commission on Technical Instruction compared technical education in England with that of certain foreign countries including Germany, and attributed the success of foreign manufactures to a better system of education in terms of both organization and content.[30] But it was in the nineties and the opening years of the twentieth century that alarm at German superiority reached high proportions.

In a report published in 1896, Sir Philip Magnus and his colleagues cited the German example to underline the significance of good schools "for the great industrial warfare." German secondary schools, in contrast to the English schools, were more accessible to the people, they were better defined and understood, and they provided better instruction.[31] Similarly, in their studies on behalf of the

Office of Special Inquiries and Reports, Sadler and his associates investigated foreign systems of education, and contrasted certain of their features with those of Britain. Sadler's reports on the German educational institutions, and his comparison of them with those of the British, brought to the attention of the English public as well as the educational policy-makers the weaknesses of English secondary education as compared to that of England's chief European competitor. Specifically, Sadler sought to impress upon his countrymen the efficiency and functionality of the German schools in a growing industrial civilization. He attributed such efficiency to the thoughtful planning on the part of the German Government and to the nature of instruction given in them. The German institutions, unlike the English, were not the outcome of a "hugger-mugger kind of growth," and technical education, as well as professional specialization, was grounded in a "sound and liberal culture."[32] The central government, through its control of methods of selection and entrance to the higher professions, and through inspection, established and maintained standards of excellence which acted as an incentive to the localities to maintain high standards.[33] Judged by such criteria, the English system was painfully weak and inadequate.[34]

This did not mean that Sadler saw no strengths in the educational system of his own country, or that he had no reservations in regard to the German system. Nor did he advocate the copying by one country of characteristics from another. Yet, he believed that many problems were the same in all countries, and that one nation, by studying the way educational problems were tackled by another, benefited in the solution of its own. Hence, although he would not sacrifice the freedom and individualism of the English system to the "large measure of State control" that obtained in Germany, he sought to explore that "debatable territory between Individualism and Socialism."[35] He was firmly convinced that the recruitment and training of the future leaders of a nation were essential, and that a machinery should be established to tap the talent from all classes of society. He, accordingly, called for better administrative methods whereby prospective leaders would have greater opportunities to obtain an education suited to them. And, like Magnus, he stressed the fact that in Germany there were more opportunities for secondary education for children of poorer families.[36]

The assumed relationship between education and the commercial prosperity of Germany at the time, and the fear of German competition, were pointed out in several other reports,[37] and by various segments of British public opinion. As one contemporary writer put it: Prussia, "Palmerston's country of d——d professors, had shown to the world that she can do other things than produce professors."[38] The same writer warned:

. . . if we are to preserve our ancient position as leaders in the race for material wealth, we must imitate our rivals. This is the lesson which Lord Rosebery endeavoured to impress upon his hearers.[39]

That the German example, more than that of any other foreign country, was an important external condition in highlighting the need for educational reform is amply sustantiated by the fact that, in the parliamentary debates over the Bills of 1896, 1899, and 1902, numerous references were made to it, not only by members of the party in power, but also by members of the Opposition.[40]

THE BOER WAR

It is difficult to establish a direct relationship between the South African War, or the Boer War as it was called, and the educational reform which followed it so closely.[41] However, the war was a test case of the overall British national efficiency, as well as of the sufficiency of the existing political and social structure and attitudes. And in this test, as Dennis Brogan has astutely noted, "Britain's defeats were humiliating and her victories unexhilarating."[42] Not only was the war a heavy drain on British resources in terms of money and manpower; perhaps more significantly, it was a humiliation, which stung poisonously the British people's conscience, broke down their complacency, and made them become self-conscious about the efficiency of their political and social institutions. The war, in the first place, revealed defects in English leadership (officers and official class),[43] in technical equipment, and in technical training; and in the second, its cost necessitated finding means to exercise greater economy.

The attention of the people, especially the reformers, was almost automatically directed to those institutions which most likely would remedy the defects, namely the schools, and particularly the secondary schools. The views of Mr. Emmott, expressed during the second reading of the 1902 Bill, were not isolated utterances. Quoting Michael Sadler as saying that "the very existence of the empire depends on seapower and school-power," Emmott pleaded for "immediate and far-reaching reform in secondary education." "This is a national and Imperial question," he added, "I am not pleading for the children, but I am pleading for the nation."[44]

The view was widely shared that effective and sound technical training itself depended on a sound general education, and that the development of technical education depended *a fortiori* on the strengthening and the wider provision of basic general education. Balfour, one of the architects of the Education Act of 1902, stated the point as follows:

> Higher technical instruction can only do its work . . . well, when that work is based on a sound general education . . . I am forced to the conclusion that ours is the most antiquated, the most ineffective, and the most wasteful method yet invented for providing a national education.[45]

Regarding the exercise of economy, the Tories, aside from their own vested religious interests, were perhaps right in maintaining that the School Boards were extravagant. Consequently they wished to see them disappear and be replaced by a different organization.[46] The elimination of these *ad hoc* bodies would not only be more economical, but would also contribute to the general national efficiency found so miserably inadequate during the South African War.

The war had yet another effect. The humiliations which the British suffered at the hands of the Boers, partly accounted for a change in the general psychological climate among the British public. This public was no longer the "illiterate," voteless populace of Bagehot's and Matthew Arnold's days. The majority of them had received the social and educational benefits that had resulted from the legislation of the last quarter of the nineteenth century. They did not all become "literate" or intelligent voters in the full sense of the word, but they could read, and, what was more important, they could read the "yellow" press, so masterfully developed by Harmsworth.[47] Furthermore, they could vote, and their voting behavior was influenced by this type of journalism. What is of significance here is the fact that what was happening in South Africa was sensationally brought to the attention of the British public via the popular "yellow" press, which was

based more on the principle of circulation than on objective truth. And the effect on the mind of the public
was twofold: on the one hand, it heightened its imperi-
alistic sentiment; and on the other, it strengthened its interest in the development of British institutions and
especially in the development of education.[48]

Thus, by the end of the nineteenth century and the
opening years of the twentieth, there was general agreement on at least three points. First, that reform of secondary education at the central and local levels was necessary;
second, that as things were, no existing authority at the
local level was legally empowered to assist secondary education, though this *was* done through grants from Parliament and from the county councils; and third, that secondary education ought to be assisted. Disagreement
revolved on deciding which authority was the appropriate
one for administering grants, and the degree of control
by both the central and the local bodies.

EDUCATIONAL POLITICS AND REFORM

The Education Act of 1899. One of the recommendations of the Bryce Commission was the creation of a central educational authority instead of the existing three,[49]
which would thus remedy the chaos and overlapping that
existed at the top of the system. The problem, as the Commissioners saw it, was "to evolve . . . one properly
constituted and organised Central Authority," to "nation-
alize" but not centralize the system of secondary education.[50] The function of this central body was not to
control, but rather "to supervise" secondary education,
not to supersede local action, "but to endeavour to bring
about among the various agencies which provide that education a harmony and co-operation which are now want-
ing."[51] The functions of such an authority would be to

"help to stimulate, guide, and supply information to all minor authorities and to all schools."[52]

After the failure of the 1896 Bill, the Duke of Devonshire in 1899 introduced a Bill in the House of Lords which was passed by both Houses and was known as the Board of Education Act, 1899. During the debates in Parliament numerous references were made to the Bryce Commission,[53] and the Bill was purportedly based on the Commission's recommendations. Actually this was not entirely the case. Instead of a Minister and an Advisory Council as advised by the Bryce Commission, the Act provided for the establishment of a Board, consisting of "a President—the Lord President of the Council—Her Majesty's Principal Secretaries of State, the First Commissioner of her Majesty's Treasury, and the Chancellor of her Majesty's Exchequer," and of a Consultative Committee, two thirds of the membership of which were to represent the views of the universities and other bodies interested in education.[54] Furthermore, unlike the Bryce Commission's unqualified statement concerning the supervision of secondary education, the Act qualified the Board's function as follows:

The Board of Education may by their officers, or, after taking the advice of the Consultative Committee hereinafter mentioned, by any University, or other organisation, inspect *any school supplying secondary education and desiring to be so inspected,* for the purpose of ascertaining the character of the teaching and health of the scholars, and may so inspect the schools on such terms as may be fixed by the Board of Education with the consent of the Treasury.[55]
(Italics inserted by the writer.)

These differences between the recommendations of the Bryce Commission and the 1899 Act should not obscure the significance of the administrative reform at the central level. In the first place, a central educational authority was created which was to take the place of the Education Department (including the Department of Science and Art), and, in time, the educational functions of the Charity Commission. Secondly, the new authority was charged with the responsibility of supervising all forms of secondary education, and no compulsion or control was stipulated. These provisions were in line not only with the best educational opinion, but also with the contemporary notions concerning the degree of State interference in education. Regarding the general character of the inspection, it was Michael Sadler himself, the man, that is, who had been largely responsible for the recommendations of the Bryce Commission, who had suggested it to the Duke of Devonshire, after he had investigated the problem, and after he had conferred with heads of Public schools, representatives from Oxford and Cambridge, and other secondary school people.[56] Voluntariness in matters of inspection was also strongly supported by the clergy.[57] There were, of course, some who objected to the generality of inspection. Bryce, for example, characterized it as "so much an optional inspection that it is not compulsory even as regards health."[58] Yet, in the same speech, Bryce himself voiced distrust at too much Government interference.[59] The main opposition to the Bill was directed against the lack of any definite statements on secondary education, its meaning, organization, administration, and content.[60] But the Duke of Devonshire and Sir John Gorst (Vice-President of the Committee of Council for Education) contended that it was not a Secondary Education Bill. Rather, as Gorst put it, it was ". . . a Bill to make *preparation* for secondary education by establishing at headquarters such an organization as will enable Parliament hereafter to confer upon those who have charge of education such functions and powers as the condition of the country in the matter of secondary education will require."[61]

The "organization at headquarters," as Gorst called the 1899 Act, prepared the way for reform at the local level. But here the task was more difficult, for it involved the by now familiar political struggle—perhaps the most important in the history of English education—between the supporters of the School Boards, and those of the local councils,[62] as to which authority should control secondary education. This issue, as noted earlier, was further complicated by the fact that the question of educational administration was enmeshed with the religious issue, whether, that is, denominational schools should be placed on the local rates or not. As will be shown later, the major religious groups (Anglicans, Nonconformists, Catholics) aligned themselves with the political groups. The Anglicans and Catholics supported the Government in its plan to establish the local councils as the educational authorities, and the Nonconformists sided with the Liberal Opposition in its efforts to perpetuate and expand the authorities of the School Boards. The victory of the Government, and the destruction of the School Boards, had significant repercussions on the development of the concept of secondary education. It is, therefore, necessary to examine and interpret this political conflict and the events that led up to the passing of the Education Act of 1902.

The Education Act of 1902. The Bryce Commission had previously suggested the restriction of the School Boards to elementary education, and the setting up of separate authorities for secondary and technical education.[63] The 1896 attempt to implement this recommendation had failed. A second possible solution was to make the School

Boards the sole educational authority for all types of education, elementary, secondary and technical. This idea was supported not only by the School Boards themselves, but also by the Liberals. However, it was strongly opposed by the Conservatives, who, as was indicated above, were against the existence of the School Boards altogether. Moreover, the establishment of the School Boards as the sole educational authority was rendered difficult by the fact that (a) they were called into existence to "fill the gaps," and consequently they controlled only a part of elementary education itself, the rest being still in the hands of voluntary agencies and specifically the Church;[64] and (b) their area of administration was small. The issue was further complicated by the fact that the Established Church, e.g., the Anglicans, came out strongly against the School Boards and threw their support behind the Conservative Party, whereas the Nonconformists supported the School Boards and backed the Liberal Party.[65]

A third solution was the destruction of the School Boards and the setting up of the county and borough councils as the units of local educational administration. Though this proposal was fraught with dangers, it was skilfully carried to fruition by the Government with the help of two outstanding figures, Robert Morant and Sidney Webb.

Robert Morant was in 1895 appointed Assistant Director of the Office of Special Inquiries and Reports, and, during the time he served in that capacity, he made valuable contributions to the work that Department produced under Sadler's directorship. In 1899 Morant left his job and became Sir John Gorst's private secretary. An imperialist by training (he had been for several years an intimate adviser of the King of Siam) and an efficient administrator, Morant put his skill at intrigue behind the Government. He saw that there was no other practical solution to the administrative muddle but the abolition of the School Boards. His first attack against these *ad hoc* local authorities came in 1899 when he summoned Dr. William Garnett, Secretary of the London Technical Education Board, and pointed out to him that it was illegal for the London School Board to spend grants which it obtained from the Science and Art Department for the support of higher grade schools. Garnett induced Cockerton, a Government auditor, to withhold payments for such schools. Though the London Board appealed, the appeal failed, and the Court of Appeal confirmed Cockerton's decision. As a result of the Cockerton Judgment, the Board of Education introduced a Minute whereby a new type of higher grade school was established which went by the name of "higher elementary school."[66] More will be said about this institution later. It will suffice to mention here that this Minute did not particularly foster the growth of "higher elementary schools," very few of which were subsequently established.

Morant then proceeded with his plan to rally support for the final abolition of the School Boards, thus paving the way for the provision of a different administrative framework for secondary education. He found ready support from several powerful groups. There were those who were firm believers in the traditional "grammar school" type of secondary education, e.g., the grammar school teachers, and the politically dominant Conservatives, especially Sir John Gorst and Arthur Balfour;[67] there was the Anglican clergy who wanted to strengthen the voluntary schools by placing them on the local rates; there were ambivalent Liberals or others who favored a national system as a function of the permanently established local administrative units; and, finally, there were the Fabians, and the National Union of Teachers.

At the same time that Morant was working for the destruction of the School Boards and the establishment of secondary education on a more permanent local basis, a short Fabian tract appeared, entitled *The Education Muddle and the Way Out*. Webb, who has been credited with authorship of this tract,[68] called for "administrative unity," and, after pointing to the inadequacy and weakness of the School Boards to supply this unity, he suggested that the county councils be made the administrative authorities "responsible for the provision and maintenance of every kind and grade of education within its area."[69]

As for London and the county boroughs, it was suggested that the School Boards "for the most part be left untouched." But, in certain county boroughs (Bury, Chester, Lincoln, Preston, St. Helens, Stockport, Wigan, Blackburn, Oxford or Worcester), the Fabian tract called for the abolition of the School Boards and the placing of responsibility for all "grades" of education in the hands of the town councils. In the remaining cases, viz., London and forty-seven county boroughs, it was suggested that the abolition of the School Boards, or the transfer of their authority, be left to their own discretion.

Concerning the central authority, the Fabian document proposed that the Board of Education be empowered to inspect, criticize and audit all types and grades of education "maintained" or "aided" by Parliament or by endowments and trust funds from deceased persons.[70]

The Education Muddle and the Way Out was widely read. Edward Pease wrote that ". . . the authorities at Whitehall were so anxious to see it that they were supplied with proofs before publication; and the tract, when published, was greedily devoured by perplexed M.P.'s."[71] And Sir John Gorst, himself, circulated it among the Ministers as a "Cabinet paper."[72] Moreover, when the Bill was introduced, and, while it was being piloted by Balfour through Parliament, Webb never ceased to give guidance and support for it. In her *Our Partnership*, Mrs. Webb talks of the frequent visits by leading members of the Government, the Opposition, and by Morant, to 41 Grosvenor Road, the "hard little house," as H. G. Wells described the Webb residence, and of their consultations with Sidney about the passing of the Bill.[73]

The Bill was introduced in the House of Commons on March 24, 1902, by Balfour, and the debate started in June. In Part I, the Bill provided that the Local Education Authority, or the L. E. A. as it came to be called, be: (1) the council of every county, (2) the council of every county borough, (3) the Council of the Isles of Scilly, (4) the council of every borough with a population of over ten thousand people, and (5) the council of every urban district with a population of over twenty thousand people.[74]

In Part II, the Bill dealt with "higher education." It provided that the county and county borough councils be made responsible for both higher and elementary education. As to higher education it stipulated the following:

> The local education authority shall consider the educational needs of their area and take such steps as seem to them desirable, after consultation with the Board of Education, to supply or aid the supply of education other than elementary and to promote the general coordination of all forms of education.[75]

Part III of the Bill was concerned with elementary education. It provided that the councils of boroughs with a population of over ten thousand people, and the councils of urban districts with a population of over twenty thousand, be the educational authorities for elementary education only.[76]

Each "local education authority" was required to appoint an education committee which would include women. The majority of this committee were to be members of the council, and the rest, persons of educational or other relevant experience.[77]

The Bill further provided that elementary Board schools (to be called council or provided schools) and voluntary (denominational) schools be brought under the control of the new authorities. The nature of the control of the voluntary schools would be as follows: A voluntary school would be eligible to receive public funds from local rates, but the provision and maintenance of buildings would be the responsibility of the managers. Moreover, the managers, one third of whom were to be appointed by the L. E. A., would maintain the right to appoint and dismiss teachers subject to the approval of the L. E. A., and would control religious instruction. On the other hand, the L. E. A. was to be responsible for and to control "all secular instruction." Although the managers were in charge of religious instruction, which in most cases meant denominational instruction,[78] the "conscience clause" would apply equally to both "non-provided" and "provided" schools, and to "higher" education as well.[79]

The character of the Bill gave rise to one of the most heated political controversies in English history. The discussion in the Commons had hardly started when it became obvious that the placing of the voluntary schools on the rates would rekindle the fierce animosities between the Anglicans and Catholics on the one hand, and the Dissenters or Nonconformists on the other. The former supported the Bill because they saw in it the salvation of their impoverished institutions; the latter objected to it because it provided that public money be spent for sectarian purposes. Furthermore, the destruction of the School Boards, which by that time had fallen under the influence of people from the Dissenting groups, meant that the Nonconformists would lose the power they had gained over popular education. The Nonconformists also resented the fact that in certain areas they were forced to send their children to Church schools because no other school existed. They had hoped that poverty would have brought about an end to this state of affairs, and non-sectarian schools would have been established in the place of Church schools. By this Bill, however, they saw a continuation rather than a termination of this situation.

The Nonconformist position was vigorously advanced inside and outside the Parliament. The Liberal M.P.'s, many of whom were religious Dissenters, had always been the staunchest upholders of the School Boards. On the fourth day of the debate, Mr. Lloyd George, a backbencher and a Baptist, with brilliant eloquence presented the Nonconformist grievance, and opened the course that the discussion was to take. In Lloyd George's words:

The Churches have over 12,000 schools in the country, which are mission rooms to educate the children of the poor in the principles of the Church. In 8,000 parishes there are no other schools, and the whole machinery of the law is there utilised to force the Nonconformist children into them.

The Church, according to Lloyd George, had "exclusive patronage to 60,000 appointments" in the Civil Service, to "one of the best, most remunerative and most honourable careers that a child can possibly enter upon." He contended that there were 1,000,000 children born of Nonconformist parents. In spite of the fact that this number included probably the best candidates for teaching, they could not advance beyond the level of a "lower grade official." No Nonconformist, according to him, could be a headmaster or enter a church-training college.[80]

Lloyd George was also quick to see in this educational measure an excellent political opportunity to bring the divided Liberal Party together, and to rally public opinion behind the Liberals by stressing the "clerical" aspects of the Bill. "This is the only country," he said, "I have ever heard of where, the community being divided up between five or six powerful sects, one sect has monopolised the control of education." According to him, the Bill was nothing else but a calculated attempt on the part of the Government and their Church allies to "rivet the clerical yoke on thousands of parishes."[81] A similar feeling was expressed by the Liberal Unionists who at this time were the allies of the Conservatives. Dr. J. G. Clover, a leader of the Liberal Unionists outside Parliament, in a letter to *The Times* wrote:

Our Conservative allies in Unionism cannot expect that we should renounce on a vital question like education the essential principle of Liberalism—representation with taxation, the soundest education of the people without waste of public money, and the liberation of teachers from ecclesiastical tests. It cannot be denied that support of the Bill which is to determine for the future our educational system would come very near to such an abandonment.[82]

Among the Liberal front-benchers in the House of Commons, who were strongly against the Bill, there was James Bryce, who called it not an Education Bill, but a "Volun-

tary Schools Relief Bill." "This settlement," Bryce asserted, "is not a compromise; it is an absolute and uncon-
ditional surrender to clerical claims." Bryce also criticized
the Bill on the grounds that it ". . . does little if anything for secondary education. . . . It does not impose
any duty on the new authorities to provide secondary education. It is purely permissive."[83]

Outside Parliament the Nonconformist position was
vigorously upheld by John Clifford, a Baptist, by Hugh
Price Hughes, a Wesleyan, and by the Reverend Dr. Guin-
ness Rogers. At a massive meeting of the Evangelical Free
Churches held in London on April 15, 1902, which, in addition to the above-mentioned Nonconformist leaders, included many Liberal Members of Parliament and
thousands of other Dissenters, several resolutions were
passed unanimously condemning the Bill "as an entire
reversal of the leading principles of 1870," and as "a violation of public justice." In Clifford's words, "It was not
like the curate's egg, good in parts, it was bad altogether."
Reflecting the Liberal-Nonconformist reaction to the Conservative-Anglican coalition, and amid "loud cheers", Clifford characterized the measure as "a Bill for Cecilizing
education and clericalizing it."[84]

Within the Cabinet itself, Chamberlain, the leader of
the Liberal Unionists, was known to be a supporter of the
School Boards and a Nonconformist. At first, in order to
pacify Chamberlain, an optional clause was inserted which
would not have made it *obligatory* on any local authority
to adopt the Bill, but later in the discussion, while Chamberlain was away recovering from an accident, this optional clause was dropped.

Not all Liberals, however, were against the Education
Bill. Richard Haldane, for example, one of the leaders of

parliamentary Opposition, did not vote against the second reading. He felt that educational reform was necessary, and he particularly welcomed the setting up of single educational authorities, for this would have helped to correlate the various educational functions.[85] He also believed that the voluntary schools should be "mended" rather than "ended," since there were too many pupils attending them.[86]

The Church position was advanced in Parliament by the Conservative Party. When Balfour first introduced the Bill, he made it clear that any educational legislation proposed by the Unionists (Conservatives and Liberal Unionists) would take into account the continuation and support of the voluntary schools.[87] This, of course, was welcomed by the Catholics as well.[88] And in order to pacify the evangelicals who feared that the High Churchmen would introduce High Church practices into the voluntary schools, the so called Kenyon Staley Clause was inserted. This clause stated that "religious instruction given in a public elementary school not provided by the L. E. A., shall as regards its character be in accordance with the provisions (if any) of the trust deed relating thereto."[89] The Church position was strengthened even more when, in the midst of the debates, Balfour became Prime Minister and took personal charge of the Bill, and Robert Morant supplanted Kekewich and became Permanent Secretary of the Board of Education. Morant was determined to reorganize secondary education, not on any radical lines or on an *ad hoc* theory, but on a compromise between the idea of the "welfare state" and the idea of voluntarism, or between collectivism and individualism.

The establishment of the county councils and county borough councils instead of the School Boards as the local educational authorities was accepted by the Conservative Party, by the supporters of the grammar school type of education, by the National Union of Teachers, by the Fabians, and by labor organizations. Furthermore, such an educational organization was in line with the trend of the period, which was not based on an *ad hoc* theory of local government, but on the councils of the counties and county boroughs, which were elected by the ratepayers and were responsible to the public for their expenditures. Similarly the establishment of the Board as a central educational authority was accepted, not only by various political groups, including, of course, the dominant Conservatives and Liberal Unionists, but also by the best educational opinion of the period.[90]

The nature of the functions of the central and the local authorities and the relation of the two in regard to the provision of secondary education were debated at the time. As it was indicated previously, there were voices raised against the "voluntariness," the "permissiveness," and the generality of the educational legislation of 1899 and 1902. By the 1899 Act the Board of Education could "inspect any school supplying secondary education," but this statement was qualified by the words "desiring to be so inspected." Furthermore, by the same Act, the President of the Board of Education was charged with the general responsibility of "the superintendence of matters relating to education."[91] By the 1902 Act the local authorities were empowered to consider the educational needs of their area and to take "such steps *as seem to them desirable* after consultation with the Board of Education, to supply or aid the supply of education other than elementary."[92] The Board exercised its influence through regulations which governed the parliamentary grants.

In the light of the provisions of the Education Act of 1944, those of the 1899 and 1902 Acts may today seem un-

important and too permissive. For in 1944 it was made
the *duty* of the Minister of Education to promote the education of the people of England and Wales, and "to secure
the effective execution by local authorities, under his *direction* and *control*, of the national policy for providing a
varied and comprehensive educational service in every
area."[93] If, however, we assessed the early legislation in
terms of the conditions of the time, it would be difficult
to envisage a situation where a greater measure of State
interference or public "control" could have been possible.
The Bryce Commission, for example, specifically recommended that the function of the central authority should
not be to *control*, but to *supervise* secondary education,
not to *dictate*, but to *stimulate* local efforts and initiative.[94]

The principle of voluntarism which underlay the concept of laissez-faire was, by the end of the century,
undermined, yet no radical shift from voluntarism to State
or public control was envisaged or advocated. Even if it
had been, however, it would not have been politically
feasible, considering the tremendous influence of the
Church, the views of the dominant Conservatives, the
traditional freedom and popularity of the grammar
schools, the number of pupils who were educated in
voluntary institutions, and contemporary educational
opinion.[95]

By providing that voluntary schools be placed on the
rates, the Education Act of 1902 strengthened voluntarism, and gave the measure the character of a compromise.
Yet, by providing that the councils of the counties and
the county boroughs assume responsibility and control
of all "secular instruction" in elementary schools, this
measure marked a significant step in the transition of
power from voluntary bodies to public authorities.

Of great importance for the development of English secondary education was the clause establishing local authorities whose task was the consideration of "the educational needs of their areas," and the taking of "such steps as seemed to them desirable . . . to supply or aid the supply of education other than elementary." This also was a compromise measure, for it was not made the *duty* of the local authorities to supply "higher education." Yet it was a very significant measure. Here, for the first time in English educational history, the State interfered in the provision of secondary education, and, although no national system was created, the foundations for such a system were laid. The "democratically" elected local bodies, which were dependent on the public for money, in cooperation with the central body, were made responsible for the advancement of secondary education.

Once the organizational and administrative foundations were laid, the development of public secondary education depended on the principles and policies of the Board of Education and the local educational authorities. As it was indicated above, the School Boards favored a conception of secondary education that was the organic outgrowth of the elementary schools, hence they were in support of the higher grade schools. But with the destruction of the School Boards and with the Cockerton Judgment, the higher grade schools were placed in jeopardy. Were their "progressive" characteristics (technical and scientific curricula) to be destroyed in favor of the "traditional" grammar school education? The answer to this question forms part of the answer to a larger question which may be formulated as follows: What was the concept of secondary education favored by the Board of Education and the newly created local authorities? The next chapter will seek to answer this question.

V

The Nature and Function of Secondary Education, 1902-6

Few regulations have had greater effect upon the evolution of English educational policy, or have aroused more controversy among historians, than those issued by the Board of Education after the 1902 Act. It has been asserted that, as a result of the Board's policies, especially those initiated by Robert Morant in 1904, the classical literary tradition of the grammar schools was imposed upon the newly established system of public education. This, according to the critics, stunted the growth of other types of secondary schools and plagued secondary education until the passing of the Education act of 1944. In view of the significance of the Board's policies, and the claims made in connection with them, it is necessary to re-examine and to assess them in the light of the contemporary social and educational conditions.

130

A SCIENTIFIC BIAS IN THE CURRICULUM

In the two years following the Education Act of 1902, the Board of Education made "scientific instruction" the dominant criterion for purposes of financial support of secondary day schools. Such schools were classified into two Divisions, A and B.[1] "Division A" schools were required to provide a thorough and progressive course in science, "together with the subjects of a general education." Specifically, the following provisions were made:

Not less than 13 hours per week must be allotted to instruction in the obligatory subjects, of which not more than five hours may be allotted to Mathematics. Not less than 10 hours must be allotted to the other approved subjects, which must include English subjects and at least one foreign language. Two of these 10 hours may be allotted to some form of Manual Instruction, and two others of them to Mathematics or Art.[2]

Following the 1902 enactment, it was also made possible for higher grade schools to be converted into "Division A" schools, thus drawing grants from the Government as well as from the local authorities, and at the same time retaining their predominantly scientific curriculum. In addition, many smaller grammar schools, owing to their impecuniosity, were converted first into "Schools of Science," and then into "Division A" schools, which in reality was another name for "Schools of Science."[3]

"Division B" schools were largely schools of the traditional grammar school type, although, starting with the year 1902, some county or municipal schools and some schools supported by religious bodies were included. But according to the provisions of the 1902 and 1903 *Regulations*, such schools could qualify for parliamentary grants only in respect to their science courses.[4] This situation created a disparity in the scale of grants. In 1902, grant-aided "Division A" schools numbered more than grant-aided "Division B" schools. According to the statistics given by the Board of Education in its report for the year 1902–1903, up to December 31, 1902, there were 214 "Division A" schools recognized for grants, as against 144 "Division B" schools, 83 of which were in England and 61 in Wales and Monmouthshire. Of the "Division B" schools in England, 69 were endowed schools; 8, county or municipal schools; and 4, schools run by religious bodies.[5] "Division A" schools continued to outnumber "Division B" schools, and continued to secure more grants by virtue of the nature of their curriculum. Speaking in the House of Commons on July 9, 1903, Sir William Anson, the Parliamentary Secretary of the Board of Education gave the following information: "I should say there are 226 schools now receiving grants in the A division and 160 in the B division; and in both we are adopting the principle of the block grant; that is to say, we are paying for curriculum and not for specific subjects.[6] It should further be noted here that, in addition to the grants given for scientific subjects of the type mentioned above, the Board of Education authorized grants for scientific and practical subjects given in "Science Classes," "Schools of Art" and "Art Classes," as well as for science scholarships, bursaries, etc.[7]

The Board's policy, which indicates a bias towards scientific instruction, was pursued in spite of previous criticisms at the neglect of humanistic studies, and in spite of the fear first voiced by the Bryce Commission in 1895 that a "lopsided development in education" might take place. Similar criticisms came from several other directions: from statesmen, Her Majesty's Inspectors, educators, clergymen and even from technologists themselves.[8]

Such criticisms and anxieties, however, should not be construed as implying that the study of science, theoretical and applied, was deprecated. On the contrary, it was generally believed that, if England were to survive as a commercial and industrial nation in the face of foreign competition, it must of necessity strengthen this type of education. What the various segments of educational and public opinion were alarmed at was (a) early specialization, without previous grounding in a general liberal education, and (b) the indiscriminate conversion of impoverished small grammar schools into scientific and practical schools. *The Journal of Education* summed up contemporary opinion as follows:

It is significant sign of the times to notice as we have done month by month, the very large measure of support given by public speakers of weight to our contention that technical education is the narrowing *coping-stone* built on the sound foundation of a general secondary education. In too many cases the harm is already done, and well meant efforts are made by well meaning people to turn scientific experts at the age of sixteen.[9]

The Board's policy heightened the criticisms and discontent against the strengthening of "scientific instruction" (theoretical and applied) at the expense of literary and humanistic education. C. A. Buckmaster, the Chief Inspector of Schools and Classes in the Southern Division, quoted the inspector responsibile for the counties of Cornwall, Devon and Somerset, as saying:

Most of these schools are undoubtedly efficient both as regards buildings and equipment and teaching power. The science subjects are well taught, but it is difficult to make the same statement with regard to English and other literary work. The time-tables are distinctly overloaded with science in several cases and insufficient attention is given to languages, history and geography.[10]

J. W. Headlam, another inspector, reported some disturbing discrepancies. He noticed that in many cases a complete reaction had taken place, and that the traditional classical principles on which grammar schools were based were completely supplanted by "scientific principles."[11] Whereas, according to him, large grants were made to students for their natural science subjects, an extra fee was charged for the study of Greek.

Headlam observed the following "undesirable" characteristics in the developing trend: (a) that Greek had practically disappeared from nearly all these schools, (b) that in many schools Latin was also disappearing, (c) that in almost every case the boys were "completely and absolutely ignorant" of elementary facts in the history and life of the people whose language they were learning, (d) that instruction in English was based exclusively on text-books and was given by inadequately prepared masters, (e) that only English history was taught, and (f) that history and geography were perfunctorily taught without any emphasis on "general principles" or "historical causes."[12] In addition, he pointed out, there was a lack of library facilities. "To teach history, language, or literature without books," he wrote, "is as absurd as to teach science without apparatus."[13]

To Headlam this state of affairs was most alarming. The neglect of literary studies and the indifference to types of instruction other than the natural sciences and mathematics could not but have "a most harmful influence on the intellect and character of the nation."[14]

Headlam's report reached the House of Commons. Sir William Anson, the Parliamentary Secretary of the Board of Education, was alarmed at the existing situation,[15] and A. H. Acland, Liberal M.P. and a member of the Education Authority of the West Riding of Yorkshire, felt humiliated.[16] Anson urged that such a "lop-sided" tendency be checked and the situation be corrected in one of two ways: either by altering the conditions under which grants were made, or by paying grants "if we are thoroughly satisfied that other studies are not being neglected."[17]

The view that literary and humanistic subjects were being superseded by scientific subjects was shared by other influential political figures. James Bryce, one of the leading members of the Liberal Opposition and a respected educational thinker, admitted that the "lop-sided development" he had feared in 1895 had already taken place.[18]

It should be noted that Bryce was calling, as indeed were all others who spoke on the subject, for a balance in the curriculum of the secondary, especially the Grade II and Grade III secondary schools, where knowledge of science would take its place along with other subjects as an essential element of a liberal education.[19] Bryce concurred with Anson's views on the significance of literary teaching, and expressed the hope that the Board of Education and the local authorities would bring secondary education "abreast of the needs of the times."[20]

It is against this background that the educational policy initiated in 1904 by the Board of Education must be examined.

THE 1904 REGULATIONS

Although the Board of Education supported schools which were referred to as "secondary," there was no official statement on what that term meant or involved. Grants were disbursed according to subjects most of which were of a scientific nature. This had created a great deal of confusion and, as noted above, uneasiness about the undue prominence of science in the curriculum. In order to bring some sort of order, the Board, under the leadership of Robert Morant, issued in 1904 the now famous *Regulations for Secondary Schools*, which embodied the first official conception of secondary education. A clear definition of the nature and function of the secondary schools had become necessary, according to Morant, if a national system was to be established.[21]

The Board found it "impracticable" to define secondary *education*, and instead defined a secondary *school*:

. . . the term Secondary School means a Day or Boarding school which offers to each of its scholars, up to and beyond the age of 16, a general education, physical, mental and moral, given through a complete graded course of instruction, of wider scope and more advanced degree than that given in Elementary Schools.[22]

Morant then, expressing the views of the Board, described more fully the characteristics and purposes of the "complete graded course of instruction." There were three "essentials" to this course: it must be general, it must be complete, and it must be graded in its various branches. By general, he meant that it should not be confined to only one branch of knowledge, or to "a particular channel," be that pure and applied science, or literary and linguistic studies. Whatever the aims of the students might be after finishing school, they should all be given a general education which aimed at the development and exercise of all their "faculties."[23]

By complete, he meant that it "must be so planned as to lead up to a definite standard of acquirement in the various branches of instruction." Students might begin the course at the age of 8 or 9, or at 12 or 13 for those who went to elementary schools, and continue up to 16 or 17.

For those planning to proceed to the universities the age limit might even be extended to 18 or 19, but "as a rule the years from 12 or 13 up to 16 or 17 will be those during which it is most important that it should be carried on in accordance with a systematic and complete course.[24] And, by "graded," he meant that instruction should be progressive and there should not be repetition of lessions already learned.

In the Prefatory Memorandum the conditions under which grants were to be made were explicitly stated and the content of the curriculum was laid down in very exact terms. Grants were to be made only to schools which provided a four-year course, and the curriculum was to include both literary-humanistic and scientific studies. Of the weekly hours, at least seven and one-half were to be devoted to science and mathematics, 8 hours to English, history, geography and one foreign language. If a student took two foreign languages, the weekly hours of the latter subjects would rise to ten and one-half. In addition, the regulations provided that if two foreign languages were taken and Latin was not one of them, "the Board will require to be satisfied that the omission of Latin is for the advantage of the School."

Such a uniform content was qualified by certain exceptions which allowed for considerable variation and elasticity. In the first place, special provisions for girls' schools were made: "In a girls' school in which the total number of hours of instruction is less than 22 per week, the time given to Science and Mathematics may be reduced to one-third, provided that at least 3 hours are given to Science.[25] In the second place, the language requirements could be waived by special permission of the Board if the English course provided adequate linguistic and literary training.[26] In the third place, provision No. 11 stated that special science courses "of an advanced character" could be organized according to local requirements.[27] Furthermore, in certain localities where a single school was the only available source of higher education it was made possible to establish "sides" in the third and fourth years of the course.[28]

In the same year in which the above *Regulations* appeared, the Board of Education addressed itself to the training of elementary school teachers. The adequate preparation of teachers for the elementary schools was, at this time, a matter occupying the attention not only of Morant, but also of those concerned with the general educational welfare of the people;[29] and, of great importance was the fact that there was a general educational concensus that a "wide and liberal course of study" or a "general education" was an indispensable prerequisite for the efficient performance of the elementary teacher's duties.[30]

The 1904 Regulations continued to be in effect for many years.[31] The ideas embodied in them have since given rise to bitter criticism among educational historians.

The salient points of these criticisms have been: (a) that the Board's policy was based on a narrow concept of liberal education; (b) that it was based on a faulty psychology, viz., faculty psychology; and (c) that, by taking into consideration only the grammar school academic tradition of secondary education, other forms of postprimary education, e.g., technical and practical, suffered from atrophy, with results little short of disastrous for the subsequent development of English secondary education. These were essentially the main points of criticism by R. F. Young,[32] the Secretary of the Consultative Committee responsible for the Spens Report of 1938, and by H. C.

Dent,[33] John Graves,[34] S. J. Curtis,[35] and H. C. Barnard.[36] Dent and Graves went further than the others by holding Morant solely responsible for the ideas underlying the Regulations. They claimed that Morant imposed an academic classical system of education upon the State system and utterly ignored the idea that secondary education "is inclusive of technical."[37]

When, however, assessment of the Board's ideas and policies is placed in its proper historical context, it is indeed difficult to hold Morant *solely* responsible for the emerging official conception of secondary education, or to blame the Board for foisting upon an unsuspecting public an undesirable pattern of schooling.

An exception to the previously mentioned historical interpretations is the research of Olive Banks, who has adduced evidence to show that the 1904 Regulations were "the result of a reaction against early specialization in technical and scientific subjects, and reflected the main body of educational opinion at the time."[38] Banks has sought to correct certain assessments by pointing out (a) that the Board's policy was a "compromise" between two traditions (the classical-literary of the grammar schools and the scientific-technical-practical of the higher grade schools), rather than abandonment of the one in favor of the other; (b) that contemporary educational opinion favored the strengthening of secondary general education; (c) that the local education authorities as well as the parents approved either openly or tacitly the Board's regulations; and (d) that the secondary schools were assigned an important role in the education of future pupil teachers, one which could not be performed adequately without a strong liberal education background.[39]

Although Banks' findings have thrown new light on this

controversy and have opened a new way to set the historical record straight, they do not present all the factors that
would fully illuminate the Board's conception, or would
account for its favorable acceptance by the local authorities, the parents, and the educationists. In order to arrive
at a full understanding of the contemporary situation, it is
necessary to inquire into the prevalent ideologies concerning the meaning and scope of secondary education, as well
as its functions in the British society of the time.

MEANING AND SCOPE OF SECONDARY EDUCATION

The 1904 Regulations did not specify the meaning of
secondary education, but limited themselves to a definition of a secondary school. For an understanding of what
this type of education denoted in terms of aims, content,
and functions, we must turn to contemporary opinions by
leading thinkers and groups.

No one devoted more time and energy to an examination of this theme than Michael Sadler. As a member of
the Bryce Commission, Sadler was responsible for the first
statement of the meaning of secondary education that appeared in an official document. The ambiguities in the
Bryce Commission's definition were discussed in Chapter
II of this study. Sadler's views become clearer when we
examine his reports written after 1902 on behalf of various local education authorities. In these reports it is clear
that Sadler considered a humanistic-literary type of curriculum as the distinctive characteristic of a liberal education and *mutatis mutandis* of the secondary schools.

In the *Report on Secondary & Technical Education in
Huddersfield* (notice here the distinction he draws), Sadler conceived the task of secondary schools as being first
and foremost "to humanize," and *then* to "impart effi-

ciency for life as it has to be lived."[40] Undue insistence on science or mathematics, he felt, was "a great defect." Speaking about a commercial community such as Liverpool, whose educational problem he called "the education of commercial England in epitome," Sadler warned against making "commercial knowledge the dominant aim of its secondary education." Rather, he said, the dominant aim should be "the real and vivid teaching of the humanities," which he identified as "the mother tongue, literature, history, geography, and two foreign languages, preferably Latin and French."[41] Sadler advocated that science and mathematics should be included in any scheme of liberal training and welcomed the Board's policy which took scientific subjects into account; but it is quite clear that to him "the linguistic emphasis," the glory of the older grammar school, should constitute the core of the curriculum.[42]

Sadler was regarded as one of the leading educational figures of the time and was frequently consulted by education authorities which were setting up plans to implement the provisions of the 1902 Act. Other statements by the county councils show that an essentially general academic curriculum with major emphasis in the humanities was what many of these authorities understood secondary education to mean. For example, the Lancashire County Council strongly endorsed the abolition of the previous classification of secondary schools into "A and B Schools" and stated that "from an educational point of view the B course is the better one for pupils up to 16 years of age." The reasons given were that: (a) "it allows for a very wide curriculum, embracing an adequate amount of literary work," and (b) it "affords a sound training in literary subjects."[43] Similar views were expressed in the

Report of the Education Committee of the West Riding County Council,[44] and by F. H. Millington, the Vice-Chairman of the Higher Education Sub-Committee of Norfolk.[45]

When these views are considered with those of Her Majesty's Inspectors and the political figures discussed earlier in this chapter, it is clear that those who expressed themselves on secondary education envisaged such an education as essentially academic and with major emphasis on the literary humanistic studies. This type of education was justified on the grounds that it disciplined the mind, which was considered a necessary prerequisite for any specialized technical or professional training. Although Thorndike and Woodworth had published a pioneer study against faculty psychology in 1901, there is no evidence to show that their findings had any impact on English pedagogical thought.

On Morant's and the Board's alleged predisposition to the "classical or at any rate the Latin tradition," it would be of interest to observe that at a meeting of the Incorporated Association of Assistant Masters in Secondary Schools, a motion deprecating "the excessive importance accorded to Latin in the Secondary School Regulations," was "negatived by twenty votes to seven."[46] The evidence shows that there were many others who staunchly defended Latin as an important ingredient of a general liberal education.[47]

THE ROLE OF THE SECONDARY SCHOOL IN CONTEMPORARY SOCIETY

In addition to such prevalent views concerning the character of the secondary school curriculum, and perhaps more important than these, one must carefully examine

the role that the secondary school was perceived to perform in the contemporary English society. The secondary
school was perceived to be a selective institution, not the
logical sequel of the elementary school. At their Liverpool
Conference, the Chairman of the Incorporated Association of Assistant Masters in Secondary Schools empha-
tically stated that "secondary education was not the
coping-stone of elementary education."[48] The secondary
school continued to be regarded as essentially a school for
the middle classes and for only those bright children of
the lower classes who gained admission to it through examinations and the granting of scholarships or bursaries.
All available evidence shows that the class idea of the
secondary schools, and indeed of other forms of education,
was deeply entrenched in the minds of contemporary Englishmen. Michael Sadler, whose views have often been
contrasted to those of Morant, drew a distinction between
secondary schools and higher elementary schools (the type
of post-elementary school created after 1900), in terms of
both the social background of students and their vocational destinations.[49]

It was previously shown that in 1895 when the Bryce
Commission issued its Report there was general consensus
that secondary education should not be free, nor should it
be for everybody. The Commission itself, which, it should
be remembered, was headed by the leading Liberal James
Bryce and included Michael Sadler, envisaged a class conception of secondary education with ample provision for
scholarships and exhibitions as a means of "enabling selected children of the poorer parents to climb the educational ladder."[50] And the term "selected children" the
Commission had defined as "candidates of exceptional
rather than average ability."[51] The middle-class associa-

tion of secondary education was taken for granted by the Board of Education as well. In the official report for the year 1908–9, Morant wrote:

> The words "secondary" and "middle class" came to be thought of as meaning the same or nearly the same thing. The idea that elementary and secondary schools represent not successive stages of education but alternative kinds of education meant for different social classes is deeply rooted, and may be said to have dominated practice until recently.[52]

This conception was taken for granted not only by the upper and middle classes, but also by the representatives and spokesmen of the working-class strata of society. There is no evidence to show that the working-class groups of the period formulated a clear-cut statement of secondary education for all, or that they envisaged different types of secondary schools from the existing ones. In their programs, both the Labour Party and the Trade Unions called for equalization of educational advantages, but by this they meant more bursaries and scholarships for working class children to climb the educational ladder and secure more positions in the secondary schools.[53] There was as yet no uniform social philosophy among the various groups which in 1900 had gathered together to form the Labour Party. The Independent Labour Party frequently advocated traditional Liberal principles and sided with the Nonconformists against the Education Act of 1902; the Fabians had sided with the Unionists in support of the Act and generally pursued a policy of their own that alienated them from other socialist or labor groups; and the Trade Unions were interested more in improving labor working conditions than in anything else.[54] As regards education, the Labour group in Parliament took a very active part in the reform for the feeding of necessitous elementary school children,[55] a measure which will be discussed later. But, so far as secondary education was concerned, there are no indications that at this time the Labour groups envisaged any radical transformation of the existing state of affairs. If this was true of the leaders, it was even truer of the rank and file of the working groups themselves. Masterman observed that what the rank and file of the laboring classes wanted most, was to be "left alone."

It was thought says Charles Booth, of a certain experiment in East London, that as the poor were not going to the churches they would attend the Hall of Science. When the Hall of Science was opened, it was as deserted as the churches. The people wanted neither religion nor its antidote. All they wanted was to be left alone . . . They don't want to be cleaned, enlightened, inspected, drained . . . They don't want compulsory thrift, elevation to remote standards of virtue and comfort, irritation into intellectual or moral progress.[56]

It seems clear that secondary education during the immediate years following the Act of 1902 was not regarded as the natural sequel to elementary education. The secondary school continued to be regarded as essentially a middle class school, and as a school preparing students for professional careers which carried higher income and prestige.

People accepted it as such, and the more ambitious working-class parents saw it as an agency for their child to enter white-collar occupations and thereby rise in the social hierarchy, rather than as an elite institution to be done away with. For, in spite of the apathy quoted previously, many skilled artisans, clerks and tradespeople sought an education beyond the elementary stage. In order to meet this demand, the Board of Education recommended the establishment of higher elementary schools. But to the parent of modest means such schools did not open the same opportunities, nor did they offer the same rewards as the secondary schools. This perhaps partly accounts for the failure of the higher elementary schools and the rapid growth of the secondary schools established by the local education authorities.

Although the secondary school continued to recruit most of its students from the middle classes, the very fact that it began to be viewed as an agency of social mobility marked a significant step in the development of secondary education. The mobility function of the secondary school is to be seen in the central role assigned to it in the training of elementary school teachers. Elementary school teachers were recruited for the most part from the lower classes and they received their training in pupil-teacher centers which offered a minimum of education beyond the elementary school. Beginning, however, with 1903 prospective elementary teachers were to receive a secondary type of education before they were admitted to Pupil-Teacher Centres.[57] The object of the Board's policy was to strengthen the liberal background of elementary school teachers. But it was also felt that a secondary school type of education would elevate the status of the teaching profession and break down the social barriers between elementary and secondary school teachers. This would create opportunities for "the sons and daughters of the laboring classes to the teaching profession in all its branches," thereby fulfilling "the widely felt desire to get up the so-called 'educational ladder' from the Elementary Schools to the Secondary Schools and thence to the Universities themselves."[58]

The social gains that a secondary school education conferred upon its recipients, relative to other types of post-elementary education, partly accounted for the popularity of the secondary schools and the failure of the higher elementary schools. Its selective nature and the career opportunities it opened made it a favored institution with the lower classes as well as with the middle classes. For it is a common phenomenon that, where society rewards various types of educational background differentially in terms of prestige, occupation and status, those institutions which confer higher prestige and position will also be the ones to which people will aspire most to send their children. The rapid increase in secondary schools between 1904 and 1906 indicates the value placed upon them by the local education authorities.

In 1903–4 there were 482 schools recognized by the Board as Secondary Schools, with nearly 86,000 students. In the following year there were 575, with nearly 95,000 pupils, while in 1905–6 the number of recognized schools had risen to 684. About 110 more schools applied for recognition at the beginning of the present school year.[59]

VI
Higher Elementary
Education

The Board's policy concerning secondary schools excluded a large number of children who wanted a more advanced type of instruction than that provided in the elementary schools. In order to meet this growing demand, an attempt was made to strengthen the system of higher elementary schools which were introduced by a special Minute in 1900. While, however, there seemed to be general agreement as to the need for such schools, there were disagreements as to what form they should take, and what their place should be in the evolving system of education vis-a-vis the secondary schools. It becomes necessary, therefore, to inquire into this type of post-primary education and to examine the various conflicts to which it gave rise at this formative stage of the development of the British system.

Higher elementary schools, established through a special Minute in 1900, were to give a more advanced type of instruction than that given in the public elementary schools. Their curriculum, "though not exclusively scientific," would, nevertheless, be given "a science basis," and they would prepare children for callings in which "scientific methods have to be employed."[1]

The attempt to establish such schools was not very successful, and their growth was very small indeed, as is clearly shown in Table I.

TABLE I
NUMBER OF HIGHER ELEMENTARY SCHOOLS
RECOGNIZED BY THE BOARD OF EDUCATION[2]

Year	Number of Schools	Number of Pupils
1900–1	18	2,872
1901–2	28	3,240
1902–3	29	6,616
1903–4	29	7,839

In 1905 the Board and the Government admitted that the attempt was a failure.[3] Sir William Anson went as far as to say that the original Minute had become "almost a dead letter."[4] Yet, re-emphasizing the fact that there were many children who could not go to secondary school,[5] especially as defined in the 1904 Regulations, the Board sought to meet the need by revising the regulations governing higher elementary schools.

In the "Code of Regulations" issued in 1905, a higher elementary school was defined as one which was intended for students who must begin an industrial employment or must enter the lower ranks of business at the age of fifteen. It would continue the work of the elementary school for a period of 3 years instead of the previous 4 (ages 12–15), but it would also provide a special and practical orientation.[6]

In this way the Board hoped that the newer type of school would fare better than the old, for the following reasons: first, the elasticity of the curriculum would lessen the cost (the former curriculum entailed elaborate buildings and equipment); and, second, the needs of different localities might be met better.[7] In setting up the curricula of the higher elementary schools, the local education authorities were advised to consider the general, the special and the practical elements of such institutions. They were asked to provide for the main types of specialization depending on whether the pupils planned to enter the "productive" or the "distributive" side of trade, and in rural areas to use this type of school for the training of teachers.[8]

In issuing these Regulations, the Board's purpose was twofold: first, to meet the growing demand for a "higher" form of education than that offered in the elementary schools; and, second, to "protect," so to speak, the standards of the secondary schools.[9]

The purpose and character of the higher elementary schools were discussed in greater detail in a special report issued in 1906 by the Consultative Committee of the Board. There it was also stated that higher elementary schools should offer a terminal three-year course (ages 12 to 15) to the higher ex-elementary school children who "as a class" will enter the lower ranks of commerce and industry;[10] that their aim should be to develop both moral and mental qualities and "the habit of applying one's mind and one's knowledge to what one has to do";[11] and that their distinguishing function should be to *prepare* for a trade, not to *teach* one. Thus, the Committee rejected specific technical instruction as the function of such schools. Rather, they should continue the general education of the elementary school, but with a "bent" towards its immediate usefulness.[12]

The Committee also drew certain distinctions between the higher elementary school and the secondary school. First, the higher elementary school was envisaged as a continuation of the elementary school: it was "an 'end-on' . . . to the ordinary elementary school." But the secondary school course was normally preceded by a primary course in a preparatory school or department which differed in character and method from the primary instruction given in the public elementary schools.[13] Second, the two types of schools differed with respect to the maximum age limit of the scholars who attended them. In the higher elementary school the age limit was fifteen, at the maximum; but in the secondary school it was sixteen, at the minimum. Third, as a consequence of the difference in the age limit, the plan of instruction differed. Fourth, the two types of schools prepared for different walks of life, "the one for the lower ranks of industry and commerce, the other for the higher ranks and for the liberal professions." As a consequence of this, the higher elementary school could only afford to teach "a limited number of subjects, and with a practical bias," whereas, the secondary school "has time for more subjects and a more theoretical and academic method of teaching." Finally, the two types of institutions differed in the social background of students.

. . . while, in the case of the secondary School, the home life may be expected to supplement and strengthen the school instruction, or, at least not to hamper it, in the case of the Higher Elementary School the home conditions, at best, do little to favour the end of school education, and at worst are antagonistic.[14]

The Committee also sought to justify the idea that the higher elementary school was the best type of institution suited to the class of students whose education would not extend beyond the age of 15 and who would seek immediate employment.[15] This school, in their opinion, would not only meet an existing need, but it would also aid the development of secondary education proper.[16]

The Board's efforts to formulate more precisely the concept of "higher elementary education" and to allow for elasticity and variation did not result in any spectacular growth of the type of school advocated. The statistics are quite unimpressive as is shown in Table II.

TABLE II
NUMBER OF HIGHER ELEMENTARY SCHOOLS
RECOGNIZED BY THE BOARD OF EDUCATION[18]

| Year | Number of Schools | | | Number of Scholars |
	Old Type	New Type	Total	
1905–6	24	4	28	7,562
1906–7	23	12	35	8,581
1907–8	19	16	35	7,670
1908–9	15	25	40	8,747
1909–10	1	44	45	9,525
1910–11	0	38	38	7,125
1911–12	0	41	41	7,706
1912–13	0	52	52	10,201[a]
1913–14	0	47	47	9,518[b]
1914–15		35	35	8,184
1915–16		33	33	7,943
1916–17		31	31	7,874
1917–18		30	30	7,874
1918–19		30	30	8,222

[a] The statistics for the year 1912–13 are unreliable. The Report of the Board of Education for the year 1912–13 gives the number of schools as 41 and the number of scholars as 8,025. See *Report of the Board of Education for the Year 1912–13* (London: H.M.S.O., 1913), p. 79.

[b] Unreliable statistics. Number of schools given in *Report of the Board of Education for the year 1914–15* is 36 and of scholars, 7,539. See *Report of the Board of Education for the Year 1914–15* (London: H.M.S.O., 1915), p. 26.

The general reaction to the Board's policy, especially after the Consultative Committee's Report, was of a mixed and at times unclear nature. In any case, local education authorities either responded coolly to the idea or rejected it outright.

In all the reports, which he wrote at the request of local authorities, Sadler recommended the establishment of higher elementary schools. Yet in his last report on behalf of the Education Committee of Essex he was critical of the Board's regulations.[17] He disagreed with the suggestion that French should be considered "solely in relation to the question of usefulness in employment." He rather felt that French could be introduced as an optional subject, but with a view to giving the children "a better understanding of their own language," and helping them "to a sympathetic understanding of the life and ideals of a foreign nation."[19] Furthermore, Sadler conceived of the aim and function of the higher elementary school in not quite the same "utilitarian" or "practical" terms as the Board did. Their "key note," according to him, should be "a general training, animated by a civic and national purpose."[20]

Sadler was specific on the differences in the curriculum of a higher elementary school and a middle secondary school. These in brief were: (a) that Latin should not be taught in the former school; (b) that, because of the shortness of the course, English literature and history should include "a different range of topics" and the sequence be treated differently; (c) that more time be given to "handicraft" in the higher elementary school than in the secondary; and (d) that in the teaching of mathematics more emphasis be placed on the practical and vocational needs of the students in the higher elementary schools.[21]

These comments, as well as those he made earlier in the report when he spoke about "the aims of secondary education,"[22] suggest that Sadler's general conception of the character of higher elementary education was not fundamentally different from his conception of secondary education, nor did he envisage the relation of the two types as distant.[23] He wanted the higher elementary school to be as good as the secondary, yet distinctive, in view of the difference in age limit, and in view of the class of pupils that would go to it. He accepted the class conception of secondary education as advanced by the Board, but at the same time he was against any possible insinuations at "cheapness" or "inferiority" or "nastiness" that might be made about post-primary instruction other than secondary.

More explicit criticisms of the Consultative Committee's conception of higher elementary education came from the National Union of Teachers (N.U.T.). In his presidential address to the N.U.T. Conference held at Oxford in April 1907, A. R. Pickles contended that the Board's sharp discrimination between the higher elementary school and the secondary school was a deliberate attempt to "fend off from the secondary schools proper all but a few of the children of the workers."[24]

At the same conference Yoxall brought forward a motion, which was wildly cheered and carried unanimously, denouncing the report of the Committee and demanding its withdrawal. *The Times* of London in its coverage of the conference recorded the following:

He (Yoxall) said that, although there were in the report good proposals, sound educational principles, and many ideas which the union had adopted and suggested, yet the whole thing was so snobbish and caddish as to make it altogether of no value, and they called for its withdrawal. They did not oppose higher elementary schools, which were no doubt a proper provision of higher education for the working man's child. He maintained that they must dignify, magnify, and glorify the upper standards of the ordinary elementary schools, and those who wished to go higher should go to the proper secondary schools.[25]

Utterances similar to Mr. Pickles' had been made two months earlier by Marshall Jackman, a past president of the N.U.T., at a conference convened by the Teachers' Guild of Great Britain and Ireland. Jackman is reported to have said that he felt bound to look upon higher elementary schools "as a dislocation of our educational system: they could only be tolerated as a stop-gap." If, according to him, there were a complete system of secondary schools, "higher elementary schools would not be wanted to any great extent," and unless care was taken he was afraid that the proposed scheme for higher elementary schools "might mean the side-tracking of the education of the children of the workers."[26]

Pickles' views, which reflected the attitude of the N.U.T., were shared by *The Journal of Education*. When the Consultative Committee's Report appeared, this journal refrained from any "wholesale condemnation," but it *did* deprecate the insinuation of "inferiority," and "class distinctions," which, it felt, were implicit in the report.[27] This criticism was renewed in an editorial note in May, 1907, in which the N.U.T. Conference's pronouncements about the "anti-democratic" views of the Consultative Committee's Report were "welcomed."[28]

The reaction, however, of the "professional" groups was of a divided nature. For example, when the question was

discussed at the annual general meeting of the Incorporated Association of Headmasters, one group approved the
Board's policy and justified it on exactly the same grounds.
This group felt that the new higher elementary schools
would occupy a place between the elementary and the
secondary school.

Another group, however, at this same conference,
viewed with "apprehension" the new Code and urged the
Board not to sanction higher elementary schools "in areas
which are already supplied with secondary schools."

It is interesting to note here that those headmasters who
attacked the higher elementary school did not do so on
the grounds that it indicated an undemocratic conception
of education, but because (a) it would overlap with the
secondary school, and (b) its function could be adequately performed in the higher grades of the elementary
school.[29]

The division among the "professional" groups is further
shown by the following resolution which was passed by
the Thirty-third Annual Conference of Headmistresses:
(1) "That it is desirable to encourage the establishment
of more higher elementary schools and fewer secondary
schools."[30]

Favorable comments to the idea of higher elementary
education came from other quarters. At the same Teachers' Guild Conference at which Jackman spoke, Professor
Adamson is reported to have said:

The only sound basis of division which could be employed
in classifying schools of different grades as part of one system
was that afforded by the length of school life of the respective
pupils; the other marks of difference were either consequential
upon that, or else were merely adventitious.

Adamson further maintained that a vigorous industrial
or commercial society needed a school "which was neither

secondary nor entirely coincident with the elementary school."[31]

In an article which appeared in *The School World*, J. L. Paton, High Master of Manchester Grammar School, praised the Board of Education for its efforts to preserve a "certain distinctive quality" regarding secondary education. Although he agreed with Pickles in repudiating "the snobbish conception of secondary education as the privilege of the respectable," he felt that the Board's attempts to maintain certain standards of quality had nothing to do with "social status or wealth."[32]

The editor of *School* commented that the N.U.T.'s accusation about "the anti-democratic tendencies at work in the offices of the Board of Education," if taken literally, "could be disproved in a dozen ways." If, on the other hand, it were taken "as an indication of the existence of the feeling of social inferiority, which aggravates the lot of elementary teachers," then one should bear in mind the truth of the following three fundamental propositions:

First, that a degree is no measure of teaching capacity; second, that even under our present defective conditions the best of our elementary scholars can climb to the top of the ladder; and third, that an education which stops at the age of fourteen differs essentially from one which carries a pupil up to man's estate.[33]

The above utterances attest clearly to the mixed reaction that followed the 1905 Code and the Consultative Committee's Report. The most outspoken critic of the Board's conception of higher elementary education was the National Union of Teachers, which represented primarily the interests of public elementary school teachers,[34] and which avowedly deprecated any devices for side-tracking the working-class children. In so far, therefore, as the

higher elementary school would do precisely that, the
N.U.T.'s criticisms were clear. But whether the N.U.T.
conceived of a radical reconstruction or reversal of the
Board's policy concerning the overall concept of secondary
education, or whether it envisaged the establishment of a
system of secondary education for all, is very unclear. The
evidence in fact points to the contrary. The notion expressed by the N.U.T. at its Oxford Conference indicates
that post-primary education envisaged for the working
class children could be better provided either by "dignify-
ing," "magnifying," or "glorifying" "the upper standards
of the ordinary elementary Schools," or by making it possible for such children to enter "proper secondary
schools."

The milder critics were equally unclear. *The Journal
of Education*, for example, while deprecating insinuations
of "inferiority" and "class-distinctions," in an editorial
note of February 1907, disagreed with Jackman's assertion
that the Board's ideal was necessarily "anti-democratic."
The editorial envisaged three types of schools "with an
age limit respectively of fourteen, sixteen, and nineteen."
And while the first "can be so schemed as to lead on naturally to either the second or the third," the second, while
admitting of transition in exceptional cases to the third,
"must be recognized as an end in itself." The editorial
continued:

The boy of fourteen who is likely to continue his education
to the age of eighteen or beyond must be taught different subjects and in a different way from the boy who will almost
certainly have to earn his own living by sixteen at the latest.
There is nothing undemocratical in such a scheme. It obtains
no less in republican France than in imperial Germany. Two
Cabinet Ministers, Mr. Jackman reminds us, have been bred

in Board Schools, but we cannot plot out our public schools to breed Cabinet Ministers.[35]

In another "editorial note" which appeared in the same issue, *The Journal of Education* stressed the point that it was the duty of the Board to see that the distinctive qualities of secondary schools were not endangered by the action of less well informed local authorities, "anxious to reduce everything to administrative uniformity."[36]

Actually, however, the local authorities responded very coolly to the idea of establishing higher elementary schools. The unspectacular growth of such schools, as shown previously, bears proof of their cool reception. A careful examination of the various proposed schemes at reorganizing education "other than elementary" shows that the efforts of many of the local authorities were directed towards secondary education as defined by the Board, rather than towards the establishment of higher elementary schools.[37] Another reason that may explain their small growth is that many parents preferred the prestige and "genteelness" that were usually associated with the name "secondary." The Cheshire Education Committee stated that "the difference between a higher elementary school and a lower secondary school appears to be that the latter sounds more genteel to parents, and is therefore preferred by them."[38] Some local authorities frequently disagreed with the Board in complying with the regulations. For example, in London, as far back as 1900, the then School Board had applied for recognition of the existing seventy-nine higher grade departments as higher elementary schools. The Board of Education objected to the establishment of such a large number of schools, and also objected to the curriculum that the London School Board proposed. Finally the School Board applied for the recognition of 15 departments and the Board of Education recognized only 7.[39] When the London County Council was established as the local education authority in 1903, it continued the interest in higher elementary education; but finally in the Education Committee's Annual Report for the year 1909–10, it was admitted that "only a small number of the Council's schools were definitely organized as higher elementary schools." The reason given was the "difficulty of fully complying with the special regulations as regards curriculum, organization, special rooms, accommodation and the admission of children."[40] The consequence of this, the Report went on, was that it was decided to consider the establishment of a different type of school for selected ex-elementary school children. This type of school was to be called "central school" and will be examined later in this study.

The failure of the higher elementary schools may be viewed in several ways. On the one hand, it indicated a lack of consensus among professional and social groups concerning the role of this institution in the society of the time and in the evolving system of education. As yet there was no clear conception of a uniform and egalitarian system of post-elementary education, that is, one that would not view education in terms of social and occupational class differences. Hence, in the struggle for survival the higher elementary school was considered to be a poor and inferior substitute for the already prestigious secondary school which completely overshadowed it and stunted its growth. In contrast, there was greater agreement on the type of education given in the secondary schools as established by the Board, and on what the role of such schools should be. On the other hand, however, the very ferment created by the higher elementary school showed the persistence of the tradition established by the higher grade schools, that is, the creation of a different form of "secondary" education. It was another manifestation of the upward thrust of elementary education which began after the 1870 Act, one that continued for several years and culminated in the "modern" school which became an integral part of the English educational system.

VII
The New Liberalism and Education

When in 1906 the reconstructed Liberal Party was returned to power, the composition of the new House and the Liberal program presaged a new era in British politics. The House of Commons revealed significant shifts in political, religious and social class groupings. For the first time a significant representation from the laboring classes managed to obtain admittance to the "best club in London." The Nonconformists, largely a middle class group, amounted to 172, the greatest number ever assembled in Parliament, including 3 Cabinet figures. There were a small number of directors of business enterprises and a large number of Liberal intellectuals, professors, journalists, and "champions of all those eccentric causes which arouse the enthusiasm of British philanthropy."[1]

The ideas and program of the Liberals reflected a change in their general social philosophy. Whereas previously liberalism denoted a laissez-faire, individualistic conception of society and non-interference on the part of the State, the New Liberalism extended its meaning to incor-

162

porate "state interference," "democratic welfare state," and "social equality." Although "freedom" had remained the essential ingredient of the Liberal creed, its meaning had expanded by accommodating positive rather than purely negative dimensions. "To be really free," the Liberal leader H. H. Asquith asserted, "men must be able to make the best use of faculty, opportunity, energy and life." These could be accomplished through "education, temperance, better dwellings," and an improved "social and industrial environment."[2] And L. T. Hobhouse, one of the leading proponents of the New Liberalism, had this to say: ". . . the struggle for liberty is also when pushed through, a struggle for equality. Freedom to choose and follow an occupation, if it is to become fully effective, means equality with others in the opportunities for following such occupation."[3]

Hence, on their accession to power, the Liberals embarked upon several programs aiming at social, political, economic and educational reforms; and, during their tenure of office in the years prior to the outbreak of the First World War, several measures were passed with that purpose in mind.[4] What is of interest to us here, however, is the Liberal views in education and the policies initiated by the new Board of Education.

POLITICS AND EDUCATIONAL REFORM

One of the issues in the elections of 1906 was the education question. Campbell-Bannerman pledged that the Liberals "desire to secure, not only public control, but improvement in the quality of education." The Liberals, and especially the Nonconformists, were dissatisfied with the 1902 settlement, in that it favored, for the most part, the interests of the Church of England. The Nonconformist position, of course, had been vigorously upheld during the debates on the 1902 Act by Lloyd George[5] who, in 1906, rose to a Cabinet position. But by 1906 the political power of the Nonconformists had been substantially strengthened. Their number in Parliament had increased to an unprecedented degree, and a Nonconformist (Augustine Birrell) headed the Board of Education.

On April 9, 1906, therefore, only three months after the Liberals won the elections, the President of the Board of Education introduced an Education Bill in the House of Commons, "to make further provision with respect to Education in England and Wales,"[6] or, as Birrell himself stated, "to amend the law of education in England and Wales."[7] This Bill, in part, aimed at abolishing the so-called dual control, thus, according to Birrell, saving "an enormous amount of time, temper and the ratepayers' money."[8]

The first clause implied that no denominational teaching would be given in any publicly supported elementary school, and another clause laid down the conditions by which voluntary schools would receive public funds.[9]

It became obvious from the beginning of the discussion of this Bill, that it was not so much the administrative structure established by the 1902 Act that was objected to by the Nonconformists, as it was that Act's provisions concerning the "religious problem." In his defense of the Bill, Mr. Perks, a Nonconformist new Member of Parliament from Lincolnshire South, asserted that the Nonconformists "were determined to put an end at the earliest possible moment to the using of these Anglican schools for the purpose of alienating the children of Nonconformists from the faith of their fathers."[10]

The Bill was defended by the other Liberal members

and by the Government, partly to satisfy the Nonconformist grievance, but also because they felt that it represented
a more democratic approach to the local administration of
education.[11] However, as J. Ramsay MacDonald, the
Labour Member from Leicester, observed, the Bill was
discussed predominantly on sectarian grounds.[12] The Nonconformist Liberal members favored nondenominational
teaching in the schools which were supported by public
funds. The Conservative members (mostly Church of England people) contended that the Bill was directed against
the Church of England in that the application of the
Cowper-Temple principle would substitute one form of
religion for another, i.e., it would substitute the Nonconformist type of religion for the type of denominational
teaching heretofore given. This, according to them, would
be a violation of the principle of religious equality and
religious freedom on the part of the parents.[13] The Catholic members opposed the Bill. "The feeling of the Catholic
people of this country," said Mr. T. P. O'Connor (Liverpool, Scotland), "is that the Bill threatens to extinguish
the Catholic character of their schools."[14] And the Labour
minority were divided on it,[15] for, according to Mac-
Donald, "we are bound to consider the Bill as being, to a
very small extent, an Education Bill, and, to a very large
extent, a sectarian Bill."[16]

The Bill was passed in the House of Commons, but the
Lords (predominantly Conservative and members of the
Church) made so many amendments that finally the
Prime Minister was forced to withdraw it.[17] This educational measure failed for several reasons. In the first place,
the Liberal Nonconformists did not indicate that they
were prepared to fight for the Bill, which leads one to believe that they had supported it with reluctance, or that

they considered other issues more fundamental at the time. Secondly, the purpose of the Bill and the whole tenor of the discussion centered on religious rather than educational matters. This, although appealing to certain radicals, did not seem to arouse enthusiasm on the part of other Members of Parliament or on the part of the public in general.[18] Finally, the veto power in the hands of the House of Lords rendered the predominantly Liberal House of Commons rather impotent.

The Liberal Government made other attempts to redress the grievances that in their opinion seemed to have arisen from the 1902 Act. In February 1907, R. McKenna, who one month earlier had succeeded Birrell as President of the Board of Education, introduced a one-clause Bill[19] "designed for the purpose of transferring from the local education authority to the managers the cost of giving denominational instruction in non-provided schools."[20] And in February 1908, McKenna introduced yet another Bill[21] similar to the 1906 one. McKenna defended the measure on the grounds that it insured the removal of the religious controversy from the schools. It seems, however, that McKenna was exaggerating this controversy. The people did not seem to be unduly discontented with the 1902 settlement. Both Bills were withdrawn and the whole question quickly forgotten.[22] The Education Act of 1902 was there to stay.

In spite of these failures, the Liberals, in cooperation with the Labourites, were responsible for certain measures which, from the educational standpoint, can never be exaggerated. In the first place, they were responsible for the passing of the Education (Provision of Meals) Bill in 1906.[23] The Bill was introduced to the House of Commons by W. T. Wilson, a newly elected Labour Member from

Lancashire, Westhoughton, and was sanctioned by the Government. In introducing the second reading on March 2, 1906, Wilson said that the object of the Bill was to provide meals for that very large number of children who went to school "without food, or underfed," and that he hoped nobody would dispute the fact that the number was great.[24]

A careful examination of the debate on the second reading of this Bill reveals some noteworthy points. First, one clearly observes that the nineteenth century notions of "voluntaryism" and "charity" as adequate means for ameliorating certain "evil" social conditions, especially the conditions of poor children, were repudiated by the Liberals and, of course, the Labourites. Wilson, for example, stating the Labour point of view, is reported to have said that "charity was not a reliable source from which to provide meals for children," hence, "the State ought to see that these future citizens were fed."[25] This would not rob the parents of their freedom insofar as the welfare of their own children was concerned, for the law would apply to those families whose weekly income did not exceed 18s (a mere pittance if there were two or three children in the family). Furthermore, according to Wilson, it would ultimately be to the best interests of the State, and society in general, if some provision were made for food to be given to those children whose parents could not afford to feed them; for by catering to the physical necessities of the learner and the future citizen, the educative process was rendered more efficient, and efficient education ultimately contributed to the general welfare of the State.[26] Birrell, the President of the Board of Education, expressing the Liberal point of view, concurred with Wilson that (a) the poor children must be fed, (b) their feeding was the responsibility of the local education authorities, and (c) better learning accrued if the physical needs of children were taken into consideration.[27] Birrell tried to elucidate the second point (which seemed to arouse controversy), namely, the degree of responsibility of public authorities. By doing so he cut at the roots of some of the similarities as well as the differences between the Labour and the Liberal points of view. For, although he agreed with Wilson that charitable efforts were not adequate to meet the demands of the day, he, nevertheless, contended that they were not "to be sneezed at."[28] The Liberals would have the transition from voluntarism to welfare state as one of gradual development, though they did imply that the State must intervene for the purpose of regulating charity and positively supplementing it. Against the Labour and the Liberal viewpoints stood the Conservative, which considered voluntary efforts sufficient on this question.[29]

Another important point that emanated from the debate on this Bill was that, for the first time in English educational policy discussions, the nonintellectual aspects of education received unanimous endorsement. "The fact," cried Wilson, "that children attended school underfed was also responsible for mental deterioration."[30] And Augustine Birrell contended that "to teach a hungry child, faint and weak, the elements of learning, either divine or human, was an act of cruelty."[31]

The question of the physical welfare of children as an important consideration in the effectiveness of education was pursued further and received statutory sanction one year later by the passing of the Education (Administrative Provisions) Bill. Clause 13 of this Bill[32] empowered the local education authorities to provide for recreational activities and medical inspection for public elementary school children.[33] This clause did not give rise to controversy during the debates on the Bill. There seemed to be unanimity of opinion on the importance of vacation schools and the medical inspection of children.[34]

The provisions of the 1906 and 1907 Acts, taken conjointly, mark an important step in the development of the conception of English education. In the first place, they were another expression of the changing attitude of Liberalism; in the second, they reflected the importance placed upon nonintellectual aspects of human nature in education. Although these Acts dealt directly with elementary education, they indirectly paved the way for a similar recognition in education "other than elementary."[35] Under the direction of Dr. George Newman, who was appointed as Chief Medical Officer of the Board,[36] a series of medical reports were issued in which one finds new notions concerning child growth and development. Very soon, medical inspection was carried on in the secondary schools, with the result that greater interest was taken in the general development of the adolescent and the conditions under which better learning took place.[37] The institution of the medical service reflected the interest shown in such subjects as physical education and general recreation in the education of students in secondary schools, about which more will be said in the next chapter.

But the Education (Administrative Provisions) Act is also important for certain provisions directly relating to post-primary education. Clause 11, for example, empowered local education authorities to "aid by scholarships or bursaries the instruction in public elementary schools of scholars from the age of twelve up to the limit of age fixed for the provision of instruction in a public elementary school," and clause 12 enabled a council to "supply or aid the supply of education other than elementary" with respect to persons not resident in their areas.[38] The importance of these provisions was that henceforth greater opportunities were created for students to obtain a more advanced type of instruction than the ordinary elementary one. But attempts to extend educational opportunity went beyond these provisions. The Liberal Government initiated yet another important measure during this period, the so-called free-place system.

TOWARD EXTENSION OF EDUCATIONAL OPPORTUNITY: THE FREE-PLACE SYSTEM

Liberty and equality were two dominant concepts to which the Liberals frequently referred during the 1906 election campaign. On their accession to power, therefore, they were expected, at least by many radical and interested groups, to put into practical application their pledges in the field of education. When in 1906 the Board of Education issued its annual report, there was every reason to believe that the Liberals would meet the educational challenge by breaking down the barriers that existed between elementary and secondary education, and thus making the latter more "democratic."

The 1905–1906 *Report* devoted an unusually large space to a discussion of secondary education, the organization and development of which it found to be "the most important educational question of the present day." "Secondary education," it averred, "is the pivot of the whole situation, as it affects the efficiency, intelligence, well-being of the nation."[39]

After elaborating on certain existing conditions, the Report announced substantial increases in the estimates for State aid to secondary schools, and stated certain educational principles upon which the regulations for the allocation of money would be based. A basic principle was closer relations between primary and secondary education and expansion of opportunities at the secondary level.[40] A different note than heretofore was struck when the Board recognized that a secondary school could also be regarded as an institution which "takes over" at a certain age and "a certain stage of proficiency" the children of the elementary schools. This did not mean that secondary education was envisaged as the logical sequel to elementary, since the Board also recognized that secondary schools could be "differently planned" without having any connection with elementary schools. But the very fact that a second alternative to the existing pattern was possible was significant in that some administrative barriers were removed, and possibly more children could pass from elementary to secondary schools.[41]

Finally, a more "democratic" ideal was stated when the Report called for the breaking down of "class" education.

A class-education in compartments after the fashion of Plato's *Republic* is contrary to the essence of democracy . . . a democracy is naturally jealous of a privileged class; and one of the dangers that have to be guarded against is that this jealousy may restrict the province or contract the scope of higher education. One of the points which demand the most careful and thoughtful treatment is how to provide State-aided Secondary education in the degree to which, and at the points at which, it is really needed, and how to ensure free access to it for children of every class according as the individual is intellectually capable of receiving profit from it.[42]

The statements in the 1905–1906 Report indicate the following points: first, that the Board of Education considered the existing opportunities for secondary education inadequate; and, second, that elementary and secondary education should be more closely connected. But the report in general is illuminating in other respects. It accepted the 1904 definition of secondary education, as well as the policy with respect to fees and grants, although it called for more grants and more scholarships.[43] The inference that can be drawn from this is that the Liberals did not entertain the notion of "secondary education for all" which would imply the further notion that secondary education was the logical second stage in the formal educational process. Rather, the Board's statements reinforced the idea of a compartmentalized type of secondary education. This, of course, did not obliterate the "undemocratic" character of secondary education that allegedly existed previously. However, the "free-place" system that followed the Board's Report can best be interpreted as marking another stage in the final acceptance of the notion of "secondary education for all," as well as of the idea that secondary education followed logically elementary education.

The Free-Place System

The appearance of the 1905–06 Report did not alleviate the discontent of certain radical groups, and discussion of the problem reached the House of Commons. On March 13, 1907, Pickersgill (Bethnal Green, S.W.) accused the Board that for many years it had been marked "by an undemocratic spirit and by a want of sympathy with the desire to place higher education within the reach of all children who were qualified or anxious to receive it."[44] Pickersgill found the scholarship system quite inadequate in that certain conditions were attached to the award of scholarships. For example, the pledge of the scholarship holder to become a teacher "seriously distracted from the value of a scholarship."

Pickersgill pointed out that some students had been refused admission to the schools and colleges, which were supported with public money, because of their "social status." He hoped that the new President of the Board of Education would introduce "a more democratic spirit" into the secondary school system by making it possible for capable poor children to have access to the "higher and the highest education."[45]

Criticisms of a similar nature were voiced by Yoxall (Nottingham W.) and by Atkins (Lancashire, Middleton). Yoxall called for greater opportunities for the children of the poorer classes:

> What was wanted was two ladders—one leading from the gutter to the wall of the University, a ladder by which the child of the poorest workman, born with capacity, could ascend to the University, and afterwards enter one of the learned professions. Such a child might be a born commentator, preacher, teacher, or writer, and the ladder from the gutter to the University should be there for him. They also wanted a ladder leading from the University to some place where technological knowledge could be obtained—a Charlottenburg or a Leipsic.[46]

McKenna, himself, the new President of the Board of Education, hoped that, because of the allocation of new grants more capable public elementary school children would gain access to "a good secondary education." However, he defended the Board's policy of charging fees as a guarantee of maintaining quality in the secondary schools. What was needed was not abolition of fees *qua* fees, but rather the provision of free places for poor children of ability.[47]

About one month later, the debate on the general condition of secondary education erupted again in the House of Commons, when Silcock (Somersetshire, Wells) moved a resolution that contained three propositions: (1) that it was desirable that "further encouragement shall be given by the Board of Education" to schools "other than elementary"; (2) that the principle of public local control "should be extended to all schools other than elementary;" and (3) that "all schools and training colleges assisted by public funds should be freed from all sectarian tests for teachers, scholars, or members of the governing body."[48]

Silcock asked the Board of Education to take steps to bring order out of the existing chaos. He cited statistical evidence to show that opportunities for secondary education for elementary school children were inadequate, and he called for the removal of the "artificial distinction between elementary and nonelementary schools."[49] However, as the debate progressed and after McKenna expressed the Board's new policy, Silcock withdrew his entire resolution.

While Silcock's resolution was still on the floor of the House, several other members (Liberal, Conservative, Labour) expressed their views on the subject. In the main, they all agreed that opportunities for secondary education should be expanded for the benefit of those who had hitherto been at a disadvantage.[50] At the same time, however, nobody wanted to alter the existing type of secondary schools or to sacrifice any of their long cherished traditional elements. Under the circumstances, Sir Philip Magnus argued, the only possible expansion of opportunity would be by means of scholarships. Furthermore, Magnus cautioned against an oversupply of secondary education in excess of demand for it. For it was his experience (and there was agreement on this point by Labour members) that there was "lack of interest and desire among the working classes for the facilities which already existed."[51]

McKenna then introduced the new policy of the Board

of Education, the so-called free-place policy, which was more fully explained in the *Regulations for Secondary Schools* issued later on in the same year.

The 1907 *Regulations for Secondary Schools* were presented to Parliament on July 1, 1907, and were to be put into effect on August 1, 1908. McKenna had previously said that the purpose of the Board's policy was "to democratize the secondary schools in the sense of raising the level and securing for the humblest in the land the opportunity of education for their children in really good schools."[52] This was to be accomplished through the "free-place" system described in the prefatory memorandum to the Regulations.

The Board have also taken measures to secure that all Secondary Schools aided by grants shall be made accessible to children of all classes. It is accordingly provided (Article 20) that in all such schools where a fee is charged, a proportion of places shall be open without payment of fee to scholars from Public Elementary Schools applying for admission. This proportion will ordinarily be not less than one quarter of the whole number of scholars admitted.[53]

Article 20 of the Regulations explained further that applicants for free places would be subject to passing an entrance test of "attainments and proficiency" of similar standard as that required for admission of "fee-paying scholars."[54]

The proportion of free places to the total number of students attending a secondary school was to be "ordinarily 25 per cent," but this requirement could be reduced in the case of particular schools, if there were sufficient grounds for such reduction.[55]

In his May speech on these regulations, McKenna had carefully pointed out that the free places "must not be confused with scholarships." They would be "for public elementary school children who would not be asked to compete with children outside, but who would only be asked to pass a qualifying examination."[56] The reason for requiring this qualifying examination was to ensure that the provision regarding free places "shall not have the effect of lowering the standard of the education provided by the School."[57]

Another aspect of these regulations that needs to be mentioned here was the relaxation of the provisions concerning fees. According to Article 19, "the school may be with or without fees, but any scale of fees must be approved by the Board."[58] McKenna is reported to have stated that schools "might have as many more places as they liked," adding, furthermore, that "where the schools were provided by the local education authority he trusted they would all be free."[59] Actually, what happened was that in certain cases[60] the percentage of free places grew higher than that provided in the regulations. The 1909–10 Annual Report gave the following information:

. . . in the year 1908–09, in the seven schools for which the Durham County Council were the responsible authority, the percentage required by the Board was 25 in each case, but the percentage actually offered was in no case less than 40, and ranged from that figure as high as 83 per cent in one school and 71 per cent in another. Similarly in Gloucestershire, where the Board's requirement in each case was only 25 per cent, the percentage actually given in the case of one school was 67 in 1907–08 and 39 in 1909–10; in another, 46 in 1909–10 and 45 in 1910–11; and in a third, 51 in 1910–11.[61]

A third important aspect of the free-place policy, implicit in the 1907 Regulations and explicitly stated in the 1909 Regulations for Secondary Schools, was the insistence by the Board that the holders of free places should be placed on the "same footing" as ordinary fee-paying pupils, in matters of "conduct, progress or attendance."[62]

The implicit notion that free secondary education, so far as the poorer classes were concerned, should not be restricted to those of exceptional ability, differed from the previous Liberal and Conservative one. The Board of Education put it as follows:

Their (Board's) object was that the education provided in Public Secondary Schools and paid for largely, if not mainly, out of public funds, national and local, and out of educational endowments, should be open to children of all classes as nearly as possible upon equal terms. Hence it follows that the tests to be applied, whether as regards capacity for entrance into, or as regards fitness for continuance in, Secondary Schools, shall be the same for children who pay as for children who do not pay fees.[63]

The free-place policy, as well as the novel ideas about secondary education underlying it, at first was not enthusiastically received by everybody. The Conservatives, for the reasons stated earlier, did not favor it.[64] *The Schoolmasters' Yearbook and Directory* was critical of what it called "the political portion of the Regulations," i.e., the "free place" portion, contending that "the Regulations will not only unnecessarily disturb the working of the school, but will also in some respects tend to perpetuate the weaknesses of the existing system."[65] *The Journal of Education*, although recognizing that McKenna and Morant effected a "veritable revolution,"[66] raised "two fatal objections." In the first place, the elementary schools could not "produce scholars in sufficient numbers . . . to make up this proportion (25 per cent) "; in the second, the secondary school "will be unable to assimilate the foreign element." The result would be that, though "it may gain in industry," it "will suffer in manners and culture."[67] At its annual meeting of January 1908, the Headmasters' Association, although in general welcoming the new regulations, passed a resolution, one clause of which read: "That it is inconvenient to lay down a fixed general rule as to the proportion of free places that should be reserved for pupils from elementary schools."[68]

On the other hand, *The School World* called the free-place scheme "a courageous attempt to provide secondary education for the people." It urged the people "to make sacrifices to keep their children at school," and hoped that the teachers "will work wholeheartedly to make it a success."[69]

Gradually the free-place policy was becoming more and more acceptable. For example, at its annual general meeting of January 1909, the Headmasters' Association accepted the 25 per cent requirement, whereas one year previously, they had not. In fact, at the discussion, the Rev. C. J. Smith (Hammersmith) objected to a suggestion that 25 per cent be considered the maximum proportion, for in his school 41 per cent of the pupils held free places, "and he had no wish to see the number diminished."[70]

The controversy, of course, over the free-place policy and the "free-placer" did not end.[71] But as time passed and as the "free-placer" was found to be industrious and could compete well with the "fee-payer,"[72] there was wider acceptance of the policy itself, as well as of the conception of education upon which it was based. The first issue of *The Times Educational Supplement*, which appeared on September 6, 1910, referred to the free-place concept and urged that it be approved by all: ". . . the principle of the free-place system, to provide a bridge whereby boys and girls of average ability who might profit by secondary education, but cannot afford to pay for it may be enabled to receive it, is one that all must approve."[73]

The *Educational Supplement* further observed that this

principle "is being more and more appreciated by the working classes." At the same time, however, the *Supplement* pointed out some dangers that might accrue if no caution were exercised and if the pace of free secondary education were not gradual.[74]

The institution of the free-place system marked, in the words of the Board of Education, "a further step in the direction of establishing a vital connection between the Public Elementary Schools and the State-aided Secondary Schools in the country.[75] Through it, a greater number of children from the less affluent classes of society could climb the educational ladder.

What the immediate effects of this change in the recruitment policy were is difficult to determine. According to the Board's statistics of 1911–12, "the total number of pupils receiving free tuition in Secondary Schools in 1911–1912 was 52,583, or 34.8 per cent of the total number of pupils, and . . . 49,120 of these had received their previous education in Elementary Schools," whereas in 1906 there were only 23,500 pupils who proceeded on scholarships from elementary to secondary schools.[76] However, it is not quite clear how many of these children came from the poorer classes. It is true, as the Board's statistics show, that a larger number of children from the elementary schools gained access into the secondary schools. But this phenomenon is clouded by the fact that the social position and composition of elementary schools "improved," and this meant that more and more parents from the middle and even upper social strata sent their children to such schools.[77] Also, as the available places in secondary schools were limited relative to the demand for them, free places came to depend more and more on severe competitive rather than on qualifying examinations, which was the intended policy of the Board. And in such competition it is not quite clear how well the children from poorer homes fared. Moreover, even though the possibility was there for a poor child to gain access to a secondary school, certain social, cultural, and economic factors acted as barriers to the full utilization of this opportunity. In spite of exemptions from certain costs, it was still a heavy financial burden for poor parents to send their children to secondary schools. It demanded heavy sacrifices, and very often parents were not ready to forego the additional income of a working son in favor of an educational investment whose practical benefits were not quite so clear or tangible, and at best questionable. To be sure, a secondary school education would probably enable a poor child to become an elementary school teacher, or a clerk, or any other white-collar lower professional, but beyond these minor occupations the chances were very few indeed, if existent at all. Added to these obstacles were, one might say, the psychological barriers present in a sub-culture whose values were quite different from the upper segments of the society. The working classes of the period were more interested in wage increases and tangible improvement of their lot than in any long-range goals. What they wanted most, as noted earlier, was to be "left alone."[78] And, even as late as 1938, many children from working-class districts refused places they had won in the secondary schools, for there was a sort of class pressure at school and at home not to accept such places.[79] To many it would have meant a cultural uprooting and an alienation from their families, relatives, and friends.

Nevertheless, in spite of these qualifications, the free-place policy represents an ideological shift in the development of the State system of secondary education initiated in 1902. It was an attempt to establish a "vital connection" between two types of education hitherto regarded as parallel. It followed from the Board's purposes that, if they were to be adequately implemented, certain adjustments or changes in the existing type of secondary education had to be made. The free-place policy, therefore, can best be interpreted as a factor in the ideological change of the nature of the secondary school in order to bring it into more organic relationship with the elementary school.

VIII

The Practical, the
Vocational, and the
Liberal in the
Curriculum

In addition to the attempts to "democratize" education, the years following the Liberal victory were characterized by an educational ferment centering in the curriculum of the schools. Changes in the political and socio-economic sectors, and a more enlightened educational opinion, highlighted the need for changes in the content of instruction. Older controversies on the relative value of subjects were revived, and one is reminded of the educational discussions following Herbert Spencer's question "What Knowledge is of Most Worth?" which had been raised about fifty years earlier. The new controversies, however, were focused more on the place of "practical" and/or "vocational" subjects relative to "liberal" subjects in the curriculum, rather

than on the claims of the sciences and the humanities. Like
the period of the sixties, it was a period of introspection,
and of a re-assessment of basic educational ideas and
practices.

CURRICULUM CHANGE AND A NEW RATIONALE

The Board's Policy

At the same time that the free-place system was being instituted, the Board sought to relax certain curriculum
provisions and allow for more practical studies in the
secondary school program. While it adhered to the previous
view that the "essential core of education" should consist
of a certain specified group of academic subjects pursued
for at least four years (from about the age of 12 to about
the age of 16), it at the same time stressed the fact that this
core should be regarded as a minimum, and that special
additional provision should be made according to location
and types of students. In the 1907 *Regulations* the prescribed minimum time spent on English language and
literature, one foreign language, geography, history and
science, was dispensed with; the modern foreign language
provision could be waived "under special dispensation";
and physical exercise and manual work were to be considered as essential elements rather than be prescribed for
certain years.[1] In the 1908 *Regulations,* it was stated that
a varied curriculum sequence different from the approved
one could be extended not only to "advanced scholars or
special classes," but to "individual pupils generally." In
all cases the aim should not be "mechanical uniformity,"
but elasticity "both in the list of subjects taught and in the
method of teaching them."[2] In all cases, according to the
Board, the essential features of a good liberal education
should not be sacrificed. The schools should not lose their

"civilizing" function by becoming unduly specialized. But it is interesting to observe that the cultivation of mind and body could be attained not only through book-work, but also through bodily-training "and the practical use of the pupil's faculties." Futhermore, one observes, especially in the 1909 *Regulations,* the view that education should be adjusted to local circumstances and requirements, and "the particular needs and capacities of the pupils."[3]

By 1909 the Board noted with satisfaction that some of the proposed changes had already taken place. Commercial subjects were taught in about 130 schools; domestic subjects were taught in practically all schools attended by girls; gardening found a place in the curriculum of 22 schools; and more than two-thirds of the schools for boys made some provision for handicraft by either a woodwork or a metalwork course. Also, it was found that English as the subject matter of a complete course of study was "winning approval."[4]

In order to facilitate the expansion of the curriculum, the Board approved the disbursement of special grants to schools which framed curricula to meet the needs of special types of students. For example, a special grant was paid to Knaresborough Grammar School, Yorkshire, which provided for the needs of students "destined for rural occupation."[5]

Several other attempts were made to introduce practical subjects into the secondary school curriculum, and to impress upon the local authorities the need to modernize the curriculum. In a pamphlet issued in 1902, the Board urged local authorities to pay more attention to French and German which was "completely disappearing," a tendency which was "much regretted," for knowledge of German was "a matter of national importance," as well as a necessary tool for scholarship and research.[6] Indeed, in the 1911–1912 *Annual Report,* the Board spoke of the possibility of the entire school course being given a certain practical bias, depending on the locality, i.e., an agricultural bias in the rural areas, and a commercial or industrial bias in the urban areas. Furthermore, it spoke of a certain amount of specialization in one direction or in several, in the higher forms. And it gave the following statistical evidence concerning the adaptation of the curriculum to meet the practical needs of students.

The information obtained has not yet been fully analyzed, but it appears from a preliminary examination that there are at present 27 schools in which the curriculum has a rural bias; 28 in which a special Commercial Course is provided (12 of these being boys' schools, 9 girls' schools, and the remaining 7 schools for both boys and girls); 16 schools offering a special course for girls in Housecraft; and 9 offering one designed for pupils about to take up Engineering or some kindred occupation.[7]

This concern for an expanded curriculum was partly due to the realization that the function of the secondary school was two-fold: (a) to provide a type of education suitable for students who would stay at school beyond the ages of 16 or 17, who would in most cases continue their education beyond the secondary school, and who aimed at higher occupations or professions; and (b) to provide a type of education for pupils who would leave school at about the age of 16, and who would proceed to posts in public offices, commercial houses, and manufactories, or enter such occupations as farming and retail trade.[8] The Board of Education painstakingly explained the principles upon which the regulations since 1907 had been based, repeatedly emphasizing the importance it placed upon both a common nucleus and a great variety of curriculum.

The nature of these two elements depended on many factors (location, teaching staff, length of school life of students, occupational goals, etc.). But the Board felt that for practical purposes it was convenient to define the common nucleus, or "a good general education," in terms of certain cardinal subjects a knowledge of which was required for entry into places of higher education and into "the professions and occupations to which pupils may be expected to pass direct from school."[9] This common nucleus was not envisaged as incompatible with variation in the curriculum. Some schools might emphasize the linguistic side, others the mathematical and scientific. And while this might best be done in the highest forms, "opportunity will also be found in the main portion of a school for giving a definite bias to the work as a whole."[10] Furthermore, whereas the main function of a secondary school would be to supply a good general education, there were cases in which the Board would approve a certain limited amount of technical work. In fact it was felt that even the general education of boys and girls would gain in effectiveness if the work at school was to some extent brought into direct connection with the students' probable occupations "in after life."[11]

It is clear that, after 1907, the policy of the Board was directed towards the expansion of secondary education, i.e., one that would accommodate, albeit to a very limited degree, "practicalism" and "semi-vocationalism" as ingredients in the curriculum. To be sure, the Board never abandoned its position that the secondary school's primary function was to supply a good general education—denoting a group of academic subjects—but one finds a concerted effort made to extend the previous conception. As Runciman, the President of the Board, put it:

We have done everything we could to make the local needs of a district one of the deciding factors in the curriculum which is sanctioned for a secondary school. . . . That a practical bent should be given to these secondary schools is all to the good. This is particularly necessary in rural areas. I am glad to be able to report that nearly forty secondary schools now give a distinctly rural bias to their education.[12]

"Practicalism" as an ingredient of the secondary school curriculum was justified in a report, now forgotten, prepared by the Consultative Committee, headed by Acland and including, among others, Michael Sadler and R. H. Tawney, a professor of economic history at the time.

A Rationale for Practicalism: The Acland Report

In the Acland Report, the Board for the first time justified rather comprehensively practical work in secondary school. Hitherto, its policy allowed for and encouraged work of a practical nature. But not until the appearance of the Acland Report does one find an educaational rationale for a type of instruction different in nature from the existing one.

The Committee was asked to consider the degree to which practical work should be "encouraged and developed" in the secondary schools.[13] It interpreted "practical work" to mean education which involved bodily activity and "learning by doing" and it focused its attention on two areas: (a) constructional handicraft and the domestic arts, and (b) the practical teaching of ordinary school subjects, especially natural science.[14]

Practical work in the curriculum of secondary schools was justified on intellectual and moral, as well as on utilitarian grounds. For example, "handiwork" could train the faculties; it could develop mind and character; and it had a "realistic" value in that it brought the work of the

school "into closer relation with the needs of daily life."
Thus, systematic work with the hands could legitimately
be considered a necessary constituent of a liberal education. It did not therefore follow that handiwork should
be confined to particular types of students, i.e., the nonintellectual. Since it could be instrumental in the mental
and moral development of the child, it should be an important branch of the general education of "normal"
children as well. For a purely bookish and intellectual type
of education which was confined to the traditional academic subjects was a one-sided education. It neglected
"to foster those activities of mind, hand and eye that are
demanded when dealing with concrete things."[15]

Practical work was also justified on the grounds that it
had bearings on certain school subjects, viz, science, mathematics, and geography. It should therefore occupy a definite
place in the curriculum of the secondary schools and in
any scheme of general liberal education, both "for its own
sake" and for its bearings upon other aspects of school
work.[16]

Although the Consultative Committee wished to advance the educational claims of practicalism as constituting
an essential ingredient of secondary education, it was not
prepared to accept definite vocational training—interpreted
as technical competency—as the function of a secondary
school.[17] This notion was brought out very clearly when
the report discussed the question of rural secondary education. There, great emphasis was placed upon the importance of making the rural secondary school perform
its essential function of providing a preliminary education
suitable to those whose future work would be connected
with the land rather than with the universities. But the
Committee did not envisage a "farm school" in the place

of a secondary school. Rather, it advocated the more practical teaching of certain subjects, e.g., natural science, and the cultivation of a scientific attitude towards the work of "the future cultivator of the land." Futhermore, even in the rural secondary schools, a just balance should be kept between "the more purely intellectual and the more 'practical' branches of school work."[18] The Acland Report summarized its position as follows:

We consider that our Secondary education has been too exclusively concerned with the cultivation of the mind by means of books and the instruction of the teacher. To this essential aim there must be added, as a condition of balance and completeness, that of fostering those qualities of mind and that skill of hand which are evoked by systematic work of the kind described in this report. We think that the time has now come when every Secondary School should provide for the teaching of some branches of Educational Handwork, should make them an integral part of its curriculum, and give them a position on the same level with other subjects studied. The value of such work, both as an element of a general education for all pupils and as a preparatory training for the special needs of some, has been amply demonstrated by the wide and representative body of evidence which we have had before us.[19]

Explanation of the Board's Policy

The Board's efforts to enlarge the concept of secondary education by advocating, and in certain cases sanctioning, practical subjects in the curriculum, may be explained in part by looking at what the Board itself called the "changes in industrial structure and in social outlook."[20] In a memorandum submitted to the Committee, R. H. Tawney set forth certain industrial changes that affected education in general. The value of the training received through apprenticeship had been destroyed owing to (a) an increase in the age limit at which apprentices were taken (in the majority of industries employers did not take apprentices until they were 15 or 16); (b) the growing specialization of industrial processes, which made it increasingly difficult for a boy who entered a workshop as an apprentice or learner to obtain a knowledge of the trade which he meant to follow; (c) the small control which under existing conditions the employer could exercise over his apprentices; and (d) the constantly changing methods of production of modern industries, which rendered mere manual dexterity inadequate.[21] These industrial conditions placed the system of apprenticeship in a precarious position. By definition, apprenticeship meant training solely in one specific workshop. Now, condition (a) had created a gap of almost 2 years in the education of a great many children between the time they normally left schools (age 14) and the time they entered apprenticeship (age 16); conditions (b) and (d) rendered the apprentice's training or learning inadequate for any post-apprenticeship employment; and condition (c) rendered even the limited training given during the apprenticeship period weak and inefficient. This necessitated changes in educational organization.[22] And, although the Consultative Committee concerned itself primarily with "continuation schools," it did imply that part of the burden would have to be carried by the secondary schools.[23] In other words, secondary schools were called upon to expand their curriculum in order to accommodate courses of study which had a wider outlook, which included much practical and "constructive" work, and which were not "fettered by ambitions to win success in written examinations." By so doing they would accomplish two things. They would, in the first place, equip those who entered the industrial or commercial fields with the necessary theoretical and practical tools to combat the four conditions stated previously; and, in the second, they would, in the long run, contribute to the creation of "a new attitude of mind towards the educational needs of the adolescence and towards the interaction of education and upon industry."[24]

The Board's policy was also in part influenced by the fact that the secondary school had acquired the two-fold function mentioned previously. This called for careful consideration of the needs of those students whose education terminated at the age of 16, and who sought certain types of employment that necessitated something more than merely a general academic type of education. The available statistics concerning the classification of occupations reveal an increase in commercial and industrial occupations that required a certain "pre-professional," so to speak, orientation in the secondary schools. For example: In the population census classified by ages, occupations, etc., conducted in 1901, there were 530,685 males ages 10 years and up listed under the category "commercial occupations." This included (1) merchants, agents, and accountants, (2) commercial or business clerks, (3) dealers in money, and (4) insurance officials, clerks, and agents. Of this number, 88,414 were between the ages of 15 and 20; 90,192 between 20 and 25; and 142,809 between 25 and 35.[25] In the next census, conducted in 1911, the number of male persons employed in commercial occupations rose to 663,316, of which 104,278 were between the ages of 15 and 20, 103,599 between 20 and 25, and 174,745 between 25 and 35.[26] Employers of those entering certain of these occupations preferred to hire boys at the age of 16 and up, who had a better education than that usually obtained in a public elementary school, and who came directly from secondary schools at the age of 16. They also felt that it would be to the advantage of such prospective employees to have had preliminary work connected with such enterprises as Banking and Commerce.[27]

Increases, sometimes of a sharp nature, were to be seen in the number of persons employed in certain skilled occupations (scientific instruments, musical instruments and apparatus for sports and games, glass manufacture, paper, prints, books and stationery, textile fabrics, cotton manufacture, etc.).[28] Finally, as the 1911 Census Report observed, there had been a continuous increase of civil servants in recent years. In 1901, for example, the civil servants employed by the national government (officers and clerks, messengers, etc.) numbered 116,439,[29] whereas in 1911, they numbered 172,352.[30] Similarly, in 1901 the civil servants employed by the local government numbered 44,904 policemen and 36,870 "municipal, parish, and other local or county officers"; but in 1911 the numbers rose to 53,160 policemen and 74,087 other local government officials.[31] This increase in the numbers of civil servants was largely brought about by putting into effect a number of statutes pertaining to social reform, specifically those engineered by the growing Board of Trade under Churchill. The Labour Exchanges Act, for example, had created new posts to which the Liberal Government appointed officials without holding the usual civil service examinations. The belief was that what was wanted was not so much special knowledge or a high standard of general education as acquaintance with industrial and labor circles.[32]

Finally, the Board's policy can further be illumined if it is looked at as an intergral part of the "social reform movement" referred to previously. The intellectual spokesmen of the New Liberalism viewed educational reform, specifically equality of educational opportunity, as an essential element in their reconstructed social philosophy. "For there is one opportunity," wrote J. A. Hobson, "upon which the efficacy of all the others, as instruments of self-development and of social benefit, depends: equality of access to knowledge." "Without this," he continued, "every other opportunity is barren for the purposes of personal or social progress. Education is the opportunity of opportunities." What was needed in education was "a broad easy stair" not a "narrow ladder," one which would make for "general" not "selected" culture. Extension of educational opportunity in the form of a "broad easy stair" necessitated a different conception of education from that offered in the secondary schools.[33] Similarly, L. T. Hobhouse, another Liberal spokesman, considered education a necessary prerequisite in the struggle for liberty and equality.

Once more the struggle for liberty is also when pushed through, a struggle for equality. Freedom to choose and follow an occupation, if it is to become fully effective, means equality with others in the opportunities for following such occupation. This is, in fact, one among the various considerations which lead Liberalism to support a national system of free education, and will lead it further yet on the same lines.[34]

Expansion of educational advantages and equality of educational opportunity, as essential ingredients of the new Liberal creed, were aims not limited to the Liberal systematic thinkers, but were shared in varying degrees by the various Liberal leaders.[35] These people, pressed by their more radical political allies, the Labourites, initiated the free-place policy, the acceptance of which called for changes in the conception of the secondary school curriculum.

It is interesting, however, to observe that the Board, in

attempting to introduce "practical" studies in the curriculum of the secondary school, was motivated first by social, economic, and political considerations and then by, strictly speaking, educational ones. In other words, what actually happened was that practical studies were first justified on social and economic grounds, and, to a certain degree, introduced into the curriculum of the secondary schools because of such factors, and then an educational theory was advanced through the Consultative Committee's Report to justify them as essential elements of a liberal education.

Now, the success of the Board's policy depended upon the degree to which it was accepted and put into effect by the headmasters, the teachers and the local authorities, as well as upon the reaction that it had on educational and public opinion in general.

THE VIEWS OF EDUCATORS

Judging from contemporary evidence, the question of the relative emphasis of the "general" or "liberal," the "vocational" and "the practical" in the curriculum of the secondary school, seemed to be a frequent topic of debate or comment among teachers, headmasters and educators, as well as professional groups and journals.

In an article published in *The School World* in September 1910, Sara A. Burstall, President of the Association of Headmistresses, drew attention to the demands made upon the curriculum of the secondary schools by (a) the growth of such schools, and (b) the early age at which pupils left. In order to meet these demands, Burstall called for a revision of the curriculum, the modification of the too academic character of secondary education, and the provision of a variety of courses for the different types of students, along similar lines as the *Realschule* and the *Oberrealschule* in Germany, and the elective and practical bias of the secondary schools in America. To the possible charge that such considerations were unworthy of those who believed in a liberal education, she answered:

. . . such courses of study may be made to contain the elements of a liberal education, especially by emphasis on literature in the mother tongue and history. It is often found in practice that the training of faculty, which is one purpose of a liberal education, can be secured more completely for certain pupils through subjects other than the time-honored disciplines of Latin and mathematics.[36]

About four years later (January, 1914), *The School World* carried a symposium on the controversial topic "Commercial Education in Secondary Schools." A group of schoolmasters and schoolmistresses who had experimented with such a type of education were invited to express their views on the subjects. Sara Burstall, Headmistress of Manchester High School for Girls, reiterated her position that so far as girls were concerned, "secretarial or commercial training, combined with general education in English and languages, was one of the most suitable forms of vocational education."[37] Caroline E. Rigg, Headmistress of Mary Datchelor School, Camberwell, S.E., expressed a similar viewpoint.[38] On the other hand, Mary Walker, Headmistress of Roan School for Girls, Greenwich, felt that there should be no difference between the education of those girls who entered "business," and the others. Although she would include such subjects as "household cookery" and "needlework," she went as far as to doubt the value of most of that which went by the name "commercial training."[39]

Similarly, Fred Charles, Headmaster of the Day School

of Commerce, City of London College, maintained that "a commercial side to secondary schools appears a mistake," while W. Bonavia Hunt, Headmaster, Kilburn Grammar School, N.W., held that "if the secondary school itself were merely to turn its pupils into a commercial department, pure and simple, it would be an unjustifiable encroachment upon the domain of these institutions."[40]

One of the contemporary organs of professional opinion was *The Schoolmasters Yearbook and Directory.* In its successive "Review of the Year" sections, *The Yearbook* made references to the various controversies centering upon the curriculum, viz., classical versus modern studies, and liberal versus vocational education. In 1909, it stated that "the literary side of education is at least holding its ground"; that "the claims made on behalf of science are growing less exaggerated"; and that "the demand for subjects of practical utility is becoming more   enlightened." Moreover, it encouragingly noted that "science is being more and more taught in close relation to the facts and needs of everyday life."[41] In 1910 the "modern" type of curriculum was defended;[42] and in 1911, after repudiating the "gymnastic theory" of classical teaching, it noted that the conviction was gaining ground "that subjects must be taught for their own sakes or not at all." It further added that the "proper welding together of the so-called practical and literary subjects" was the "next great problem of the Curriculum to be solved."[43]

In spite, however, of the encouraging note that there was great interest in a type of education that prepared for livelihood, the *Yearbook* observed that the teachers still held fast to the traditional theory of a liberal education, for it seemed that Macaulay's schoolboy was still the ideal. Apparently, according to the *Yearbook,* there was fear lest premature specialization for industry subordinate the individual to the interests of the State.[44]

"Vocationalism" and "practicalism" were discussed at meetings or organizations by educationalists and by educational journals. *The Journal of Education* discussed liberal and vocational education with respect to Germany, the United States and England. It deprecated the American tendency of excessive vocationalism in its secondary schools, but it seemed to it that Germany was most successful in providing vocational instruction without injuring or encroaching upon liberal education. It emphasized the fact that in England the dominant view was that liberal education should precede and form the basis of any type of vocational instruction.[45] For ultimately "a nation of men will always triumph over a nation of plough boys, artisans, and shopkeepers."[46] Three months later, the same journal speaking on the possible effects of the free-place system, agreed with Runciman (the President of the Board) that modern subjects should be substituted for "small Latin and less Greek" in the case of students who would terminate their formal education at the age of 16. At the same time, however, it agreed with Sir William Anson that there was a danger lest schools offering "bookkeeping, shorthand and the like should be found masquerading as secondary schools."[47] Its persistent target seemed to be the United States. It criticized American secondary schools for the emphasis placed upon vocationalism and carefully pointed out that liberal education was "the making of a man," while vocational education was "the making of a tradesman." According to it, the secondary schools should stress the former rather than the latter.[48] This viewpoint continued in 1912.[49] Yet, in the same issue, this same journal carried an editorial entitled "vocational education," in which it supported Burstall's view that vocational and liberal education "intermingle in every school system." Furthermore, it asserted that "general education can be given through vocational and vocational through general."[50] And one year later it supported the inclusion of "housekeeping" in the curriculum for girls.[51]

The Educational Times, another contemporary organ of educational opinion, took from the start a more favorable stand toward vocational education and practical studies in the curriculum. In a leading article in 1911, it noted with approval that schools tended to move away from the aristocratic concept which implied a classification of students into the "Thinkers" and the "Doers." The curriculum should be supplemented by studies and activities "fitted for that other type which learns best when it is *doing* or *producing* most."[52] Two years later, the same journal welcomed the Board's views on a "wider curriculum" and maintained that "the physical and emotional natures need as careful training as has in the past been given to the intellect."[53]

One of the strongest defenses of the idea of practicalism in the secondary school curriculum was advanced by Isabel Cleghorn, President of the National Union of Teachers, at the association's Forty-second Annual Conference in 1911. In fact, at this meeting Cleghorn advanced a new concept of secondary education, viz., secondary education for all. This is the first time that such a concept was carefully explained and, so far as this writer can ascertain, expressed at all.

. . . after the age of twelve years I want a system of ladders by means of which all can climb not necessarily to the University or the training college, but to the goal of their own individual ambitions. Secondary schools or classes of varying types, to meet the demands of the localities, should be organized to fulfill the essential duties of secondary schools; that is, to add to the education given in the primary schools, but in a more specialized manner. . . . Why should we by means of our school system cater only, or mainly, for those who are to be clerks, or teachers, engineers or electricians? Why should we educate for the Civil Service or the Post Office, and omit to educate for the farm or the garden? Why not supply the education necessary for the plumber, the painter, the bootmaker—the dressmaker, or the domestic servant?[54]

This was an ideal to be aimed at. Under the existing conditions, Cleghorn called for experiments such as the addition of trade centers to existing ones, the introduction of classes "with vocational bias," the making of the day school curriculum "more practical," and the extension of the central schools which had recently been established by the London County Council.[55] However, there is not enough evidence to show the extent to which Cleghorn's views were shared by all the members of the N.U.T.

The views of other people concerned with secondary education were rather divided and sometimes unclear. At the annual meeting of the Secondary Schools Association[56] held on April 4, 1911, Sir Philip Magnus, the president, called for the establishment or encouragement of different types of secondary schools with varied curricula adapted to the different classes of future occupations of the students. But in a paper delivered at the same meeting, Dr. Gow maintained that the existing academic curriculum was well chosen to perform the proper function of a secondary school, which was the "training and developing of the judgment, the taste, the power of logical reasoning, the curiosity in regard to cause and effects.[57] And at their Thirty-seventh Annual Meeting, the Headmistresses passed a resolution which stated that: "Training in domestic subjects should supplement and not replace the

general subjects of a liberal education as given in public
secondary schools for girls."[58] It might perhaps be of interest to note here that, although, generally speaking,
there was a good deal of agreement among the headmistresses and schoolmistresses concerning the importance
of certain practical subjects in the curriculum for girls,[59]
it was reported that the Association of Women Clerks
and Secretaries was in favor of postponing professional
training until the age of sixteen. They urged that, where
possible, the period of general education should extend
up to the age of eighteen.[60]

In addition to the above, certain other contemporary
educational thinkers voiced their views on "vocationalism."
For example, Cloudesley Brereton, in a paper read at the
Hague Moral Education Congress, deplored the fact that
the professional or vocational side of education "has been
lost sight of" and that it had been provided for in special
schools "with a more or less direct utilitarian bias." He
called for a close union between schools of general education and schools of special education, and maintained
that vocational education should view the curriculum not
only as preparation for the student's life work, but equally
as a harmonious whole of both liberal and technical studies.
Brereton also favored modification of the existing courses
of study such as the creation of special branches and bi-
furcations within the schools of general culture so that the
pupil might be given a "foretaste" for his future career.[61]
Similarly, A. H. Angus, Headmaster of the Dixon Secondary School in Birmingham, listed seven advantages in his
support of "handiwork" in the curriculum. These ranged
from "manual dexterity" and "character building" to training in observation, correlation of subjects, and "timetable
variety and relief."[62] On the other hand, Frank J. Adkins,
a schoolmaster, stressed that education in the use of leisure

was more important than education whose chief end was merely to enable people to earn their own living. He, accordingly, urged that it would be more fruitful if the national system of education "made more of ideas and matters of general historical, social, aesthetic, and literary interest."[63]

Our analysis shows that opinion on "vocationalism" and "practicalism" was by no means of a uniform nature. Neither the Board, nor educational opinion in general, conceived of the secondary school as strictly speaking a vocational institution, i.e., a place where the pupil would learn a trade, or directly prepare for a specific vocation. Rather, the general opinion was that, in addition to the usual subjects which constituted the staple of the secondary school curriculum and which purportedly furnished a liberal type of education, certain other "practical" subjects might be included. These could be useful not only for their educational value, but also for the future vocations of the students. The degree of emphasis on such practical subjects would depend on the length of time spent in the school, and on the occupational goals of the students, as well as the needs of the locality where the school was.

Now to what degree did the Board's policy, as well as the various pronouncements concerning expansion, actually bring about changes in the curriculum of the secondary school?

THE EFFECTS ON THE SCHOOLS

Under Article 39 of the 1907 Regulations, the Board could augment its grants to schools for experiments which, in its opinion, would be of value to general educational progress. Certain local authorities made application and received such augmented grants. For example, Perse School in Cambridge received grants for the new oral method of teaching classics; Knaresborough Grammar School in Yorkshire, for a curriculum especially designed for boys and girls who planned to enter rural occupations;[64] Manchester High School for Girls, for a course fitted for those who intended to enter secretarial businesses;[65] Sexey's School, Blackford (Somerset), for an experimental course in agriculture; James Allen's Girls' School, Dulwich, for an experiment in the teaching of Botany;[66] and the Central Secondary School in Birmingham, for its non-classical curriculum which would be suited to boys intending to enter the various professions.[67] Other sources of information are the scattered statistical evidence given in the Board's annual and statistical reports. For example, the 1911–12 Report gave the following information: out of the 885 secondary schools eligible for grants, 27 had "a rural bias," 28 provided a "special Commercial Course," 16 had "a special course for girls in Housecraft," and 9 one course "designed for pupils about to take up Engineering or some kindred occupation." Note, however, that 757 of those schools, or 85 per cent, included Latin in their curriculum, while 183, or 20 per cent, included Greek also.[68] The 1912–13 Annual Report stated that out of 898 secondary schools eligible for grants, 74 had a definite vocational bias. Of these, 34 provided a rural or agricultural course, 25 a commercial course, 14 a domestic course (for girls), and 8 an engineering course (for boys).[69] Further data on the existing offerings were given in the *Educational Statistics* of 1911–1912 as summarized in Table III.

The available evidence shows that the response to vocational courses, or practical courses with quasi-vocational bias, was not as encouraging as one might have expected. The *Educational Statistics* published annually by the Board revealed that a large number of students who were leaving secondary schools after the age of twelve, were entering commercial, clerical, industrial, manual, agricultural or rural occupations. For example: in the year 1908–1909, out of the 38,200 pupils in that age category who left school during the year, (a) 12,838, or 33.6 per cent, "went to a place of further education," or became teachers, or entered training colleged for elementary school

TABLE III
CERTAIN PARTICULARS CONCERNING THE CURRICULA OF SECONDARY SCHOOLS FOR THE YEAR ENDING 31st July 1912[70]

Courses or Subjects	Number of Schools in which they were offered	% of Total Number of Schools listed as 885
Specialized Courses:		
(i) Commercial Courses	25	2.8
(ii) Domestic Economy Courses	14	1.6
(iii) Rural or Agricultural Courses	33	3.7
(iv) Engineering Courses	8	.9
Languages:		
(a) Latin	757	85.5
(b) Greek	183	20.6
(c) French	879	99.3
(d) German	373	42.1
(e) Spanish	5	.56
Number of Languages:		
(a) No language	1	.11
(b) 1 language	104	11.7
(c) 2 languages	386	43.6
(d) 3 languages	256	28.9
(e) 4 languages	137	15.4
(f) 5 languages	1	.11

teachers; and (b) 15,493, or 40.6 per cent, entered the occupations mentioned above. The rest (9,869, or 25.8 per cent) were listed under such categories as (a) remained at home, (b) went abroad, (c) left, illness or died, and (d) occupation unknown or unclassified.[71] In the year 1910–11, out of 39,923 pupils, 11,051, or 27.7 per cent, were listed under category (a), whereas 17,956, or 45.0 per cent, were listed under (b).[72] And in the year 1911–12, out of 44,705 pupils, 12,707, or 28.4 per cent, came under the second.[73]

The explanation of this half-hearted response, however, cannot be sought exclusively in the Board's policy or in any academic biases that the individuals on the Board had. For, in terms of the extensive analysis of the Board's policy presented earlier in this study, it is difficult to see how the Board inhibited the secondary schools from fulfilling their functions. The explanation, therefore, must also be sought elsewhere.

One of the contemporary conditions that in part explains this phenomenon was the variety of external examinations commonly taken in the secondary schools. In a thorough and comprehensive report published in 1911, the Consultative Committee dealt with the entire system of such examinations.[74] The report noted that, although only 2.70 per cent of the pupils went to the universities as a whole, the curriculum of the upper forms of many schools was modelled largely on the needs of this small percentage of students. Thus the school studies of the majority were regulated by the special requirements of the few, and the examinations generally used in secondary schools ignored "certain important parts of the curriculum," such as handicrafts, domestic science and needlework.[75]

The report explicitly stated that the system of examinations might seriously endanger the efforts of the State and the local authorities at widening and modernizing the curriculum. Certain witnesses testified that the existing system of examinations tended to squeeze out of the curriculum such subjects as handicraft and domestic science.[76]

Another contributing factor in the nonexpansion of the curriculum of the majority of the secondary schools was the reluctance on the part of parents, local authorities, the teaching profession, and others, to accept the notion of vocationalism as an essential element of secondary school education, or of practicalism as an ingredient of a general liberal education. Although, as shown earlier, various individuals and professional groups—especially those concerned with education for girls—called for reform, the rank and file of the teachers still adhered to the notion that vocational education must start after the foundations for a general education were laid, such general education denoting for the most part academic branches of knowledge. This may have been due to the widely-held belief in faculty psychology and its associate doctrine of formal discipline,[77] as well as to the fact that it was the only type of secondary education they had been used to. The parents seem to have been more interested in the occupational future of their children and their acquisition of certificates through the passing of examinations.[78] Moreover, they saw a more prestigious future for their children in the existing type of secondary education. Lastly, even labor groups did not conceive of the secondary school as an institution of vocationalism, but rather as one whose function was general liberal education.[79]

The Central Schools: A Successful Experiment

The failure of the secondary schools to accommodate on a sufficient scale the new demands made upon them, coupled with the unfavorable reception accorded to the higher elementary schools already discussed, prompted certain progressive authorities, specifically those of London and Manchester, to turn toward the establishment of another type of "post-primary" education, namely the "central" school.

The inception of the central school idea is to be found in the London County Council Education Committee's *Annual Report of the Education Officer* for the year 1909–10. There it was stated that the Board and the London County Council had failed to reach an agreement on the spread of higher elementary schools. As a consequence of this, a scheme for a new type of school, providing a superior elementary education for selected pupils, was outlined. This was to be called "central school" and was to provide for both the intellectual development of students and a definite bias toward industrial or commercial work. The central schools would occupy a distinct position from that of the secondary schools, since they would be part of the elementary school system and the leaving age would be 15.

The curriculum of the central school would be practical in character. The aim would be to equip students to enter the commercial or industrial world, but at the same time to proceed, if they wanted, to further training for some particular industry at a polytechnic or similar institution. In all cases handicraft for boys and domestic subjects for girls would form an essential part of it. Subsequently it was stated that the pupils for these schools would be selected on the same lines as those who gained scholarships to attend secondary schools, the implication being that the central school should in no way be regarded as inferior to the secondary school.[80]

The establishment of central schools was hailed by

certain members of the London County Council as "little short of a revolution."[81] About five and a half months later, the London Education Authority opened seven central schools in St. Pancras, Hampstead, Deptford, Brixton, Hackney, Kensington and Mile-end.[82] The experiment was almost simultaneously copied by the city of Manchester.

The influential London *Times Educational Supplement* reacted favorably to the central school. The central schools, it wrote, which would take the place of the higher grade and higher elementary schools, "may do much to improve the education of children in London," and the experiments "will be carefully watched by educational authorities all over the country."[83] In the same vein the Board itself expressed sympathy with the experiment, watching "its progress with interest."[84] The Board also explained the character of such institutions and cited the statistics of their growth. According to its 1911–1912 Annual Report, the London Education Authority had established 31 central schools, containing 42 departments, 19 of which had a commercial bias, 16 an industrial bias, and 7 "a dual bias." The Manchester Education Authority had instituted six District Central Schools, including 3 boys' departments, 2 girls' departments and 3 mixed departments.[85] In a subsequent annual report, the Board of Education noted that in London their number had increased to 49 (16 for boys, 14 for girls, and 19 mixed) with an accommodation for 16,163 scholars.[86]

The distinctive feature of the central schools is to be sought in the word "bias," which could be commercial, industrial or a combination of both. The degree of "bias" in a school determined its characterization, whether, that is, the school was vocational in a narrow sense, semi-vocational, or secondary. Although later, many central schools sought to ape the existing type of secondary school and thus obviate any "bias," the intention of the pioneers of the system was clear. It was the establishment of a type of institution different, yet equal, to the existing secondary school. It was to be non-vocational, i.e., not vocational in the sense that a technical or trade school was, yet oriented in such a way that when students finished at the age of 15 or 16, they could, if they wanted to, directly embark upon a commercial or industrial career. Schools with a specific "bias" had to conform to certain minimum curriculum requirements. Thus, the following minima were laid down for a "commercially-biased" department:

French or other modern foreign language, 4 hours per week. . . . Experimental Science, 2 hours per week for at least the first two years of the 4 year course. . . . Drawing, 2 hours per week. . . . Handicraft, 1 session (half-day) per week for the first 2 years. . . . Domestic Economy, 1 session per week for 3 years. . . . Shorthand, 1½ hours per week for 3 years. . . . Typewriting, where there is sufficient demand, 1 hour per day, in or out of school hours, for 3rd and 4th years. Optional on the part of children.

In an "industrially-biased" department, the curriculum included 12 hours per week of "practical work of all kinds," e.g., science, drawing, clay modelling, wood and metal work, domestic economy, etc.[87]

These "biased" courses, it should be borne in mind, were to be taken *in addition to* the ordinary subjects of the public elementary schools, i.e., in addition to subjects such as English, arithmetic, nature study, geography, history, singing, hygiene and physical training.[88] The purpose of these subjects was akin to the general purpose of the elementary school, i.e., "to form and strengthen the character and to develop the intelligence of the children entrusted to it."[89]

In conclusion, it should be stated that the central school was initiated by London and Manchester to fill the gaps created by (a) the failure of the secondary school to expand adequately its curriculum, and (b) the rejection of higher elementary schools. It was not intended to be a vocational school in the narrow sense that the technical and trade schools were, but rather a practically oriented institution whose function was the extension of the educational purposes of the elementary school, *plus* a certain "bias" for selected pupils between the ages of 11 or 12 and 15 or 16. It was, in other words, more like an annex of the elementary school, as the higher grade and higher elementary schools had been. Like these, it was another institutional expression of what earlier was referred to as the upward thrust of elementary education. But unlike these, its fate was different. For the central school continued, its idea expanded, and in the twenties it was incorporated into the secondary modern school. It is on these grounds that its examination in this study is justified. It is the opinion of this writer that the reason for the subsequent success of this type of school *vis-a-vis* the higher elementary school was its *selective* nature. In a class-conscious society, as the English society was at this time, the value placed upon education was in no small part related to the parents' ability to send their children to certain types of institutions. Selection meant that not everybody could go to such schools. It meant more prestige, perhaps a better position, and, who knows, it *could* mean the same advantages as the other secondary schools.

IX

The First World War
and the Ferment
for Reform

DISLOCATION AND ADJUSTMENT

The immediate effects when war broke out were dislocations in all sectors of the society, including education. Soon after the outbreak of hostilities, the Board of Education issued various circulars to the effect that in certain areas military requirements had necessitated, or might necessitate, the requisitioning of school buildings.[1] This factor, coupled with the increasingly growing shortage of teachers (many were called to arms, others changed their occupations), imposed a heavy strain on the normal functioning of the schools. "For the time being," remarked *The Education Times,* "everything is dominated by the war. Schools feel it in the absence of teachers and in the lack of material."[2]

In spite of severe hardships,[3] school authorities, teachers, pupils, the public and the Government exerted great efforts to keep the educational machine going, and, as far as possible, intact.[4] Judging from the successive reports by the Board,[5] the efforts made by everybody to meet the war exigencies (shortage of teachers, labor, materials, classrooms) were quite admirable.

The war exigencies also called upon the secondary schools to make readjustments of the curriculum and to contribute to the general war effort. Here again the schools responded admirably. The Board's 1914–1915 Annual Report noted that work on munitions, shells, and hospital equipment was being done in various schools;[6] the 1915–1916 Report echoed the same idea, and, as an example, it cited Bradford Secondary School where "more than 1,200 articles, including splints, crutches, bedboards and rests, screens, rollers, trays, etc., have been made in the Manual Training department during the year";[7] and the 1916–1917 Report stated that "a large number of schools have given effective help towards the organization of food production."[8]

In spite of the great difficulties that were created, during the war years there was an unprecedented general interest in education, a steady increase of students attending secondary schools and of schools coming within the Board's purview, as shown in the following table.

TABLE IV
NUMBER OF EFFICIENT SCHOOLS AND PUPILS
DURING THE WAR YEARS[9]

Year	Number of Schools	Number of Pupils
1913–1914	1,027	192,374
1914–1915	1,054	203,540
1915–1916	1,056	212,520
1916–1917	1,056	224,095
1917–1918	1,073	242,024

The increase in schools and enrollments as well as the interest in education can in large part be explained by certain social, political and economic changes or conditions created by the war. One such change was the substantial rise in family earnings on the part of certain groups among the working classes.[10] Although when the war broke out there was immediate labor unemployment, within a few months it ceased, and the problem was shortage rather than surplus of labor. Work started in many factories which had been closed down, and industries engaged in the production of war materials demanded more and more labor. In order to meet the growing labor shortage (more and more men were leaving their jobs to fight the war), employers began recruiting men from other trades, as well as women for jobs hitherto regarded as suitable only for men. Certain war conditions (e.g., commandeering of vessels, importing and exporting goods for military use, labor shortage in dock areas, monopolistic "rings," etc.) brought about a rise in prices, especially of foodstuffs.[11] Labor, accordingly, demanded wage increases and price and profit regulations by the Government. In 1916 the Government set up a Ministry of Food to regulate prices. In the meantime, however, the persistent pressure of labor groups and their occasional striking, in spite of the Law (Munitions of War Act, 1915) which forbade it, were instrumental in bringing about a steady increase in the wage rate. This, coupled with full family employment and overtime, increased—in certain cases quite substantially—total family earnings. In a special study conducted just after the war, Bowley wrote:

Those who continued at their former work got more pay; many were promoted in the scale of work; women and girls' wages approximated more nearly to men's, and in some cases they undertook men's work at men's rate of pay. Nearly every able-bodied or partially able-bodied person was able to get work and to get it continuously. At the same time multitudes of families received government allowances on account of their absent men folk. Even if rates of wages increased less rapidly than prices, the household earnings often increased more rapidly.[12]

Partly as a consequence of this factor there was a blurring of class distinctions by the process of "upward" and "downward" social mobility. A contemporary civil servant noted the following:

Class distinctions . . . are much more blurred—the working classes much better off and better informed . . . the upper classes are poorer, and perhaps the upper middle—professions, etc., while the lower middle—shopkeepers, etc.,—are perhaps better off.[13]

And an Oxford graduate echoed a similar idea:

. . . This tendency towards uniformity shows itself also in the breaking down of barriers which formerly existed between class and class and group and group. War-time economy and ration tickets did much toward bridging the gulf which was fixed between the way of living of rich and poor, and both the new rich and the new poor have learnt that the old social orders were not immutable, that the roles of Lazarus and his patron *are* interchangeable.[14]

In addition to income increases for the working classes and for some of the middle-class people (contractors, investors, etc.), there were other factors which helped blur social classes. The heavy taxation introduced by the war budgets resulted in decreases in the income of the upper and upper-middle classes. Consequently, it was not unusual to see a duke's daughter "hoeing turnips" while her hitherto "social inferiors" were buying "fur coats" out of their earnings in the munition factories. Furthermore, during the war, particularly after the introduction of conscription, the dukes' sons fought side by side with their gardeners' sons, and sometimes they even served under them. Officers' uniforms were worn by young people of all classes, and Public school graduates served in the ranks.[15]

In the political sphere the war years witnessed the reorganization and consolidation of the Labour movement and the extension of the franchise. The Lloyd George-Asquith rift proved to be irreparable, and after that the Liberal Party was never able to organize itself into a united party. But if the war and its politics were detrimental to Liberalism, they gave the Labour Party an opportunity to establish itself as another major party in British politics. Many rank and file Liberals who were disappointed at the early inertia of certain of their leaders and became disenchanted with their own party, joined the Labour ranks. After initial disagreements, the Labourites presented a united front as an independent party.

Although during the war years the working classes rallied to the support of their country, they did not cease their struggle with capital and the Government. Especially after 1916 they pressed for improvements not only in health, housing and labor relations, but also in educational opportunities; and in 1917 their political power was strengthened when a Representation of the People Bill was enacted increasing the total electorate from 8,000,000 to about 21,000,000.

In view of the aforementioned social, economic, and political changes, it is not suprising that the latter years of the war were characterized by a ferment for educational change. H.A.L. Fisher, the distinguished historian, who, in the midst of the war crisis was called upon to head the Board of Education, observed an unusual general interest

in education, especially among the hitherto complacent
laboring classes.

For the first time in our national history education was a
popular subject and discussed in an atmosphere cleared of
religious acrimony. Large audiences were attracted to educational meetings and listened with interest to addresses on the
school age and physical training and how best to fit the
younger generation for the strain and burden of modern life.[16]

FERMENT FOR REFORM: WHO SHALL BE EDUCATED?

In its leader of January 6, 1914, *The Times Educational
Supplement* wrote that "our education is astir with new
ideas." Such ideas, however, were seen to be "discordant
with one another" because they had sprung up from different and diverse roots.[17] Yet in another leader, published
three years later, the same newspaper struck a different
note.

Schemes of educational reform amounting in fact to educational revolution, pour to-day into the Press. The New Year
opens with a demand for reform from every variety of educational body, from statesmen and cranks, experts and amateurs,
headmasters and assistant masters, directors of education, education committees, associations of teachers, and leagues of
reformers and reactionaries, humanists and men of science,
Montessorists, Froebelians, bishops, priests, and the dwellers
in America. Every man and woman in his or her own fashion
has received the wonderful message of reform.[18]

During this period it was generally believed that the
existing educational opportunities were inadequate and
that the State should by legislation extend them. A large
section of the student population was debarred from receiving any educational benefits beyond the elementary
stage (normally ceasing at the age of 14). But, even within
the elementary group, the laws governing child employment were such that many children were forced to work,
and hence they were deprived of the full benefits of that

type of instruction. The nature of the proposals for extending educational opportunities, and the various discussions on the problem, presented certain differences, in certain instances of a quite radical nature.

Education and Labour

Foremost among the various groups and individuals calling for reform were those representing working-class interests, especially the Labour Party and the Workers' Educational Association. In their Fourteenth Annual Conference, held in Glasgow in 1914, the Labour Party Education Committee called for (a) the raising of full-time attendance by progressive stages, (b) the provision of continued education for the vast majority who did not pass to a secondary school, through "a system of compulsory half-time attendance at a continuation school," and (c) the gradual extension of the free-place system.[19] Three years later the Labour Party passed certain resolutions that were quite radical. They called for the abolition of all education fees, the raising of the school leaving age to 16, compulsory part-time attendance for all boys and girls under 18, and universal free compulsory secondary education. Mr. F. Titterington, of the Bradford Trades Council, moved that there should be no specialization until the last year of the secondary school, when a bias could be given in some direction—technical, professional, or commercial—as a part of a general education. He urged that the entire system of education "must be overhauled and enthused with new ideas," and that there should be free and compulsory secondary education which should be organically related to elementary.[20]

At its Seventeenth Annual Conference held in 1918, the Labour Party felt that, although Fisher's first Bill marked a great advance in education, it fell "far short of the minimum that is adequate to the needs of the country." Consequently, a resolution was moved and passed which *inter alia* included the raising of compulsory school age to 16.[21] Subsequently, another resolution which was carried stated that secondary and technical education should be free and open to all capable students, and that vocational training as part of the general system of education should be opposed.[22]

In the same month, i.e., February 1918, the Labour Party adopted a new constitution which expressed a more "socialistic" philosophy,[23] and in June 1918, various resolutions on reconstruction were carried, one of which was addressed to education:

That the conference holds that the most important of all the measures of social reconstruction must be a genuine nationalization of education, which shall get rid of all class distinctions and privileges, and bring effectively within the reach, not only of every boy and girl, but also of every adult citizen, all the training, physical, mental and moral literary, technical, and artistic of which he is capable.[24]

One of the most active organizations campaigning for educational reform on behalf of the interests of the working classes was the Workers' Educational Association (W.E.A.). In July 1916, the W.E.A. submitted a memorandum to the Board of Education concerning the "abnormal employment" of children during the war, and suggested certain reforms immediately after hostilities ceased. The fact that local education authorities relaxed the educational by-laws, thus permitting thousands of children between the ages of 11 and 14 to enter industry, affected the future well-being of these children, and failed to equip them sufficiently for the task of becoming "efficient, self-supporting citizens of a Democracy." Consequently, the memorandum suggested that special facilities be provided for part-time education for children who were employed.[25] In addition, it was suggested that unemployed children should be compelled to attend an elementary or another type of school on a full time basis.

Another important educational idea expressed in this memorandum was that no type of education below the age of 16 should be solely concentrated on special employment "without provision for the general training of the faculties." Even in a technically oriented situation, the aim should be technical *education*, rather than technical *instruction*, viz., "an education of a general character with a special bias towards the interests and occupations in which the child is interested."[26]

The W.E.A.'s campaign in education continued with accelerated speed. In the September 1916 issue of *The Highway*, the "monthly journal of education for the people," J. A. Mactavish, the W.E.A.'s general secretary, hailed the enthusiastic response on the part of several groups representing the interests of labor for "a big move forward." *The Highway* was purchased in large quantities and discussed at meetings and conferences. There were numerous requests for speakers "from many quarters."[27] Mactavish also noted that, at a three-days' conference held at Oxford, there was "unanimity of our conclusions," which included the raising of the school leaving age, the reduction of the size of classes, compulsory part-time education for adolescents, and the opening of secondary schools and universities to all "who are fitted by character and ability to proceed to them."[28]

Three months later, and through the pages of *The Highway*, the W.E.A. presented a comprehensive program for educational reconstruction, recommending certain minimum national requirements, the only road "to social and individual salvation." The ideal set was called "the highway of education." The recommendations were presented in the form of resolutions which were formulated with the cooperation of "Trade Unionists, Co-operators, Socialists, Liberals and Conservatives—men and women, workman and don, teacher and preacher." The resolutions called for the acceptance of the broad principle of education in all its stages, for universal full-time education up to the age of 14, for the raising of the school leaving age to 15, and for compulsory part-time education of 20 hours per week for those deprived of full time education.[29] As regards "full-time secondary education," it was recommended that admission to a secondary school be based on the ability of the student to follow the curriculum; that free provision be made for all students who were "eligible and desirous" to enter such schools; that the number of secondary schools be increased and the curriculum differentiated to meet the needs and interests of individual students; and that liberal education "be regarded as paramount in the organization of every type of secondary school."[30] Essentially the same proposals were made at the W.E.A. National Conference convened on May 3, 1917,[31] and at the meeting of the Central Council held on September 25, 1917.[32]

In summary, the various bodies representing working-class interests espoused and advocated the following. First, compulsory full-time education should extend to the age of 14 (W.E.A.) or 16 (Labour Party). Second, both the W.E.A. and the Labour Party maintained that secondary education should be free and accessible to all who were "capable," or "eligible and desirous." In 1917, the Labour

Party for the *first* time promulgated the doctrine of secondary education for all, which in and of itself marked a great advance in Labour thought. However, it did not describe adequately what this doctrine entailed. It stated that there should be "universal free compulsory secondary education." It did not seek to define secondary education, and the term as understood at the time did little to accommodate what the general doctrine implied. Moreover, the statement "secondary . . . schools shall be free and open to all *capable of making use of the opportunities provided to develop their individual aptitudes,*" which formed part of the resolution adopted in 1918, rendered the Labour notion rather unclear. Third, both bodies emphasized the notion that the primary function of the secondary school should be the provision of a general liberal education, rather than of any vocational (always interpreted in the sense of preparation for a specific vocation) training, although some form of "practical bias" directed towards employment might be given.

The Views of Other Groups

There were various other organizations which expressed their views on the educational situation and suggested lines of action. For example, the Education Reform Council, founded in 1916 at a conference called by the Teachers' Guild, presented a comprehensive program of reform[33] "to widen educational opportunity." It, accordingly, recommended compulsory full-time education in elementary schools up to the age of 14 and, thereafter, part-time education until seventeen. It then suggested a recasting of the elementary school system into (a) primary departments or schools (ages $5\frac{1}{2}$–$11\frac{1}{2}$); (b) middle departments or schools, (ages $11\frac{1}{2}$–$14\frac{1}{2}$); and (c) continuation departments or schools with a vocational bias.

Beyond the elementary stage (the Council used the term elementary but did not imply approval), it was suggested that enough junior scholarships and free places should be provided for capable students. Furthermore, it was proposed that the transfer from elementary to secondary schools take place between the ages of eleven and twelve, and that the number of efficient secondary schools of varying types should be increased.[34]

At its September 6, 1916, meeting at Newcastle, the British Association urged the replacement of the "educational ladder" by an "educational highway."[35] And the Teachers' Registration Council "as representative of the teaching profession," called for (a) compulsory schooling until the age of 14, (b) complusory attendance at one or other of whole-time secondary schools or part-time secondary schools "of varying types," (c) abolition of fees in secondary schools maintained by the local education authorities, and (d) provision of free places in secondary schools which were partly maintained by State grants.[38]

The question of educational reform was taken up by two influential publications, namely, *The Athenaeum*, a literary and scientific journal, and *The Times Educational Supplement*. In a supplement to the September issue, *The Athenaeum* proposed to issue a series of papers, the object of which was to indicate various war changes as well as the modifications in "thought and outlook." In its first article on "The War and Education," it referred to education as "the greatest need of the nation at this time." After commenting on various contemporary viewpoints, *The Athenaeum* asserted that "the times are ripe for the introduction of universal secondary education," but this must be done "through a system of compulsory part-time day continuation schools."[37] In subsequent issues it discussed various aspects of educational reconstruction. But its general position was not novel; it was similar to that of the Workers' Educational Association discussed previously.[38]

On the other hand, *The Times Educational Supplement* adopted a more radical doctrine, namely, secondary education for all. As early as May 1913, the *Educational Supplement* published a letter by J. E. G. DeMontmorency, in which the author called for the recasting of the national system of education, so that every child should have the benefit for a shorter or a longer period of secondary education. DeMontmorency, accordingly, suggested that elementary schools be replaced by preparatory schools for every child up to the age of 10. Thereafter, all children should automatically pass on to secondary schools, or, as he called them, "intermediate schools" (ages 10–14). The purpose of such schools would be "to give an outfit for life, not a technical, nor necessarily a scholarly outfit, but an outfit that would reveal to the child mind something of the general principles that guide mankind." After the fourteenth year the children would either leave for some form of technical study, or continue their education until the seventeenth year.[39]

The two interesting points in DeMontmorency's proposals worthy of note were (a) that secondary education is a *stage* in the educative process, and (b) that everybody should have it.

Soon after war broke out, the *Supplement* opened in its columns what it later called "a campaign for revolution in national education . . . with an urgent demand for immediate action."[40] The reforms advocated and the concept of secondary education were similar to DeMontmorency's.[41] The *Supplement* rejected the notion of continuation schools which Fisher and many others wanted to establish.

The *Supplement*'s campaign continued after the war and the passing of the 1918 Act. In a leader on March 20, 1919, it optimistically looked into the future when "some local authority will have the courage to break definitely with the past and offer preparatory education up to eleven years, and then secondary education for all up to the new age limit."[42]

Official Opinion and Reform

The question of "who shall be educated?" occupied the attention of official circles, and educational reform figured prominently in the government program of reconstruction. Back in 1913, the Consultative Committee was instructed to report on the state of affairs governing the opportunities for transfer from lower to higher educational institutions. The war, as the Committee admitted, necessitated prompt investigation of this problem, and, accordingly, an interim report on "Scholarships for Higher Education" was issued in 1916. The report dealt primarily with the question of scholarships from the secondary schools to the univerties or other places of higher education, and its aim was largely the improvement of scientific and technological efficiency in Britain. However, it expressed certain principles which are directly relevant here. It stressed, for example, the significance of education in the "national recuperation," and the necessity for expanding educational opportunities. Of special significance was the Committee's interpretation of the doctrine of "equal opportunity." To the Committee equal opportunity did not mean equal or "equivalent" education for all. Rather it meant equal opportunities for public education for every one up to a certain age, and thereafter, for only those who "proved themselves fit." Secondary education would be included in this latter category.[43]

In April 1916, Arthur Henderson, a Labour leader, and at the time a member of the War Cabinet, appointed a Departmental Committee whose report appeared in April 1917. Many of the proposals in this report were incorporated in the Education Act of 1918.

The Lewis Report, as the report came to be known, characterized the existing situation as one of "educational and industrial chaos." According to its estimates, only 13 per cent of the pupils enrolled in public full-time day schools (elementary, secondary and junior technical) were likely to have received "any fragment of full-time education after the age of 14," and not more than 5 per cent "can have received this in secondary schools." Of all "juveniles" between 14 and 18, 81.5 per cent were not enrolled either in day schools or in evening schools. Furthermore, a large number of children were "in blind alley occupations," rather than for the purpose of practising a trade as adults.[44] This chaotic state of affairs militated against an efficient social and moral reconstruction of the nation after the war.[45] Something had to be done, especially with the "age of adolescence." In order to solve the problem, the Lewis Report proposed, among others, (a) the enforcement by statute of "a uniform Elementary School leaving age of 14," and (b) compulsory attendance for a certain number of hours per week or year at "Day Continuation Classes" between the ages of 14 and 18.[46]

The significant point for the purposes here was the fact that official opinion recognized the importance of the reform of education, especially that of the adolescent. To the question "who shall be educated?" the official opinion seems to have been: everybody up to the age of 14, and from there on, everybody "more or less" up to the age of 18. There was no conception of "secondary education for

all," or "free secondary education," but there was the notion that everybody must receive some form of education
beyond the national minimum, and that there must exist
some coordination among the various existing types.

The official position on this question was explained further by H. A. L. Fisher, the newly appointed President of
the Board of Education, in his speeches on educational
reconstruction. The State, Fisher stressed, must never
shrink from its responsibility "of diffusing knowledge and
intelligence among the people." Neither the amount of,
nor the opportunities for education were adequate. The
entire system was "half-hearted."[47] Secondary education
"should proceed upon a democratic scale." The free-place
policy must continue, but the State should see that the
great number of children whose education ended at fourteen "secure a minimum of continued education."[48] All
people should be rescued "from the dump helplessness of
ignorance," not only because it was politically prudent,
especially after the enfranchisement of several million of
new voters (Representation of the People Act), but also
because it was the right of human beings "to be considered as ends in themselves."[49]

These views permeated Fisher's speeches in Parliament
and underlay the Government's program of educational
reconstruction. On the floor of the House, he exposed the
lack of opportunities at the secondary level and urged that
secondary education should be available to every boy and
girl who is capable of profiting by it. However, although
he sympathized with the ideal of a system of free secondary
education, he felt it would be impracticable at the time.
Instead he suggested the continuation of the free-place
policy and an increase in scholarships and grants.[50]

Fisher launched his campaign for reform on April 19,

1917, when he asked Parliament to grant £13,565,780 to £5,450,000, already voted on account, "for the Salaries and Expenses of the Board of Education, and of the various establishments connected therewith."[51] In addition to these increases in expenditure, which also included secondary education, he laid down some of the lines upon which he planned to proceed with the reform of the entire system of education. According to him, every child should receive an education "most adapted to fashion its qualities to the highest use"; and the county authorities should devise schemes for an adequate and systematic provision of all types and grades of schools.[52]

The program of reform, and the principles upon which it was based, were elaborated in the speech of August 10, 1917, when Fisher introduced a Bill "to make further provision with respect to education in England and Wales."[53] The measure, Fisher explained, was prompted by deficiencies revealed by the war, and it was framed "to repair the intellectual wastage which has been caused by the War." Moreover, the war had created an "increased feeling of social solidarity" and a new way of thinking among the more reflecting members of the working classes, thus giving impetus to the establishment of an educational democracy. "The same logic," according to him, "which leads us to desire an extension of the franchise points also to an extension of education."[54]

The proposals for reform which Fisher outlined and explained to the House were essentially the same as those of the Lewis Committee. First, the administrative organization established by the 1902 Act would, in the main, remain unaltered; second, all exemptions between the ages of 5 and 14 would be abolished, so that there would be full-time school attendance during that period; third, and, according to Fisher, "the most novel, if not the most important provision of the Bill," every young person "shall attend such continuation school as the local authority of the area in which he resides may require for a period of 320 hours in the year, or the equivalent of eight hours a week for forty weeks;" and lastly, adequate and suitable provision would be made with respect to central schools.[55]

Fisher anticipated that the greatest objection to his proposals would come from employers who depended on child and adolescent labor. His efforts "to sell the idea" to these people remind one of Horace Mann's fight for the public support of education in the United States in the nineteenth century. In his parliamentary speech and in subsequent speeches around the country, Fisher pressed hard the idea that ultimately such educational reforms as he suggested would be for the benefit not only of society in general, but also of industrial efficiency and *pari passu* of industrial output. "We are proposing," he said, "not a form of military conscription, but a form of educational investment," and he asked employers "to reflect how greatly the success of industry depends on the character of their employees."[56] And in his Bradford speech on November 2, 1917, after comparing the situation in England and America, he exhorted his audience to press ahead with educational change, otherwise, "we shall be committing industrial suicide."[57]

In order to have greater chances of success, and in order to alleviate certain objectives, Fisher was advised to recast the Bill, and the new version was read for a second time on March 13, 1918.[58] The main features were vigorously debated and the principles upon which the proposals were based were more clearly brought out. Chief among the points discussed was whether the provisions on compulsory attendance, especially compulsory attendance at continuation schools (ages 14–18), were injurious to industries and agriculture.[59] But Acland noted that public opinion on the whole had been consolidating behind the Bill and was in favor of it.[60]

During the debate on the second reading, Fisher was careful to point out an essential feature of the Bill that seemed to have been neglected in the heat of the discussion. This was the prescription to the local authorities that in their schemes for educational development and organization they should consider all forms and levels of education as parts of a single whole.[61] In addition to central schools, special classes and the like, the local authorities were directed to make adequate arrangements for further education in schools other than elementary, for the transfer of students to such schools, and for the support of such a type of education.[62]

This Education Bill passed into law on August 8, 1918, and came to be known as the Fisher Act. To the question "who shall be educated?" the Fisher Act furnished the following answer: everybody up to the age of 14, and from there on everybody up to the age of 18 but on a part-time basis, except in the case of certain groups of students attending full-time or part-time institutions. The Act did not establish "secondary education for all," nor "free secondary education." These doctrines, though advanced by certain groups, were not as yet accepted by official opinion. Rather, the official view seems to have been that opportunity should be extended by means of scholarships and free places, and that free secondary education should be given, as the Act stated, to those "capable of profiting."[63] However, the Act established these principles: (a) that there should be a co-ordination among the various grades of education; (b) that the education of the adolescents (interpreted as young persons over the age of 14) should be a necessary public concern; and (c) that central schools and senior classes—the direct outgrowths of the upward thrust of elementary education—should be recognized as intermediate schools and should be co-ordinated with secondary schools.

X

The Functions of
Secondary Education
and the Conflict
of Studies

The social and ideological upheaval created by the war
directed public attention to the essential role of the secondary school in relation to the individual and the
society. The issue that seemed to figure most in contemporary discussions on this subject revolved around the question of the liberal versus the technical functions of
secondary education.

One viewpoint expressed largely by industrialists and
other employers was based primarily on economic considerations. According to this view, if every school were
turned into a form of workshop, then the industrial deficiencies revealed by the war, as well as the labour shortage, would be remedied. Such a conception of secondary

230

education would of necessity give scientific, technical and practical studies a predominant place in the content of the curriculum.[1]

There were, however, strong voices against such a utilitarian view. In its 1917 "Review of the Year," *The Schoolmaster's Yearbook* asserted in no equivocal terms that the *raison d'être* of the secondary school was to provide "a liberal training." Specific or technical instruction in professional or commercial studies was "no part of its task."[2] This view did not imply a rigid narrow curriculum. Nor did it imply a bookish type of education that would seek primarily to impart knowledge without having any relation to the pupil's interests or to "the things about him." A "good general education" could take one of several forms, and schools should be free to select the curriculum and the method of treatment. The curriculum should not be made "narrowly technical," and ample scope should be given to develop it according to the interests of the pupils. If this could be accomplished, then it would solve the problem of the "free-placer," for it would aid the student to understand the things about him and in which he is interested. In other words, secondary education was envisaged not in purely intellectual terms, but also in social terms.[3]

Technical instruction as an ingredient of secondary education was objected to by the working classes. It was previously noted that both the Labour Party and the Workers' Educational Association deprecated the idea of including any form of technical or vocational training in the secondary schools, but insisted on the requirements of "a liberal education." *The Times Educational Supplement* observed that Labour favored "the cultural aspect of education" and desired that their sons should have the chance of becoming "all-rounded educated men and not be exploited as expert specialists on some narrow line of work."[4] Essentially the same idea was echoed in the Interim Report of the Committee on Adult Education appointed by the Ministry of Reconstruction. Adults favored an education which was "non-vocational in character." Working classes regarded "technical education" with suspicion, on the grounds that its economic advantages would "accrue mainly to employers of labour."[5]

One of the most vitriolic attacks against the "materialistic" conception of education that viewed the education of the working class solely in terms of economic utility came from *The Athenaeum*. It vehemently attacked the Memorandum on Education issued by the Federation of British Industries (F.B.I.), as advocating nothing else but the old aristocratic conception of education. Such a view, according to it, assumed a dichotomy in society between the well-to-do and the poor, betweent the laboring classes and their superiors, and a different kind of education for each group. For the well-to-do, education was necessary and produced its best results only in the case of the few who were to enter the professions or occupy positions of authority. In so far as it was provided for the masses, "it should be directed mainly towards economic ends." This, *The Athenaeum* called the "capitalist theory of education."[6]

Instead of a "commercial view of education" intended for the cultivation of the intellects of the few, "we must learn to conceive of education as a continuing process as necessary to the full growth of the average person as to the developments of the super-businessman." Education, according to this journal, must not be viewed in terms of "vocational goals," but in terms of the individual and the citizen. The worker is not merely a worker, but a citizen with rights. Hence, education is a privilege which should be enjoyed "by every individual of every class, whether he is 'more promising' or 'less promising.' "[7]

This social purpose was also expressed by the Board of Education and by the Committee on Adult Education. According to them the success of a democratic society depended upon wider educational opportunities, a "wide diffusion of a sense of responsibility," and upon "the intelligent participation in public affairs by the rank and file of the population."[8]

Judging, therefore, by what was said and written at the time, the general opinion was that the function of secondary education was still a liberal or general education, the two terms being used interchangeably. However, the "materialists" would restrict such a type of education to the very few and would interpret "liberal" in a narrowly academic sense. On the other hand, the ideas advanced by the others necessitated a different understanding of "liberal education," for obviously the narrowly academic conception would be inadequate for the purpose of accomplishing the social end of education.

LIBERAL EDUCATION

The ferment of educational discussion during the war extended to the curriculum, where all sorts of vested interests and prejudices were aroused. The growth of schools providing a practical type of education, and the increased importance of applied science brought to the fore by the war, revived the controversies concerning the value of this or that subject in the liberal education of youth. Furthermore, the expanded role of the secondary school, and its concern with the interests of a wider section of the community, necessitated a re-examination of its curriculum as a whole.

The Conflict of Studies

During the war, controversies over the curriculum took one of two forms. On the one hand, there was considerable discussion over the broad categories of the merits of the "humanities" and the "sciences," and on the other, over the educational claims of various subjects. As regards the latter, the battle raged over the value of the classics, which were gradually being pushed out of the curriculum of the secondary schools, and over that of "modern studies" and the sciences, which were advocated as being an essential element of a liberal education.

One of the most vigorous defences of the humanities in general, and the classical tradition in particular, was made by none other than R. W. Livingstone in a widely read book published in 1916. Speaking about the relative merits of the humanities (literature, history, and philosophy), as against physical science, Livingstone maintained that the former "reveal to us man," whereas, paradoxically, "science . . . tells us hardly anything about man."[9] Literature, according to him, views man "as a being with feelings and prejudices, virtues and vices, ruled by intellect or perverted by passion"; philosophy views him "of his own origin, nature and destiny," and history "as a political and social being."[10] Furthermore, a "literary-philosophic-historical education" trains flexibility of mind, sympathy and imagination.[11] Turning then to the classics, Livingstone defended their place in the curriculum of the secondary schools and the universities because of their peculiar qualities of completeness, simplicity, lucidity and directness, and their established importance as

the best introduction to modern problems of life and politics. In fact, Livingstone gave the classics the highest priority in the content of a liberal education, and justified
their study on disciplinary grounds as well.

The classics were also defended by the venerable Bryce,
but Bryce's position was not as extreme as Livingstone's.
He distinguished between two classes of knowledge, i.e.,
"the world of nature," (physical science), and "the world
of man" (humanities), and asserted that "plenty of knowledge in both is needed to produce a capable and highly
finished mind."[12]

Livingstone's defence of classical education, and his contention that such a type constituted the essence of a liberal
education, were rebutted, at times rather pungently, by
H. G. Wells. Wells advanced the claims of the mother
tongue as a better medium for the Englishman in the
study of such subjects as philosophy and history.[13] Then
he cited examples, including Livingstone himself, to support the view that the study of the classics did not necessarily result in better use of the English language.
Assuming the role of "Paterfamilias," Wells would have
his boy educated humanistically, but, bearing in mind
that his boy was English, he would have him exercise himself "in every possible use of our most flexible, beautiful,
expressive, and very difficult tongue."[14] He saw in the exclusive study of the classics a narrow, aristocratic conception of education unsuitable for a democracy, and "cut-off
from the market-place."[15]

The claims of the classics were also advanced by other
individuals.[16] However, the nineteenth century argument
that a classical education not only formulated the question "what is liberal education?" but also had specific answers for it, was no longer an unquestioned, self-evident

assumption. Although they were still required for entry into Oxford and Cambridge, and for the Higher Division Civil Service Examinations, it was admitted that their study "was seriously threatened." A special committee, appointed by the Prime Minister to inquire into their position in the educational system of the United Kingdom, found that the numbers of students taking classics was gradually diminishing, and in some instances Latin and Greek were almost disappearing.[17]

The claims of the modern studies were advanced in a comprehensive report issued by another special committee appointed by the Prime Minister in August 1916. The Leathes Committee, as it was called (after Stanley Leathes, its chairman), defended modern studies (historical, economic, literary, critical, philological), and others which were directly approached through modern languages, on practical, disciplinary and cultural grounds.[18]

This aim, which the report called "the idealistic aim," had hitherto furnished the educational and psychological rationale of classical education. In fact, classical studies held the monopoly as instruments in its achievement. But, the Leathes Report maintained, although the discipline of the two areas—modern and classical—might not be identical, it might nevertheless be equivalent.[19]

The Leathes Committee was careful to point out that the need for modern studies became clearer and more insistent during and because of the war. The ignorance of the English people about foreign countries not only hampered them in their preparation for such national crises as the war, but also impeded the effective prosecution of the war. In addition, therefore, to being useful for industry and commerce, as well as for cultural uplifting, modern studies were a national necessity, indispensable for a post-war "instructed democracy."[20]

The third curriculum area that was brought to the fore of educational discussion was science. Early in 1916 a self-organized committee comprising a group of noted scientists drew up a memorandum in which they ascribed certain war failures to the neglect of science in the schools and the universities of England. The committee, accordingly, urged that "physical science" (mechanics, chemistry, physics, biology, geography, and geology), and the scientific method, be given more attention, especially in the training of leaders and administrators.[21] Three months later, Lord Rayleigh, presiding over the committee, urged that "time for the teaching of science must be found by displacing classics from the privileged position they now occupy." At the same meeting, E. Schafer moved a resolution, which was adopted unanimously, urging that natural science be made an integral part of the curriculum of all schools, and be included in the entrance examinations of all universities.[22]

A Synthesis of the Scientific and the Humane

In August 1916, the Prime Minister appointed another special committee, headed by Sir J. J. Thomson, "to enquire into the position of Natural Science in the educational system of Great Britain." The report issued two years later presents a comprehensive viewpoint on the same lines as the Modern Studies Report. Like the latter, it admitted that the war and its needs highlighted "the nation's weakness in Science," and that improvement in the scientific education of the country was a matter of national necessity and post-war reconstruction.

At the outset, the Thomson Report contended that the teaching of science should not be looked at solely in terms of "material and mechanical aspects," but also in terms of its "humanizing influence." Subsequently, certain "distinct kinds of educational value" were formulated, which attest very clearly to the educational rationale upon which science was advocated, as well as to the persistence of the psychological doctrine of mental discipline.[23]

The Committee eulogized the "material" and the "educational" values of science as follows:

How necessary Science is in war, in defence and offence, we have learnt at a great price. How it contributes to the prosperity of industries and trade all are ready to admit. How valuable it may be in opening the mind, in training the judgment, in stirring the imagination and in cultivating a spirit of reverence, few have yet accepted in full faith.

The Thomson Report then considered science in the curriculum of existing secondary schools, public and grant-earning, and made specific recommendations for its improvement. It noted that through the control exercised by the Board of Education since the beginning of the century, science teaching occupied a position "in no way inferior to that of any other subject." The Committee, however, felt that in certain areas, especially in the more thickly populated ones, more attention could be given to "Science, Mathematics, Manual Instruction and Drawing."[24] Subjects of this nature, according to it, should be regarded as an essential part of the general education of boys and girls up to the age of 16. Referring to secondary education, it echoed the commonly held conception that the best preparation for any occupation or profession was a general education in "English, History and Geography, Languages other than English, Mathematics and Natural Science."[25] It is within the context of such a broader framework that the report advocated the study of science, i.e., within the framework of a liberally educated individual and a citizen.[26]

During this period there were other attempts made to

view the curriculum as a whole, rather than to push the claims of one subject at the expense of others. In a letter signed by a group of noted men of letters, including such figures as James Bryce, J. B. Bury, H. A. L. Fisher, Frederick G. Kenyon, Gilbert Murray, W. Osler and G. O. Trevelyan, an attempted synthesis was sought. Emphasis was placed on education as a preparation "for the whole of life" rather than for "practical efficiency" or "technical know-how." More than anything else, the nation required training in "scientific method" and a belief in mental training which could be accomplished through classics, history, politics, etc., as well as "physical science."[27]

The letter was published in *The Times* of London on May 4, 1916. In September 1916, *The Journal of Education* published a communication drawn by a conference representing the Classical, English, Geographical, Historical and Modern Language Associations. The communication included six resolutions which were intended "to form a basis for common action between the five associations and . . . for cooperation with representatives of the natural sciences as well as with those of other elements in education." The categories "humanities" and "sciences" were used rather apologetically and for the sake of "brevity," as "all would agree that 'humanistic' studies should be scientific, and 'scientific' studies humane." The five resolutions marked the greatest compromise in a battle dating as far back as the 1860's, and are worthy of being quoted in full.

(i) It is essential that any reorganization of our educational system should make adequate provision for both humanistic and scientific studies.

(ii) Premature specialization on any one particular group of studies, whether humanistic or scientific, to the exclusion of all others, is a serious danger, not only to education generally but to the studies concerned.

(iii) Humanistic education implies the adequate study of language and literature, geography and history, which in each case should, at the appropriate stages of education, go beyond the pupils' own language and country.

(iv) The representatives of humanistic studies would welcome from the representatives of the mathematical and natural sciences a statement with regard to those studies similar to that contained in (iii).

(v) In all reform of education it must never be forgotten that the first object is the training of human beings in mind and character, as citizens of a free country, and that any technical preparation of boys and girls for a particular profession, occupation, or work must be consistent with this principle.[28]

Two months later, the same journal editorially observed that the above "manifesto" had received "the adhesion of a large number of organizations, including several which represent Natural Science and the teaching profession."[29] The Association of Public School Science Masters expressed "cordial agreement" with the principle stated in the manifesto; so did the Mathematical Association in an announcement signed by A. N. Whitehead, its president.[30]

In the meantime, on October 13, 1916, a Council of Humanistic Studies was formed with Viscount Bryce as president and Sir Frederick Kenyon, as chairman. This Council immediately entered into relations with the Joint Board of Scientific Studies, which was brought into being through the efforts of the Royal Society (representing mathematics and natural science), and the Neglect of Science Committee referred to previously.[31] At a conference convened on December 8th in the rooms of the Royal Society, representatives of the different groups agreed that in all schools the curriculum up to the age of 16 "should be general and not specialized," and that it should include an integrated course of languages, English and history, mathematics, natural sciences including geography, and artistic and manual training.[32] This conference was followed by another held on January 26, 1917, again in the room of the Royal Society, by several groups representing the various subject matter areas. Here again various resolutions were passed based on essentially the same principles and recommending the same curriculum.[33]

Against such a background it was not surprising that the Board of Education in its 1917 secondary school policy regulations merely echoed the above climate.

> In order to be recognized as a Secondary School . . . a School must offer to each of its pupils a progressive course of general education . . . of a kind and amount suitable for pupils of an age range at least as wide as from 12 to 17. . . . The curriculum must provide instruction in the English Language, and Literature, at least one Language other than English, Geography, History, Mathematics, Science and Drawing. A curriculum including two languages other than English, but making no provision for instruction in Latin, will only be approved where the Board are satisfied that the omission of Latin is for the educational advantage of the School. The instruction in Science must include practical work by the pupils.[34]

It was further provided that "organized games, physical exercises, manual instruction, and singing" be included.

These provisions pertained to secondary education up to the age of 16 or 17. Beyond that, a new policy was initiated whereby an advanced course could be provided in one or other of three groups of subjects, viz., science and mathematics, classics, and modern studies.[35]

Conflicts over the content of the curriculum, and controversies over the relative value of the various subjects, were not new. In his famous St. Andrews Inaugural Address about fifty years earlier, John Stuart Mill had referred to "the great controversy of the day" as "the vexed question between the ancient languages and the modern sciences

and arts; whether general education should be classical
. . . and say literary—or scientific."[36] Indeed one is struck
by the similarities in the arguments used in the two periods
in support of certain subjects. On both occasions the
"mental gymnastics argument" figured prominently. "As
an intellectual exercise," wrote the Thomson Report, in
language that reminds one of Herbert Spencer and T. H.
Huxley, science "disciplines our powers of mind." In
pushing the claims of the modern studies as essential ingredients of a liberal education, the Leathes Committee
echoed the same idea when it said that "language teaching
in schools has and should have a disciplinary and educative
aim." And, of course, so did Livingstone in his justification
of the classics.

A second argument that was used both in the 1860's and
during the war period was the cultural value of studies.
The Leathes Committee defended modern studies as being
"an instrument of culture," and the Thomson Report contended that in addition to its utilitarian value, science has
a "humanizing influence."[37]

Yet from the historical standpoint there were also important differences. It was evident that by the time of the
First World War the classics were no longer the unquestioned champion of liberal education. Indeed, by then they
were clearly on the defensive. Science had not only secured
a firm position in the curriculum of the secondary schools;
its practical and utilitarian value was openly acknowledged,
and no longer did its advocates have to take cover under
the protective wings of "culture" and "mental discipline,"
as was the case fifty years earlier. Finally, the controversies
during the war were followed by actual concrete programs
and by statutory sanction.

In this changing attitude the war itself was an important

contributing factor as was shown earlier. Time and again the arguments on behalf of scientific and modern studies were tied up with questions of "the promotion of national efficiency," of prosperity and power for the individual and the society, of "defence and offence," and the like. Indeed, it is not uncommon to observe that when nations undergo a period of crisis and reconstruction, education in general and the curriculum of the schools in particular become the centers of attention and controversy.

The heated arguments over the relative values of subjects in creating liberally educated men and women and useful citizens for a changing society were not limited to England. Echoes were heard in Europe and the United States. At the same time as the various individuals and organizations were conferring and issuing their reports and resolutions, similar conferences were held in the United States and the same issues were discussed. The most notable of these gatherings was the Princeton Conference, a most diverse assemblage of personages ever to discuss matters affecting education and its relation to the welfare of the individual and the society. There were classicists and scientists, businessmen, professors and presidents of universities, presidents of business organizations and newspaper editors; there were statements by senators, by ex-Presidents of the United States, by the Secretary of State, and by President Woodrow Wilson himself. Heartened by this august assemblage to discuss such a "dull and uninteresting subject as education," James Bryce sent the following telegram: "Rejoice to hear energetic efforts being made in America to vindicate place of classical studies."[38] An ironic twist, one might say, to the fortunes of a long standing and glorious tradition.

XI

Post-War Developments and Outlooks

EDUCATION AND POLITICAL TENDENCIES

Soon after armistice was declared, the eight year old Parliament was dissolved, and at the general elections of December, 1918, the Lloyd George new coalition won a decisive victory. Of the 706 members elected, the coalition parties (Conservatives, Lloyd George Liberals, National Democratic) won 484 seats, against 222 won by the noncoalition parties (Labour, Noncoalition Conservatives, Asquith Liberals, National Party, Independents, Sinn Feiners, Irish Nationalist).[1] Although the Lloyd George Liberals numbered 136, the elections were a victory for the Conservatives, who numbered 338. The Lloyd George-Asquith split, which began soon after the outbreak of the war, proved disastrous for the Liberal Party, which in the later elections of the twenties was almost annihilated. On the other hand the Labour Party increased its parliamentary representation from 38 to 59 and became the official party of the Opposition.

244

The postwar Coalition Government (1918–1922) was beset by political and social commotion. The war boom lasted for a very short while and was followed by a slump. Labor unrest increased and there were even appeals to "direct action" though they were never put into operation.[2] Until 1920 the amount of unemployment was very little, although it was still higher than that of the war years. But towards the close of the year 1920 there was a collapse of trade accompanied by a rapid decline of employment. By June 1921, 20 per cent of the workers were unemployed, and, although the percentage declined somewhat the following year, it was still very high. In May 1922 it was 16 per cent. Then it dropped to 14 per cent, and from 1923 to 1929 it ranged from 12.5 per cent to 9.7 per cent, representing a little over a million workers, or double the pre-war average.[3] Labor commotion was heightened by the fact that the Government, instead of continuing the policy of "control" of the war years, adopted a "decontrol" policy, thus frustrating any Labour hopes for the nationalization of industries.[4]

In addition to these economic and labor troubles, and largely as a consequence of them, there was confusion in party politics. The Coalition Government, especially after 1920, was growing unpopular even among its own members. This unpopularity stemmed in part from the character of Lloyd George, who had assumed almost dictatorial powers in the direction of Cabinet decisions.[5] But it was also due to the fact that most of the issues that had hitherto separated the Conservative and the Liberal Parties had disappeared. In Mowat's words, "On social policy, on education, on questions of empire or foreign relations nothing now separated them."[6] Some entertained hopes of a fusion similar to the Unionist fusion of the eighteen nineties, but the Conservatives, especially the die-hard political bosses, wanted to dissociate themselves from a possible Liberal-Conservative rapprochement. The spark to the dissolution of the idea of "fusion," and in fact to the fall of the Coalition Government, was given by the Chanak crisis, for which Lloyd George and his Liberal policies were blamed. Soon after, Lloyd George resigned and Bonar Law formed a Conservative Government. Party politics were re-aligned on the old Conservative, Liberal, Labour pattern. At the general election held on November 15, the Conservatives were returned, with a majority of 73 over all other parties combined.[7]

Two significant things can be said about the results of this election. In the first place, the Liberals, who were still divided and who fought as two parties (Liberal under Lloyd George and National Liberal under Asquith) were pushed to the background; in the second, the Labour Party won a striking success, having secured 142 seats, and thus became, as the *Annual Register* recorded, "the second strongest Party at St. Stephens."

Although in the elections that followed one year later the Liberals looked as if they would make a comeback, their strength as a major political force was sealed. This can be ascribed in part to the lack of a unified leadership caused by the long Lloyd George–Asquith rift. More important, however, was the fact that Liberalism had lost certain of its distinguishing characteristics. On the one hand, its policy of social reform was in many respects indistinguishable from that of the Tories; on the other, the element of radicalism, which had hitherto rallied many of the workers to its support, had been wrested from its hands by the Labour Party.

The Tory Government did not last long. Its electoral slogan of "Tranquillity and Stability" was, as Hutchison put it, "an aspiration, not a policy."[8] Affairs, both domestic and foreign, were neither "tranquillized," nor "stabilized,"[9] and in the autumn of 1923 the country was subjected to another general election. The results showed, as the *Annual Register* for that year recorded, "a strong drift to the left" on the part of the electorate, "so that the Liberals gained at the expense of the Unionists (Conservatives) and Labour at the expense of both."[10] The same source gave the Conservatives 258 seats, Labour 191, and Liberals 158, a few Independents comprising the rest. No party had an over-all majority. But, with the support of the Liberals, Labour was called upon to form a Government, the first Labour Government in British history, with J. Ramsay MacDonald as Prime Minister.

The Labour Party assumed office under precarious conditions. The problem of unemployment was still unsolved. In Parliament Labour it was crippled by the fact that it was a minority party and depended on Liberal support for the effective execution of its policy. Moreover, the party leaders were divided on the degree of socialism they were to follow. By the 1918 constitution[11] and the manifesto *Labour and the New Social Order*,[12] the Labour Party was committed to an outright policy of socialistic reconstruction. On Labour's accession to power, the "left-wing" Clydesiders (29 M.P.'s elected by the Clydeside workers in Scotland), represented in the Cabinet by John Wheatley, the newly-appointed Minister of Health, were constantly discontented with the moderate policies of MacDonald and the other members of the Cabinet. Discontent also arose between the Executive Committee of the Party and the Cabinet.[13]

In general, the first Labour Cabinet was a composite of moderate, right-wing, bourgeois "Labourites," including, furthermore, some aristocratic deserters from the Liberal camp, e.g., C. P. Trevelyan, who was given the presidency of the Board of Education; Haldane, who became Lord Chancellor; and Noel Buxton, who was given the Ministry of Agriculture.[14] This composition, although disconcerting to certain groups, was not an unexpected one considering the diverse elements that went by the name of "Labour," which ranged from socialist evolutionary intellectuals (MacDonald, Snowden, Webb), to Trade Unionists (Clynes, Shaw), and Clydeside radicals (Wheatley).[15] Moreover, it was reassuring to many sections of the general public that no socialist revolution of the Russian type or a complete socialist reconstruction was forthcoming.

The Labour victory, however, was short-lived. Within less than a year MacDonald's Government fell, and the Conservatives assumed the reins of Government under Baldwin. Labour's defeat, however, did not imply its extinction from British politics. Its place as the other major party has continued to the present time. Its emergence in that capacity indicated the consummation of the upward thrust of the "lower" strata of society for a voice in British politics and social policy. And, although in the twenties its social philosophy contained elements of the Conservative-Liberal tradition it sought to supersede, it was essentially progressive and novel. An outstanding example of this was Labour's conception of secondary education.

Post-war Secondary Education and Labour Policy

The Fisher reforms raised high hopes in the plans for postwar educational reconstruction. Many features, e.g., the raising of the school leaving age to 14, the medical inspection of pupils, and the School Certificate and Higher School Certificate examinations, remained, but the provision concerning the establishment of continuation schools did not take firm roots. The heaviest blow that fell upon them, and which to a degree set back temporarily the growth of secondary education, was the so-called "Geddes Axe."

Owing to the post-war slump, Government supporters and many representing business interests demanded drastic cuts in expenditures and a stringent economy. Accordingly, in August 1921, the Government appointed a committee of business men under Sir Eric Geddes, the Minister of Transport, "to make recommendations to the Chancellor of the Exchequer for effecting forthwith all possible reductions in the National Expenditure on Supply Services."[16] Geddes promised to do that "with an axe"; hence, the three reports published in 1922 have come to be known as the "Geddes Axe." One of the major victims of this "axe" was education. In the area of secondary education, the report recommended substantial increases in fees and reductions in expenditures for the support of secondary schools.[17] Furthermore, it recommended that free secondary education be confined "to children whose mental calibre justifies it and whose parents cannot afford to pay for it."[18]

Although the educational recommendations of the Geddes Committee were not carried out in full, what cuts were made[19] were by no means insignificant in view of the rising demands for more education. They checked the growth of the continuation schools recommended by the Fisher Act, and inhibited the full application of an important principle established in the same Act, namely, that "children and young persons shall not be debarred from receiving the benefits of any form of education by which they are capable of profiting through inability to pay fees."[20]

TABLE V
INCREASE IN NUMBER OF FREE-PLACE PUPILS[24]

Year	Number of Free-Place Pupils	Percentage of Total Numbers
1909–1910	44,652	31.4
1914–1915	57,933	32.1
1919–1920	82,632	29.3
1924–1925	112,710	34.4
1925–1926	117,171	35.6
1926–1927	124,588	36.4
1927–1928	131,309	37.6

In spite of the Government's post-war economy drive, there was a continued increase in secondary schools and in the number of children attending them. In 1918–1919 there were 961 secondary schools eligible for grants, educating a total of 245,993 pupils. In addition, there were 134 schools recognized as efficient, which educated 27,400 pupils.[21] By 1923–1924 the number of schools eligible for grants had increased to 1,137, and the number of pupils to 327,601.[22] The "other schools" recognized by the Board as efficient numbered 254, and the pupils in them, 49,438. In 1926–1927, there were 1,177 secondary schools eligible for grants with 342,304 pupils in them, and an additional 305 "efficient schools," which by October 1927 had increased to 311, with 57,655 pupils in them.[23]

In addition to the increase in schools and students, there was, as the above table indicates, an increase in the number of "free places." Yet opportunities at the secondary level were felt to be limited relative to the existing demand. Speaking in the House of Commons on August 12, 1919, Fisher exclaimed: "All over the country I find the cry goes up: More secondary schools, and, again more secondary schools! We cannot build them fast enough to hold the pupils who want to go into them."[25]

The inadequacies of the existing state of affairs just after the war were brought out in a comprehensive report written at the direction of the President of the Board by the Departmental Committee on Scholarships and Free Places, headed by E. Hilton Young.

The Young Report recorded that the number of children in grant-aided secondary schools, junior technical and similar schools, was 8.7 to each 1,000 of the estimated population of England for the year 1919–1920.[26] In London and other areas the tendency was to accept "10 school places per 1,000 of population." This ratio the Committee found inadequate and it suggested 20 per 1,000 instead, "a figure mentioned to us in evidence, and not, we believe, inconsistent with the view now taken by many Authorities."[27] It was further shown that the so-called educational ladder was rather narrow, in spite of the free-place policy. Of a total of 627,826 pupils in public elementary schools in 1919, between the ages of 10 and 11, only 59,666, i.e., less than 10 per cent, were admitted to some kind of grant-aided post-elementary schools.[28]

It should be remembered that the Fisher Act had established two significant principles: first, that the local authorities were obligated to contribute towards the establishment of a national system of public education "available for all persons capable of profiting thereby";[29] and, second, that no person should be debarred "from receiving the benefits of any form of education" by which he or she is capable of profiting "through inability to pay fees." In seeking to answer the question: "What does 'capable of profiting' mean?" the Young Committee concluded that "practically *all* children, except the subnormal, are capable in the limited sense," i.e., about 75 per cent.[30] This percentage, of course, represented a far greater number of children who could profit from a secondary education but did not have the opportunity. A great many pupils were denied secondary education because of "inability to pay fees"; but, according to the provisions of the Act, this should not have been the case. The local authorities should have seen that enough scholarships and free places were provided. Again the Committee found that the situation with respect to "free places" was inadequate, although the number was higher than at any previous time. It, accordingly, recommended that free places be increased from 25 to 40 per cent.[31]

The Young Report contained certain educational ideas which foreshadowed the trend of educational thought in subsequent years. It emphasized the significance to social well-being of secondary education for the greatest possible number of children, and argued that the same logic that had made the State accept full financial responsibility for elementary and part-time post-elementary education, applied with equal force to secondary. If this were not accepted, then the State assumed "an artificial and unsound distinction between the several stages of the educational process." The ideal envisaged here was free secondary education. Owing, however, to the "urgent need for national economy," the Committee did not recommend it as an "immediate policy," but as "a prospective policy."[32]

Another notion expressed in the Report was that the best age of transfer from the elementary to the secondary school was between 11 and 12, an assertion that was made after consultation with people concerned with "the nature of human development." It further recommended that all pupils at that age "should be examined for scholarship purposes," because "the country cannot afford to miss intelligent children."[33] Lastly, it called for a variety of post-elementary schools, the known secondary constituting only one type, and suggested that the transference to such schools take place at the age of 11 or 12.[34]

The evidence accumulated by the Departmental Committee's report on scholarships and free places, and many of its underlying ideas, were skillfully utilized and woven into a masterful exposition of Labour policy by R. H. Tawney. In his *Secondary Education for All: A Policy for Labour*, Tawney presented the most comprehensive statement on Labour's position concerning secondary education, and indeed on the doctrine of secondary education for all.

The course of Labour thought up to 1918 was discussed in the previous chapters of this study. The contention thus far has been that Labour did not envisage a reshaping of the concept of secondary education on the lines of secondary education for all, but rather the extention of opportunity so that working class children of ability would not be debarred from climbing the educational ladder. Labour thought, however, shifted in the twenties.

At its Eighteenth Annual Conference held in London, June 1918, the Executive Committee of the Labour Party approved the Fisher Bill as being "comprehensive" and as embodying "so many of the things that Labour has advocated for a long time."[35] Yet, the conference, although appreciative of the educational advances proposed by the Fisher Bill, declared that "the Labour Party cannot be satisfied with a system which condemns the great bulk of the children to merely elementary schooling." It, accordingly, called for "genuine nationalization of education," which would get rid of all class distinctions and privileges and bring within the reach of everybody all aspects of education "of which he is capable."[36]

At its Nineteenth Annual Conference held at Southport the following year, Labour upheld its previous position and went further. One of the resolutions passed stated that "all grades of education shall be free, from the primary school to the University," whilst another read:

That secondary education shall be placed within the reach of every child by a non-competitive system of maintenance scholarships, sufficiently liberal to enable every child who can reach a certain degree of efficiency to remain at school longer than the present system allows.[37]

At subsequent conferences, Labour protested against the curtailment of educational opportunities brought about by the economy drive of the Geddes Committee, and called for the implementation of the principles embodied in the 1918 Act.[38] And at its Twenty-third Annual Conference held in London, in June 1923, it upheld the same principles, calling for the implementation of the Labour's educational policy.[39]

It was at this juncture that R. H. Tawney "edited" his manifesto for the Education Advisory Committee of the Labour Party. The opening lines boldly enunciated the doctrine of secondary education for all and the corollary notion, i.e., that primary and secondary education should be organized "as two stages in a single and continuous process; secondary education being the education of the adolescent and primary education being education preparatory thereto." Such a conception, according to Tawney, was "educationally sound" and "suited to a democratic community." He stated Labour's objective as follows:

Its objective . . . is both the improvement of primary education and the development of public secondary education to

*such a point that all normal children, irrespective of the in-
come, class, or occupation of their parents, may be transferred
at the age of eleven from the primary or preparatory school
to one type or another of secondary school.*

Secondary schools could be of different types, but they
should all form a system of "free and universal secondary
education."[40]

This was the *first* time that such a statement was made by
a Labour committee. It expressed a revolutionary ideal in
Labour thought; one that would, according to Tawney,
take time. In the meantime, however, and as a step towards
that ideal, he recommended the abolition of fees in grant-
aided secondary schools, "either at one stroke or by increasing the number of free places from year to year."
Pending such a reform, he urged that the recommendations
of the Departmental Committee on Scholarships and Free
Places be carried out.[41]

To Tawney, the existing division of education into
elementary and secondary was "educationally unsound and
socially obnoxious." He called for a regrading of the educational system into (a) *primary,* "for all children up to
eleven to twelve," and (b) *secondary,* "for boys and girls
between the age of twelve and sixteen-eighteen."[42]

Tawney elaborated that the most vital question of educational policy was how to establish "a living and organic
connection between primary and secondary education."
Although tremendous progress had been made in that
direction since 1895, it was not as it should have been.
Only a small fraction of capable elementary school children
could receive a full time secondary education. Secondary
education was not, as it should be, "the education of the
adolescent," nor, "primary education preparatory education." The former too often was "a landing without a

staircase," and the latter "a staircase without a landing."[43]
He clamored for the greater democratization of secondary
education, which he defined in terms of three general
characteristics, viz., age, curriculum, and purpose. The
novelty in his definition was his conception of secondary
education as the education encompassing the period of
"adolescence," which he envisaged as starting at the age of
11. As regards curriculum and purpose, he accepted the
Board's definitions. The aim of secondary education was
not specialized training for any particular trade or profession, but the development of all the faculties of man;[44]
and he agreed with the Board that "English, one foreign
language, geography, history, mathematics, science, and
drawing" should provide "a common nucleus of study,"[45]
although "the degree of emphasis laid on the linguistic,
as compared with the mathematical and scientific side,
will naturally vary from school to school." In addition,
Tawney contended, there will be schools which, without
neglecting their main function, i.e., the provision of a
good general education, will develop "a rural or an industrial 'bias,'" and which "will make a generous use of
the interest of boys and girls in 'practical' work."[46]

This then was the essence of Labour thought in the
early twenties. The goal was free secondary education for
all, and all measures taken at the time should aim at that
goal. Tawney justified his position on educational and
social grounds. In fact this was the first time that *educational* opinion was brought in to lend further validity to
Labour contentions.[47]

Tawney's manifesto was later accepted as the official
Labour statement on secondary education.[48] Early in 1925,
Labour introduced a parliamentary motion which was
agreed to by all parties, and which embodied most of the

immediate proposals recommended by Tawney and the Departmental Committee on Scholarships and Free Places.[49]

Labour's conception of secondary education was another expression of Labour's progressive yet moderate social philosophy. The notions that secondary education should be interpreted as a stage in the educational process, and that it should be free for every boy or girl entering the period of adolescence, were certainly progressive. And insofar as Labour alone was concerned, they were, one might say, revolutionary. For, although resolutions had previously been passed calling for universal free secondary education, such pronouncements were not only vague and general, but they also lacked the necessary program of action. Tawney's memorandum was the first comprehensive statement embodying definite lines of action. The significance of this becomes greater when one considers that the power of Labour in the twenties had increased to an unprecedented degree. When it came, however, to defining the content and purpose of secondary education, Labour relied heavily on the ideas and values of the conservative-liberal tradition it sought to supersede. Moreover, it was content to accept intermediary steps, realizing that it would take time to achieve the ideal it set. This is another indication of the general character of the Labour movement, namely, the emphasis on an evolutionary sort of social development, one that would be accomplished through parliamentary and constitutional means rather than outright revolutionary reconstruction.

The earnestness of Labour in its interest in secondary education was shown by the fact that, when it came to power, C. P. Trevelyan instructed the Consultative Committee to investigate the problem of the education of the adolescent and to implement the Labour scheme. The result was the report entitled *The Education of the Adolescent*, which will be fully discussed later in this study.

EDUCATION AND SOCIO-ECONOMIC TENDENCIES

The evidence given by the Departmental Committee on Scholarships and Free Places and by R. H. Tawney indicated that educational provisions for all the students "capable of profiting" were insufficient. The base of recruitment into secondary schools was rather narrow and only certain classes of people could be benefited. In another socialist manifesto, published in 1924, Tawney called the educational period after the age of 14 "an educational desert, with a few small and scattered oases."[50] These views were further corroborated by the sociological findings published at the time by Carr-Saunders and Jones. Speaking of the years 1921–4, Carr-Saunders and Jones concluded that 80 to 85 per cent of all children did not and were unable to obtain full-time education after the age of 14.[51] To be sure, the percentage of pupils climbing the ladder (about 12 of every 100) was much higher than in 1895 or 1902, but in the opinion of many social and educational reformers it was inadequate in the post-war period.[52] The inadequacy of educational provision was further accentuated by certain changes in the socio-economic condition of England, such as changes in the laws and conditions affecting the employment of children, in the social stratification, and in the occupational structure of the society.

"Boy-labor" had been a characteristic of the British industrial system since its inception. As time passed, various laws were enacted to protect children from economic exploitation, until, by the Fisher Act of 1918, stringent restrictions were made on the employment of young children, especially at the age of 14 and under.[53] But after the age of 14, i.e., after the age at which compulsory attendance ceased, the majority of children entered upon wage-earning occupations. A committee appointed by the President of the Board of Education and the Minister of Labour estimated that about 600,000 "juveniles" left the various types of schools annually and entered "some kind of employment other than occupations at home."[54] Many of these children entered occupations in industries at which employment ceased at the age of 18, with the result that they had to look for new jobs, in many cases in different industries. Many of those who intended to become apprentices had to wait for a year or two and, even after the expiration of the contractual relationship, they could still be jobless for there was no job guarantee by the employer.[55] Hence, the question of choice of occupation presented problems, and juvenile unemployment was quite high, a factor which was conducive to an increase in juvenile delinquency.[56] Reformers contended that a way to remedy this situation was to raise the age of compulsory attendance and to create enough free places and scholarships for more children to be educated beyond the elementary stages. In this way they would become better qualified to enter other than "blind-alley"occupations.[57]

In addition to this situation, many heavy industries such as iron, steel and chemicals, required some preliminary training, which, as things were, was given in the form of "apprenticeships" or "learnerships." However, the training was "noneducative" and too narrowly vocational. To remedy the situation, it was suggested that the concept of secondary education be enlarged to accommodate prepration for the changing industrial world.[58]

The demand for equality of educational opportunity

was also strengthened by certain equalitarian tendencies which gained accelerated momentum in the post-war period. One such tendency was the further blurring of the "social classes." "We hear less than formerly," wrote Carr-Saunders and Jones, "of the 'upper,' 'middle,' and 'lower' social classes." On the notions of "class-consciousness" and "class warfare," they had this to say:

The belief in the existence of social classes, or even of one social class, the interests of the members of which are identical, or nearly so, and opposed to the interests of the rest of the community, is the result of studying social theory of doubtful value and of neglecting social facts.[59]

By 1925, according to Mowat, "It was taken for granted that the old order of high society of the glittering Edwardian days had gone for ever."[60]

Another tendency towards social equality was the continued effort by the State to improve the general standard of living and to continue the collectivistic policy in certain services, e.g., insurance, housing, pensions, education, etc.[61] Gradually the individual looked more and more to the State to satisfy his needs and promote social equality; and educational opportunity was envisaged as the *sine qua non* of social opportunity. Moreover, as real wages increased,[62] the desire for better education also increased.

In addition to these equalitarian tendencies, the attention of reformers was directed to the *kind* of schooling that would best serve the complex structure of a democratic society. Would, that is, an essentially intellectual type of secondary education adequately prepare for the multifarious responsibilities of a complex democratic society? Lindsay exclaimed:

The results of elementary education and the "ladder" idea are important, but the future of democracy is even more important . . . while the cry for more and more secondary education finds a willing response in these pages, based on the evident public needs, secondary education may become as unrelated to the present world as University education has tended to become, unless there is a philosophy of democracy on which it is based.[63]

The framers of the Hadow Report bore this consideration in mind when they advanced their novel conception of secondary education.

Finally, the post-war society saw also an increase in certain occupations, notably those which absorbed most of the young persons who received a secondary school education, namely, the professions, the civil service, and certain kinds of skilled labor.[64] This situation called for changes both in the conditions under which access to secondary schools might be facilitated, and in the type of schooling appropriate for such occupations.

EDUCATION AND NEW OUTLOOKS IN PSYCHOLOGY

The foregoing political, economic and social forces exerted fundamental demands on both the quantitative and qualitative aspects of secondary education. In the evolving conception of secondary education, however, one must not ignore certain intellectual outlooks, and specifically certain outlooks in psychology, especially those formulated by William McDougall, Sir Percy Nunn, and the American G. Stanley Hall.

Back in 1908, only two years after he had established a psychological laboratory at Oxford University, a place generally antagonistic to the scientific study of psychology, William McDougall published a widely read book entitled *Introduction to Social Psychology*.[65]

McDougall's object was to develop a more "positive science of conduct or behaviour," one that would displace the "static, descriptive, purely analytic psychology" by a "dynamic, functional, voluntaristic view of mind."[66] A narrow conception of psychology, according to him, of the former kind, of which the traditional associationist theory[67] furnished an example, was of little use to the social sciences (ethics, economics, political science, philosophy of history, sociology, cultural anthropology, religion, law, education and art). Its scope did not extend beyond the level of consciousness, nor its method beyond that of introspection. It neglected the "orectic" aspects of the mind, i.e., affection and conation, and dealt primarily with the intellectual processes or cognition. The result was that social scientists were compelled to construct their theories and practices on *ad hoc* psychological assumptions to suit their purposes. Instead, McDougall contended, the social sciences must be based on "a comparative and physiological psychology relying largely on objective methods," and taking "the largest possible view of its scope and functions." It must be "an evolutionary natural history of mind" and must provide an accurate account of "the innate tendencies to thought and action that constitute the native basis of the mind."[68] Consequently, McDougall developed a psychological theory based on the biological doctrine that man, like all other animals, inherits certain "instincts" which are the mainspring of his behavior in all its aspects, cognitive, affective and conative.[69]

While insisting on "instincts" or "innate psycho-physical dispositions" or "innate propensities," as he later called them, as determinants of human behavior, McDougall by no means disparaged the importance of the social environment in the development of mental life. Various instincts, he maintained, become organized with reference to particular objects by means of sentiments, which bring order and consistency in our "orectic" life. The organization of the sentiments in the developing mind is determined by experience, that is to say, "the sentiment is a growth in the structure of the mind that is not natively given in the inherited constitution."[70]

McDougall's psychology of instinct spread rapidly. It was accepted in the main by psychologists in general and educational psychologists in particular.[71] It was not, however, until after 1920 that his psychological views penetrated educational thinking. This was done primarily through the work of Sir Percy Nunn, of London University, a well-known figure in educational circles.[72] In his treatise *Education: Its Data and First Principles,* Nunn utilized extensively the psychological views of McDougall and wove them into the pattern of his own philosophical and educational doctrine.

Nunn developed his theory on the biological and teleological concept of "hormě," a Greek word meaning an urge or impulse to action, and a term which at Nunn's suggestion McDougall used to describe his own theory. McDougall called it "the hormic theory," which he elaborated further in his *Outline of Psychology* published in 1923.[73]

Nunn, like McDougall, criticized any mechanistic conception of the human mind and the Cartesian doctrine of "psycho-physical parallelism." Instead, he propounded an "organismic," biological doctrine that viewed animals, from the amoeba upwards, as centers of energy "in constant dynamical relations with the world," yet each shaping its own course "in accordance with its natures and its powers" and developing its own "rudimentary or complex individuality."[74] Nunn interpreted the history of life as a purposive, teleological striving "towards the individuality which is expressed most clearly and richly in man's conscious nature."[75] While insisting on the importance of the development of the self or individuality as the cardinal aim of life, Nunn, like McDougall, was far from denying the influence of the social environment, or from minimizing the responsibility of society in the shaping of the individual's life.

> *This view does not deny or minimize the responsibilities of man to his fellows; for the individual life can develop only in terms of its own nature, and that is social as truly as it is 'self-regarding.' Nor does it deny the value of tradition and 'discipline' or exclude the influence of religion. But it does deny the reality of any super-personal entity of which the single life, taken by itself, is but an insignificant element.*[76]

Nunn's treatise was an elaboration of this doctrine which he sought to ground in the facts of human development and make the basis of a stable educational policy. The importance of *Education: Its Data and First Principles,* lay in the fact that it represented a pioneer attempt by an "educationalist" to develop a psychological and philosophical rationale upon which future educational concepts and policies might be based; and, in so far as the views expressed in it contributed to the intellectual foundations of the Hadow Report, its importance is vital.

One important aspect of educational theory discussed by Nunn was the aim of education and the school's responsibility with regard to the individual and the society. According to him, the concept of individuality, which was germane to his entire doctrine, should also be the criterion of all educational effort, for such an education is the only education "according to nature." "Individuality" is an affair of the *whole* organism, or "body-mind,"[77] and as such it develops "only in a social atmosphere where it can feed on common interests and common activities." On such a conceptual basis, he postulated that the school's aim should be the unimpeded encouragement of the growth of "individuality" through the provision for everyone of the conditions under which it is "most completely developed."

Nunn envisaged individuality in dynamic terms, constantly modified by the results of its own activity, and, in its striving toward a higher and more unified structure—McDougall's "self-sentiment"—constantly interacting with the social environment.[78] He did not see any contradiction in the statements, e.g., "the true aim of the school is to cultivate individuality," and "a main function of the school is to socialize its pupils."[79]

In order for such an aim and function to be achieved, the school must be envisaged as both a "natural" and an "artificial" society. It must, on the one hand, be natural in the sense that there should not be a violent break between the life inside the school and that outside, and no hampering or "stifling of the citizen's energies." On the other hand, it must be an artificial society in the sense that, in so far as it should reflect the world outside, it should reflect "only what is best and vital there." Hence, the school, while conserving the best in a nation's heritage and transmitting it to the younger generation, must at the same time re-examine its ideals, revitalize the nation's energies, and help guide its future.[80]

Nunn discussed other concepts central to educational theory and educational policy, such as "discipline," "punishment," "interest," "freedom" or "the play-way in education,"[81] as he called it, and the question of the "grading" of education. He repudiated the doctrine of "mental discipline" or "formal training" as understood previously, which presupposed a conception of the mind in terms of "faculties." In line with his own interpretation of discipline, he maintained that a person *can* be disciplined through "organized studies" or "occupations," i.e., he can be trained in such a way that he may acquire a facility "in applying certain ideas and methods to situations of a certain kind, and in a strong tendency to bring the same ideas and methods to bear upon any situation akin to these."[82]

Thus he defended certain studies, e.g., mathematics, science, classics, language, handicraft, history, geography, not in terms of the traditional "formal training" doctrine, but in terms of his own interpretation of "discipline." In addition to such forms of activity, however, which to him constituted "the solid tissue of civilization," Nunn considered other forms of activity, e.g., "care of health and bodily grace, manners, social organization, morals and religion." Both groups should be represented in the school curriculum, and the school where they are studied must be conceived not as a place where they are learnt as a body of knowledge, but "as a place where the young are disciplined in certain forms of activity."[83]

Lastly, Nunn addressed himself to the problem of the "grading" of education. Basing his arguments on psychological ideas derived from both McDougall and Freud, he conceived of education below the university level as a continuous process, the main constituents of which were three natural stages, viz., (a) infancy (ages 1–6 or 8), (b) childhood (age 6 or 8–11 or 12), and (c) adolescence (ages 11 or 12–18), each stage having its distinct problems and requiring its own peculiar educational methods. According to Nunn, the education carried during the period of childhood should be called primary education, and that during adolescence secondary education, the latter to include "all forms of post primary education."[84]

Nunn's position, bolstered, as it were, by psychological information, paved the way for a fundamental shift in the meaning of secondary education as well as in the meaning of equal opportunity at the secondary level. The clue was quickly taken by Tawney as furnishing an educational rationale for the doctrine of "secondary education for all." Secondary education was now conceived in terms of the *adolescent* with his differing "ability, *ingenium* and needs," rather than in terms of essentially academic studies. Furthermore, secondary education was thought of as a *phase* in a single universal scheme; and equal opportunity, as the right of all who came to be offered what would be of value to them.

The view that sound pedagogical theory and practice must be based on an understanding of the laws governing the growth of child development was further bolstered by G. Stanley Hall and his pioneer work on adolescence. Hall's researches and their implications for education were known to the English psychologists before the war, but it was not until after the war that their influence was felt in the educational world. The textbooks of the period attest clearly to the acceptance and further extension of Hall's concepts concerning the general mental development of children during the adolescent stage, especially the emotional stresses they undergo.[85]

Hall's views on adolescence reached official and policy formulating bodies such as the Consultative Committee. In 1923 the Consultative Committee issued a report on "Differentiation of the Curriculum for Boys and Girls Respectively in Secondary Schools." In its attempts to re-evaluate the curriculum of the secondary school and to suggest courses of action, the Committee drew from various sources, including Hall's work on the nature of the physical and psychological development of the adolescent.[86] Incidentally, this was the first official attempt made to base educational policy concerning the curriculum on more scientific data of child growth. The general tenor of the report reflected a changing outlook concerning the education of the adolescent. To use Hall's terms, education was envisaged more in *pedocentric* and less in *scholiocentric* terms. It was urged, for example, that more scope should be provided "for the individual divergence of interest and ability," and that "the curriculum should be arranged to meet . . . variations between chronological, mental and physiological age."[87] Furthermore. it was suggested that, in the light of available psychological evidence, the pressure of an uncongenial subject might be removed "if the teacher considers that no further educational benefit is to be got from it."[88] The curriculum of the schools should therefore be remodelled and adapted to the succesive stages of child development.[89]

Lastly, the post-war period saw a revolt, albeit rather feeble if compared to the educational scene in America, against faculty psychology and its associated doctrines of mental discipline and transfer of training. "Faculty Psychology," it should be remembered, attempted to explain mental phenomena by referring them to certain corresponding, relatively independent, agencies or "faculties." The mind was thus conceived in terms of certain "faculties," each of which was assigned as a cause or as a real condition of a mental state or process. As a corollary to such a psychological hypothesis, it was maintained that education should concern itself with the "training" of these faculties through "exercise" or "discipline." From this the educational theory developed that certain subjects, e.g., classics, mathematics, or science, had the peculiar attributes of best performing the function of "training" such faculties as memory, verbal accuracy, reasoning, observation, imagination and so on.[90] From this "formalist" assumption there was the further corollary, namely, that once a specific "faculty" was "trained" by a specific subject, that capacity as a whole was thereby strengthened and its results could be transferred to any other situation.

In England "faculty psychology" was attacked in the nineteenth century by John Adams[91] and the British Associationists. Indeed, by 1899, G. F. Stout, for many years editor of *Mind*, could rather too optimistically say that "Faculty Psychology may be pronounced obsolete."[92] And in America the problem of "transfer of training" was put to an experimental test by E. L. Thorndike and R. S. Woodworth in a well-known pioneer piece of research which appeared in *The Psychological Review* of May 1901. The mind, according to them, on its dynamic side, "is a machine for making particular reactions to particular situations." Functions such as memory, observation, etc., are "mythological, not real entities," and any spread of practice from one situation to another "occurs only where identical elements are concerned in the influencing and influenced functions."[93]

Discussion and experimental research on "formalism" and its corollary doctrines continued with increasing vigor in both America and England. But in England, as P. B. Ballard pointed out in 1925, "the formal training controversy has been almost entirely carried on by theorists." Administrators "did not know that there was anything to argue about," and teachers "have only just realized that there has been a battle."[94]

That controversy on this problem remained confined to "theorists" and psychologists partly accounts for the longer persistence of the traditional notions of "formal training" in the field of education, if the time element were compared with that in America. As late as 1918, as shown in the previous chapter, classics, science, and modern languages were defended on "formalist" grounds. Another reason for such a persistence was the fact that the new psychology was late in entering the group of academically respected subjects as a separate branch of study, especially in the two older universities.[95] This hampered the ready acceptance of new psychological notions. Added to this was the fact that "professional" training of teachers as one of the functions of the university did not really start until after 1911, and even after that not all the universities accepted the proposed four-year scheme. Thus, most of the secondary school teachers did not have any so-called professional training, and it was the opportunity afforded by such training which could bring them into contact with the educational implications of the new psychological theories. The natural result was that secondary school teachers believed in and followed the traditional pedagogical ideas and methods through which they themselves had gone.[96] Formalism was also supported by certain social groups who had found in it a justification for advocating a "limited curriculum" to whose study they had easier access, and which traditionally was associated with higher status and prestige.[97]

By the twenties, however, the revolt against formalism was exercising a subtle pervading influence in the evolving conception of secondary education. The growing demands for a broader curriculum, a reinterpretation of "liberal education," a greater concern for the child's interests and needs, and the view that studies must be brought into closer relation with life were all partly due to the gradual weakening of the doctrine of formal training as it was traditionally understood.[98]

XII

Toward a New
Prospect in Education:
The Hadow Report

In May 1924, the Consultative Committee of the Board
of Education began its consideration of the question referred to it by the Board of Education under its President,
C. P. Trevelyan. The final report entitled *The Education
of the Adolescent* appeared in December 1926. The Hadow
Report was immediately heralded as an educational landmark, a judgment which to a large degree has persisted up
to the present time.[1] As in the case of the Bryce Commission, the purpose here will be to examine the educational
ideas embodied in this document. By contrasting the views
of the two reports, it will be possible to identify the shifts
in ideology within the period under consideration. This
will be followed by a brief discussion of the relation between the views of the Hadow Report and those which
underlay the educational reconstruction of the forties.

The composition of the Committee was different from
that of the Bryce Commission. This, of course, is not surprising, since the Consultative Committee from the beginning was essentially an educational body. Also it was not
an *ad hoc* agency set up by a special government in power,
but its tenure was more permanent. Thus there was a total
absence of political figures and a large number of what
might be called professional educationalists. All in all
there were twenty members, but it was possible to secure
information on only eleven of them.

Of these eleven, eight were directly engaged in administration or teaching at the secondary and higher educational levels. Sir W. H. Hadow, the Chairman of the
Committee, was at the time Vice Chancellor of the University of Sheffield; P. W. H. Abbott was headmaster of
the Polytechnical School in Regent Street; S. O. Andrew
was headmaster of Whitgift School, Croydon; Miss E. M.
Tanner was headmistress of Roedan School; Mr. W. W.
Vaughan was headmaster of Rugby; Sir Ernest Barker was
principal of King's College London; and R. H. Tawney
and Lynda Grier were university professors. There were,
in addition, the Rev. Dr. D. H. S. Cranage, the Secretary
of the Board of Extra-Mural Studies; Sir Percy D. Jackson,
the Chairman of the West Riding Education Committee,
and Dr. A. Mansbridge, the founder of the Workers' Education Association.

Of this sample, five (Hadow, Barker, Tawney, Mansbridge and Vaughan) were men of distinction in their
respective fields both at home and abroad. Hadow was
noted not only for his work in the field of national educa-

tion, but more so for his scholarly accomplishments in the history of music. Educated at Worcester College, Oxford, where he won a First in classical moderations and in *literae humaniores,* and where he served as scholar, lecturer, fellow, tutor and dean, he has been described as a brilliant lecturer, a scholar and an administrator of remarkable academic range.[2] Vaughan was the first lay headmaster of Rugby and served as the President both of the Modern Language Association and the Science Masters' Association. Tawney's work in the field of English education was discussed earlier and his reputation in the fields of economics and social theory is well known. Furthermore, both he and Mansbridge played an important role in the development of Labour social and educational thought during the decades preceding the appearance of the Hadow Report. Indeed, there is a surprising similarity between Tawney's manifesto examined earlier and the Hadow document. Finally, Barker remains one of the most distinguished of the twentieth century English political theorists, especially of the classical Greek period.

The Committee examined 95 witnesses representing local education authorities, government departments, teacher organizations, employers and workers, and religious bodies. In addition, various sub-committees were appointed. Among these was the Drafting Sub-Committee consisting of eight Committee members, with Ernest Barker as Chairman, and with powers to co-opt any other members from outside. In this way, the Drafting Sub-Committee secured the services of Professor T. Percy Nunn of the University of London, who, according to the Report, "placed at its (the Committee's) disposal his wide knowledge and sound judgment, and who has rendered invaluable help in the preparation of the Report."[3]

Neither the minutes nor the evidence and the memoranda submitted by the various witnesses and organizations are available in full as in the case of the Bryce Commission. However, the Report frequently refers to such sources of information, and thus it was not impossible to assess the climate of opinion at the time and to make inferences on the sources of influence. A close examination, for example, of the views of the Report and those of Nunn discussed earlier, shows an astonishing similarity between the two. Considering the role assigned to Nunn by the Drafting Sub-Committee, and the references made to him in the main body of the Report, it would be justifiable to infer what Nunn's influence was.

The Consultative Committee was asked to address itself to the following problem:

> To consider and report upon the organisation, objective and curriculum of courses of study suitable for children who will remain in full-time attendance at schools, other than Secondary Schools, up to the age of 15, regard being had on the one hand to the requirements of a good general education and the desirability of providing a reasonable variety of curriculum, so far as is practicable, for children of varying tastes and abilities, and on the other to the probable occupations of the pupils in commerce, industry and agriculture.[4]

SECONDARY EDUCATION FOR ALL

One of the most significant ideological principles embodied in the Hadow Report was the view that secondary education should not be considered as a selective type of schooling for a small portion of the population, but for *all* children after the age of 11+. In a now famous passage, the Report stated that secondary education should encompass the period of adolescence which begins at the age of 11 or 12. At that stage of human development all children should be transferred to different types of schools: to those which were then called secondary, or to central schools, or to senior and separate departments of the existing elementary schools. If such a transfer took place and an environment were provided which would be adjusted to the interests and abilities of the students, then they could "thrive to a new height and attain a sturdier fibre."[5]

Such a concept of secondary education necessitated a change in the existing terminology of "elementary" and "secondary." Hitherto the two levels of education were socially and pedagogically divided and the relation between them was not "organic." The problem had been how to select a minority of students to pass from one type of school to another. Selection, in short, was taking place through elimination based on social, economic and intellectual factors. The Hadow Report found this notion quite inadequate and not in accord with "the temper of the times" or the social and intellectual developments of the last decades. Instead of the elementary-secondary division with all its social connotations, the Report suggested a change in nomenclature: education up to the age of 11+ to be called primary, and later education to be called secondary.[6] This was not a mere change of names. The Report went to great pains to vindicate the point that education should be viewed as a continuous process with one stage following logically the other and one phase organically connected with the other.

This ideological shift entailed a different interpretation of the concept of selection. The focus now was not on selection of a minority into a separate system, but selection of all "normal" adolescents or all children after the age of 11+ into appropriate types of institutions all bearing the name "secondary" and all based on certain uniform general principles. To use the Report's own words, "selection by differentiation takes the place of selection by elimination." The Board continued:

We regard the general recognition that the aim of educational policy must be, not merely to select a minority of children for the second stage, but to secure that that second stage is sufficiently elastic, and contains schools of sufficient variety of type, to meet the needs of all children.[7]

Such a concept of education was quite novel insofar as official opinion was concerned. The contrast between it and the views of the Bryce Commission discussed in Chapter I is too clear and marked to require further elaboration. Such an ideological shift, however, would have no substantive meaning if it were not viewed against the historical background and the interplay of forces of the period separating the two bodies, a task which has been the major concern of this study. It is true, as will be shown later, that this concept did not receive statutory sanction and did not become a reality until after the passing of the Education Act of 1944. But our main concern here has been primarily with changes in *ideology,* and a full account of what followed the Hadow Report would more appropriately be the subject of another study.

The central idea that *all* children should receive the benefits of some form of secondary education gave new meaning to the concept of "equality of opportunity." Equality of opportunity has frequently been used in at least two senses: (a) as access to education, and (b) as a type of education according to the individual's needs, interests and aptitudes. Clearly the Committee's view that at the age of 11+ all normal children should proceed to a secondary school, regardless of their social, economic and intellectual background, represented an ideological departure from tradition. Hitherto, equality of opportunity was interpreted to mean access to a narrowly conceived type of secondary education for those "capable of profiting." In addition to this, however, the Hadow Report sought to give practical meaning to the second interpretation of the term "equality of opportunity." The differentiation of students after the primary stage was to take account of the pupils' interests, needs and abilities.[8] Herein, therefore, lay another important ideological shift. The role of secondary education and the school was not conceived solely in terms of the claims of society, how, that is, "to equip the pupils for service as workmen and citizens in its organization," but also in terms of the development of one's individuality. In the post-war period there was an ideological controversy between those who stressed the claims of society and viewed the school as a social agency for the exclusive purpose of recruiting people for services demanded and determined by the society, and those who laid greater stress upon education as primarily based upon the claims of the individual. The first view was represented by E. T. Campagnac and Fred Clarke,[9] and the second, to some degree by Sir Percy Nunn, although, as shown previously, Nunn sought a synthesis between the two. This ideological dilemma, as T. H. Marshall has pointed out, continued and is in fact the dilemma of the modern welfare state in Britain. On the one hand, in its educative policy the welfare state emphasizes an "intense individualism," i.e., an education according to the child's needs, interests and abilities; on the other, it also emphasizes a "collectivism," i.e., an education aimed at the social good, which requires "a balanced supply of persons with different skills and aptitudes who have been so trained as to maximize the contribution they can make to the common welfare."[10]

The Hadow Report referred to both schools of thought,

and, in words echoing those of Nunn, attempted an ideological synthesis through what it termed "social individuality."

A well-balanced educational system must combine these two ideals [the claims of the individual as against the claims of society] in the single conception of social individuality. The general aim should therefore be to offer the fullest possible scope to individuality, while keeping steadily in view the claims and needs of the society in which every individual must live.[11]

What form the Committee gave to this idea will be discussed later. Suffice to mention here that the view that secondary education should consider the individual's or the adolescent's "rights" was made quite explicit and has been maintained up to the present time. The secondary stage, according to the Report, should be envisaged "as far as possible as a single whole," and, although there should be different types of schools, such an education should nevertheless be marked "by the common characteristic that its aim is to provide for the needs of children who are entering and passing through the stage of adolescence."[12] Such a concept set the views of the Hadow Report in sharp contrast with those of the Bryce Commission.

SELECTION AT ELEVEN-PLUS

The process of selection or allocation of students into different types and amounts of education at the age of 11+ has been, especially since the Second World War, and continues to be one of the most hotly debated questions in English education. The arguments for or against the break at 11+ have been based on psychological, sociological, pedagogical and political grounds. Those, for example, who have espoused the eleven-plus

policy have justified it on the grounds that the age of
eleven marks another phase in the child's psychological
development, which necessitates a different organizational
and pedagogical treatment; that it is possible at that age
to gauge the individual's capacities and interests; that
since human aptitudes and interests vary it is quite equitable and democratic to identify them at an early age and
"stretch" them to the fullest by separating students into
relatively homogeneous groups; that, since a democratic
society needs leaders and since selection of such leaders is
indispensable, the earlier they are identified the better;
and, finally, that no better alternative has been found.[13]

On the other hand, the 11+ policy has been severely
criticized by individuals, organizations and political
parties, e.g., the Labour Party, and more recently by the
apparently rejuvenated Liberal Party. The critics maintain that selection at that stage is inequalitarian; that it is
based on false psychological assumptions; that it has created parental neuroses; and that it is unpedagogical. Thus,
for example, A. D. C. Peterson, Director of the Oxford
University Institute and Department of Education, speaking at the inaugural meeting of the Oxford Branch of the
Liberal Education Association, is reported to have said:

(The Eleven-Plus) . . . is a sin against the three great principles in which liberal-minded people believe—against the
freedom of the individual; it sins against equality and it sins
against fraternity.[14]

The principle that the transition from an elementary
type of education to a secondary should take place at the
age of 11+, or thereabouts, was not a phenomenon of the
post-Second World War period. In his answer to the ques-
tionnaire given by the Bryce Commission, M. G. Glaze-

brook stated that there should be a diversified system after the age of 12 according to the type of occupation that the student will enter. And he added: "One of the most responsible functions in the educational system of a large town is the task of sifting boys at the age of 11 or 12, and distributing them into their right categories."[15]

Similarly, in his memorandum to the Commissioners, J. G. Fitch suggested that if a child were to receive the full benefits of a "secondary" type of education, he "must be discovered earlier—say at the age of 11 or 12—otherwise there will be an awkward break in the continuity of his studies."[16] Referring specifically to the children who would be selected from the poorer classes in order "to climb the educational ladder," the Bryce Commission itself recommended that such children "should have the opportunity of proceeding at the age of 11 or 12 from the elementary to the secondary school."[17]

The difference, of course, between these views and those of the Hadow Report is that the latter's meaning of secondary was broader than that of the Bryce Commission, and selection at the age of 11+ was to apply to all students in the public system of education. Nevertheless, the idea, albeit in a rather limited form, that at that age a transition should take place from elementary to secondary is to be found in the Report of the Bryce Commission.

The London County Council indeed adopted this policy for scholarship competitions.[18] In fact, since 1902 when the foundations of a public secondary school system were laid, it was increasingly realized that the secondary school could not perform its function adequately unless the children remained in it for at least four years before the leaving age, i.e., before the age of 16. Hence, as the scholarship and free-place systems developed, the elementary school children who moved on to the secondary schools were usually required to make the transfer between the ages of 11 and 12. This policy was followed by London and the other local education authorities, even in the case of those which had established central schools, and in all cases it seemed to work well. In a circular dated January 28, 1925, and sent to the local authorities, the Board itself accepted the age of 11 as the dividing line between "junior" and "senior" education.[19]

Similar views had been expressed a few years earlier by the Departmental Committee on Scholarships and Free Places in 1920,[20] by Sir Percy Nunn[21] in 1921, and by R. H. Tawney in his Labour manifesto of 1922.[22]

The Hadow Report referred to such a climate of opinion and to what it called the "empirical precedents," and recommended that primary education should be regarded as ending at the age of 11+. At that age, a second stage should begin which for some would end at 16+, for others at 18 or 19, but for the majority at 14+ or 15+. In a footnote to this proposal it was further stated that the age of 11+ was not intended to be used in a precise chronological sense, but that "the mental as well as the chronological age of the pupil must be taken into account."[23]

It is noteworthy to observe that the 11+ policy of selection and transfer from the primary to the secondary stage was felt, at that time, to be quite democratic and equalitarian, even by Labour. The Hadow Report, however, justified this policy on psychological grounds, as well, a rationale which had not impregnated pedagogical thought until after the First World War. In the Bryce Commission there was a total absence of a psychological rationale for the transition from the elementary to the secondary schools. Where the Commission spoke of mental discipline as a function of education, it referred essentially to the formalist theory in psychology which was prevalent at the time, a theory which emphasized the disciplining of the mind through certain subjects. The formalist theory, it should be remembered, was based on certain metaphysical assumptions about the human mind, and the theories of learning and education associated with it were based primarily on logical inferences from these assumptions. Secondary education was interpreted in terms of subjects, the number of years a child could remain at school, and the vocational destinations of students. Essentially the same psychological assumptions underlay the educational policy initiated by the Board in 1904. The view, as stated earlier, that there were successive cycles in the physical, mental and emotional development of children, each of which presented peculiar problems that must be taken into consideration in pedagogical differentiation and "grading," was a post-war phenomenon in England. The first evidence of this, as shown in Chapter XI, in so far as official pronouncements are concerned, is to be found in the Consultative Committee's Report of 1923 entitled "Differentiation of the Curriculum for Boys and Girls Respectively in Secondary Schools." Nunn, whose ideas, according to Curtis and Boultwood, "had a profound influence on the generation of teachers who entered the profession in the period between the two great wars,"[24] envisaged secondary education in terms of the *adolescent* with his differing "ability, *ingenium* and needs."

In the report under consideration and the subsequent report on the primary school,[25] the Hadow Committee was very much aware of the work of the psychologists, especially that of Nunn. In justifying the break at 11+, the Report significantly stated that at the age of 11 or 12, when a transition takes place from childhood to adolescence, children display differences in interests and abilities which must be taken into consideration in any scheme of educational organization. The two stages (childhood and adolescence) are successive and one must naturally lead into the other.[26] This was a reinforcement of the psychological arguments of the years after the First World War, and the subsequent psychological justification of the 11+ policy was a mere extension of the position of the Hadow Report, as well as of its assumptions.

In this statement, however, there is another significant element in the ideological stance of the Hadow Committee. In addition to the view that secondary education should coincide with the psychological stage of "adolescence," it was further stated that the differing capacities and interests of the students would be catered for better "by means of schools of varying types." Thus, so far as the institutional expression of this basic psychological principle was concerned, the Hadow Report envisaged a differentiated secondary school pattern, rather than a "comprehensive" or "multilateral" one.

A DIFFERENTIATED INSTITUTIONAL PATTERN

Throughout the Report there are constant references to the necessity for different types of secondary schools: not only should there be a transition at a certain point, i.e., at 11+; at that point also, there should be selection aimed at placing students into schools which would be related "to the actual requirements of the children themselves." Such requirements were dictated by the fact that there were "diversities of gifts" and diversities in vocational aspirations and destinations of students. Moreover, the Committee justified this stance on the grounds that equality of opportunity did not imply identity. Secondary education for all meant larger numbers of students with different types of character and intelligence. Therefore, secondary education should provide "a range of educational opportunity sufficiently wide to appeal to varying interests and cultivate powers which differ widely both in kind and in degree."[27]

Such a rationale for differentiation cannot be explained solely in terms of the intellectual climate of the post-war period, although the Committee again cited Percy Nunn to bolster its position.[28] The notion of diversity and variation, in so far as official bodies were concerned, went back to the Schools Inquiry Commission and the Bryce Commission. It was also expressed in the Report of the Departmental Committee on Scholarships and Free Places in 1920. But in the latter document, and in a more explicit form in the Hadow Report, the universe, so to speak, to which this principle would apply was considerably larger, for it included all normal children. Moreover, the Hadow stance on differentiation must be viewed in relation to the British social ideology concerning the concepts of "equality of opportunity," and "leadership." When the Report stated that "equality is not identity," it was reflecting a most significant element in British social and educational thought, an element which, at the time and later, partly accounts for the rejection of the comprehensive and "multilateral" school. Equality of opportunity in the Hadow Committee's interpretation meant access to different kinds of schools according to aptitude and interests. To put it in another way, equality of opportunity signified access to unequal education. This ideological principle was also implicit in Labour's stance *at the time,* and indeed, as will be shown later on, underlay the recommendations of the Spens Report of 1938, of the Norwood Report of 1943, and of the tripartite institutional arrangement which followed the 1944 Act and which exists today.

The second point that must be made here is the emphasis which the English have placed on the role of the schools in education for leadership. Different types of schools, and different amounts of education, have always been regarded as necessary prerequisites for the creation of a leadership class; and a democracy without a well-trained group of leaders who would "set the pattern," so to speak, was a travesty. Accordingly, an educational framework which smacked of "uniformity," or which aimed at the "average," has been held suspect, and this is, to a large degree, true even today. In the nineteenth century the leaders were recruited almost exclusively from the great Public schools and the better grammar schools. But after the 1902 Act, the public "secondary" school began to assume a greater role in such a function; and, what is equally important, intellectual considerations gradually replaced social considerations in education for leadership.[29]

In their seminal form both of these ideological factors entered into the deliberations and institutional recommendations of the Hadow Report. At the age of eleven and after an examination, which might also include a psychological test, children were to be selected for the various types of secondary schools. These would include (a) grammar schools which would carry their education to the age of at least 16+; (b) modern schools with a leaving age of 14+ or 15+; and (c) senior classes with again a leaving age of 14+ or 15+. Grammar schools would cover

not only the "old foundations," but also the "larger number of County and Municipal Secondary Schools which
have been founded since 1902"; modern schools would be
of two types and would replace the existing "selective"
and "non-selective" central schools; and senior classes
would include the existing "senior classes," "central department," "higher tops" and "analogous arrangements."[30]
In addition, some junior technical schools could be considered as secondary schools.

Some of the constituent elements of this institutional
framework were in some respects rooted in the past. For
example, the newly recommended secondary grammar
schools were an outgrowth of the older grammar schools;
the others were an outgrowth of the upward thrust of popular education that characterized the period after the 1870
Act, which had taken the intermediary institutional forms
of higher grade elementary schools, "higher elementary
schools," and "central schools" discussed earlier. But this
should not obscure the fact that the types of schools proposed by the Hadow Report were in certain respects conceived in different senses. Grammar schools were no longer
conceived as coextensive with secondary education as was
the case in the nineteenth century; nor were they conceived as constituting an exclusive, separate system providing an essentially classical type of education. A grammar
school in the Hadow Committee's sense was still exclusive
in that only certain intellectually capable students could
attend it, but "non-exclusive" in that theoretically all
those who had the requisite intelligence could go. It was
still separate in the sense that it did not function, as the
other schools, under the same roof, but nonseparate in the
sense that its work was organically related to that of the
primary school, and in that students from other post-pri-

mary schools could be transferred to it. For the Hadow Committee explicitly stated that "arrangements should be made" to allow for transfer at the age of 12 or 13 of pupils from "modern" and other schools to grammar schools, and conversely from grammar schools to the other schools.[31] Finally, as will be shown in the following section, the Hadow Report had a different conception of the curriculum.

The modern school, which was the other major constituent element of the institutional structure recommended by the Committee, was no longer envisaged, as its precursors were, as a branch of elementary education. It was to be a secondary type of school in its own right, again organically related to the primary school and to some extent to the grammar school. In addition, and perhaps rather too optimistically, the Hadow Report recommended "parity of esteem" among all the secondary institutions. To be sure "parity of esteem" may be, and indeed has proved to be, but "a consummation devoutly to be wished." For where different types and amounts of education are rewarded differentially in terms of income, prestige, status and educational value placed upon them, "parity of esteem" has been found to be more of a myth than a reality. Nevertheless, this is a problem that England, with its own social and occupational structure as well as its own value system, has been and is confronted with even now. Our purpose here, however, is not to pass judgments on the goodness or badness of the situation, but rather to describe and illuminate a historical phenomenon, and to assess, as in the case of the Hadow Report, the impact upon subsequent phenomena. The institutional framework recommended in the Hadow Report represented a consummation of previous tendencies and laid the ideological foundations for the institutional arrangements that followed the 1944 Act. In this sense it was historically important for good or for ill.

The Hadow Committee did not bring all the technical schools, the trade schools and other "vocational" schools under its purview of secondary education. For this it has been criticized, specifically because it allegedly did not take fully into account the recommendations of the Bryce Commission.[32] Such a criticism, however, is somewhat exaggerated. In the first place, as it was shown in Chapter II, the views of the Bryce Commission on the relationship between secondary and technical education were not as clear as they have been made to be. In the second place, the Hadow Committee *did* include certain types of junior technical schools, provided they fulfilled certain conditions which were in accord with its conception of what the aims and content of secondary education should be. Finally, in assessing the historical significance of the Hadow Report, it is also necessary to consider its views on this subject in relation to its over-all concept of secondary education, as well as to the contemporary climate of educational opinion.

The Hadow Report rejected the idea of a secondary school performing a specific technical or vocational function. While it strongly emphasized the need for a "realistic" or "practical" bias "in the latter years of the course" of modern schools and senior classes, it flatly rejected the idea that the role of any secondary school should be training for a *specific* trade or occupation. A rather fine distinction was drawn between specific vocational training and a more general training with a practical orientation which would make it possible for someone to adapt to a variety of occupations. The former was the responsibility of technical and other vocational schools; the latter, of secondary schools of the modern variety.[33]

It is significant to mention also that employers for the most part preferred the latter more general type of preparation for employment after school, rather than the former more specific one.[34] Also there is no contemporary evidence to show that the views of the Committee were contrary to educational and public opinion.

In this connection it would also be of interest to note that even with the attempt later, especially after the 1944 Act, to elevate the status of technical schools, they have not taken as firm a root as the other secondary schools. In 1959, the Report of the Central Advisory Council for Education, commonly known as the Crowther Report, recorded that "over 40 per cent of the local education authorities do not provide technical schools." It added:

. . . we do not have, and never had, a tripartite system. . . . Instead of a tripartite system we have (if we may generalise about England as a whole) a two-sided system, based on the assumption, where maintained schools are concerned, that all boys and girls alike go to undifferentiated primary schools, and that from the age of 11 onwards all go to a modern school unless they can show cause to the contrary and there is a place for them in a school giving a different kind of education.[35]

Except for the schools referred to as "senior classes" which, in any case, were to be established where neither a grammar nor a modern school was practicable, the current institutional pattern is essentially similar to what the Hadow Report recommended.

AIMS AND CONTENT OF EDUCATION: THE GENERAL, THE PRACTICAL, AND THE VOCATIONAL IN THE CURRICULUM

The acceptance of the general idea that all children

should receive some form of secondary schooling according to their capacities, needs and interests inevitably raised questions about the aims of education and the nature of the curriculum. Indeed this has been found to be a theme debated constantly throughout the period under consideration.

As it was pointed out earlier, the debate over the general, practical and vocational aspects of the secondary school curriculum figured prominently in educational discussions after the initiation of the Free-Place System in 1907. It was shown there that the Board sought to inject some degree of "practicalism" into the curriculum of the secondary schools, but that the results were not spectacular. Furthermore, it was shown that the reaction to the Board's policy was rather lukewarm and ambivalent. The Board, of course, had at the same time reaffirmed its position that the essential function of secondary schools should be the provision of a general type of education, mostly literary and scientific in content. It was assumed that such a type of education was quite adequate both for those students who intended to continue their education and enter the professions and for those who would go "direct into employment" at or about the age of 16.

In the light of the then prevalent views about the meaning and scope of secondary education, both the form it took and its rationale are easy to understand. But, by 1926, the ideological climate, as well as the political, social and economic conditions discussed earlier, rendered the rather limited and uniform conception of the curriculum inadequate for all types of secondary schools.

Perhaps the most significant element in the Hadow Report's general conceptual framework on the meaning and content of secondary education was its famous description of "liberal" education.

A humane or liberal education is not one given through books alone, but one which brings children into contact with the larger interests of mankind; and the aims of the schools . . . should be to provide such an education by means of a curriculum containing large opportunities for practical work and related to living interests.[36]

In its embryonic form this idea, so far as the Board is concerned, is to be found in the Consultative Committee's Report of 1913 discussed in Chapter V. But it was not until the appearance of the Hadow Report that one finds a cogent rationale for practical education as an aspect of a "humane or liberal education." In spite of its attempts to blur the distinction between "liberal" and "technical," the Bryce Commission leaned heavily towards the literary-scientific components of a liberal education, and when it spoke of "humane and generous studies" it referred to the traditional classical-humanistic subjects. Moreover, in the Bryce Commission's ideological framework there was a distinctly higher value placed upon a "literary-humanistic culture." During the war years when the debate over the value of studies was at its height, those advocating the claims of nonclassical studies as essential ingredients of a liberal education were referring to scientific and modern studies which they sought to justify on the grounds that they were as "humane" as the "humanities." The Hadow Report, on the other hand, viewed a literary-scientific type of instruction as not necessarily solely coextensive with a humane or liberal education. Other types of education could be "humane" or "liberal" to the degree that they took into account the pupil's "natural and social environment" and to the extent that school work was connected with the interests "arising from the social and industrial environment of the pupils."[37] "Education," according to the Report, "fails in part of its aim if it does not prepare

children for a life of active labour and of social cooperation."[38] The ideal of "social individuality" implied that
the school should not be regarded as an "isolated unit,"
but that it should be related to the "mainstream of life."[39]

This ideological position becomes clearer when one considers the Report's views on "practical" or "realistic" bias
which, as pointed out above, must not be confused with
"vocational education." First of all, "bias" was to be introduced in the latter years of the modern school course.
In the earlier years (ages 11 to about 13) the curriculum
would be similar to that of the grammar schools, so that
transfer could take place from one to the other. Secondly,
the "bias" would be "general" in that it would not be
aimed at preparation for specific trade or occupation but
rather at a variety of occupations. Thus, for example, for
prospective trade apprentices in engineering firms, schools
would emphasize habits of careful observation and "a
readiness to think things out by a process of scientific reasoning." In such instances it would emphasize elementary
mathematics and science as well as "a literary training sufficient to enable them (the children) to express themselves properly."[40] In county schools, i.e., schools in
agricultural districts, the science syllabus would be largely
based on "biological interests" and arranged in such a way
that it would have bearing on horticulture and agriculture.[41]

The subjects recommended for the curriculum of modern schools and senior classes included: (1) English
language and literature plus one foreign language, which
could be French, Spanish or German depending on the
locality of the school; (2) history, which would be mainly
general English history "with some idea of its world setting," but which should also include some social and eco-

nomic history; (3) geography; (4) elementary mathematics; (5) elementary science (chemistry, elementary physics and simple mechanics, fundamental principles of biology and elementary physiology and hygiene); (6) handwork, including drawing and applied art, and the various branches of practical instruction; and (7) music.

These subjects are predominantly literary and scientific, which was the case with the more academic secondary grammar schools. But in the detailed description of each, the Committee stressed the fact that they should be approached both for their theoretical or artistic value and for their practical or utilitarian bearings. In the case of mathematics, science, and drawing, for example, the aim was stated as not only the acquisition of mathematical and scientific knowledge and principles, but also the practical bearings of such knowledge and principles on the occupational destinations of students and "the problems of our everyday life." Similarly, English would be approached for the purpose of developing understanding, appreciation, and love of literature as a form of art, and of equipping the individual with the necessary linguistic tools to be able to express himself properly both orally and in writing. History would also aim at a two-fold general purpose: (a) the acquisition of historical knowledge, the understanding of and appreciation for past events, and the interaction of events and their development; and (b) the relevance of history to the present, the pupil's immediate environment, and his future occupation.[42]

In addition to these subjects, however, the Report recommended the inclusion of "practical instruction" in handicrafts for boys, and needlework, handwork and "housecraft" for girls.[43]

The Hadow Committee did not elaborate on the content of instruction in the secondary grammar schools because such institutions were outside its scope of investigation. But it did make sporadic references in order to show the similarities and differences between these schools and the others (modern and senior classes). The curriculum of the secondary grammar school would continue to be predominantly literary and scientific; the leaving age would be 16+; the objective would be the First School Examination and presumably the universities and ultimately the professions. Practical instruction would not figure as much in grammar schools, and examinations in the other schools would be of "a much less rigid character."[44] Thus, the two major typologies of schools were differentiated in terms of school-leaving age, types of school-leaving examinations, vocational aspirations and destinations of students, and curriculum "biases," especially during the latter years of one's schooling (ages 14 to 15 or 16). On the other hand, during the first 2 years all schools would offer essentially the same course so that transfer from one to the other could take place; the First School Examination could be taken by other than grammar school children if they attained the required standard; and, conversely, grammar school children could take the less rigid examinations usually intended for modern school students.

The two major institutional typologies were justified on two major student typologies, the literary-scientific and the "practical," and were considered to be psychologically and pedagogically valid and socially equitable.

Whether such a rationale and the form it took are valid or justifiable is not a question that falls within our purview here. Our major purpose is to describe and illuminate its development and transformation in the light of the mainstream of English history. The general major conclusion of our inquiry is that, although the types of schools envisaged by the Hadow Committee were in some respects functionally equivalent to previous institutions, the Committee brought them within a different and more comprehensive ideological framework. And, whether valid and justifiable or not, this, as will be briefly shown below, was essentially the framework which furnished the basis of what ensued.

THE AFTERMATH OF THE HADOW REPORT

The reaction to the Hadow Report was immediate and in the main favorable. The Report was discussed by individuals and groups representing practically every section of public and educational opinion. In its new year *Educational Supplement*, the *London Times* summarized the main points of the Report and editorially called it "a masterly document." According to the *Supplement*, the Consultative Committee had finally adopted the scheme which in essence it (the *Supplement*) had been advocating "some ten years ago." The scheme was "secondary education for all."[45] In another leading article in the following issue, the *Supplement* urged the adoption of the Hadow proposals.[46] The only feature in the Report criticized by the *Supplement* was the recommendation that children at the age of 11+ be subjected to psychological tests in addition to oral tests and the headmaster's evaluation. Similarly, the National Federation of Class Teachers felt that the Report followed in the main the lines of advance advocated by the N.F.C.T. and the N.U.T., but, like the *Supplement*, was critical of "the elaborate examination system at 11+."[47] *The Journal of Education* expressed "general satisfaction with the report," and thought that the substance of the Hadow Committee's recommendations "seems to us conceived in the very spirit of wisdom."[48] Meanwhile, an independent committee of educationists headed by the venerable Lord Haldane had reached similar conclusions as the Hadow Committee and it urged the adoption of the Report's recommendations.[49] In its annual report for the year 1926–1927, the Board of Education called the Hadow Report "the most important event during the period under review."[50] In 1928 the Board issued a pamphlet entitled *The New Prospect in Education* in which it officially sanctioned the basic ideological principles of reorganization in the Hadow Report and urged their implementation.[51]

However, Hadowism, interpreted as the cluster of ideas in the Report, was not fully implemented by successive governments. The Board, although it approved the general principles of the Report, refused to sanction its recommendation that the school-leaving age be raised to 15. Yet in the thirties several local education authorities devised schemes for the organization of modern schools along the lines recommended by the Hadow Committee.[52] Government attempts to raise the school-leaving age to 15 in order to make modern school education a reality failed. The full implications of Hadowism were not fully realized by many people and adjustments in outlook concerning the functions of the various types of secondary schools proceeded at a slow pace. Some people, in fact, were apprehensive lest the prestige attached to the academic secondary "grammar" school should suffer if other schools were given secondary status.[53]

Nevertheless, as Richmond has pointed out, "a considerable remodelling of the statutory system *was* being effected, and, if Hadowism did nothing else, it administered a much needed jolt to stick-in-the-mud mentalities."[54] It was more than an ideological "jolt," however. For Hadow-ism exerted a subtle pervading influence throughout the thirties and was reaffirmed in another monumental report which the Consultative Committee issued in 1938 under the chairmanship of Sir Will Spens.

XIII

Hadowism And the "Re-Formation" of the Forties

THE SPENS REPORT

Seven years after the appearance of the Hadow Report, the Consultative Committee was instructed to address itself to the following question:

> To consider and report upon the organisation and interrelation of schools, other than those administered under the Elementary Code, which provide education for pupils beyond the age of 11+; regard being had in particular to the framework and content of the education of pupils who do not remain at school beyond the age of about 16.[1]

Since the types of institutions examined by the Hadow Committee continued to be conducted under the Elementary Code despite the Hadow recommendations, the terms of reference of the Spens Committee applied, strictly speaking, to the grammar schools. But the Spens Report also discussed the general question of secondary education and the interrelationships among the various types of post-primary institutions. Indeed, it explicitly stated that since it was ideologically committed to the Hadow Committee's views that secondary education should be envisaged as "a single whole," it could not wholly exclude modern schools from its considerations. Furthermore, it considered the examination of technical and other "vocational" schools as legitimately falling within its frame of reference.[2]

The Spens Committee devoted an entire chapter of its report to show that between the ages of 11+ and 16+ there are distinct changes in the physical, mental and emotional development of children. This period, known as "adolescence," presented its own peculiar physical, psychological and educational characteristics and problems, which should be carefully considered by parents, teachers and educational reformers. In words which were but a mere echo of Hadowism it stated: "We consider that the prime duty of the secondary school is to provide for the needs of children who are entering and passing through the stage of adolescence."[3] Affirming the general principle of its predecessor, the Spens Committee proposed a "secondary code" which would break down the administrative division into "elementary" and "secondary" education and thus establish in practice the principle of secondary education for all children after the age of 11+.[4]

The Spens Committee endorsed the view that education after the age of 11+ should be called "secondary" and should be an organic outgrowth of primary education.[5] In its institutional recommendations it accepted the two main types of "secondary" schools proposed by the Hadow Committee, viz., the grammar and the modern, but, in addition, it recommended the establishment of selective "technical high schools" which "should be accorded in every respect equality of status with schools of the grammar school type."[6] Thus, the principle of secondary education for all which was implicit in Hadowism took the form of the well-known tripartite arrangement into grammar, modern and technical secondary schools. It is of interest to observe that the proposed technical secondary schools were in no way to be narrowly vocational. Their purpose was stated as: (a) to provide a good intellectual discipline, altogether apart from its technical value, and (b) to have a technical value in relation not to one particular occupation but to a group of occupations.[7]

The Spens Report, as much as the Hadow Report, rejected by implication the view that the role of the secondary school was "vocational" in the sense of preparing its students for *specific* trades or occupations. Indeed it explicitly reaffirmed the Hadow Committee's statement about trade schools, namely, that "within their own province (they) are doing most valuable work and should be developed as far as is possible in accordance with the needs and requirements of certain local industries."[8] The claims that the Spens Committee in this respect deviated markedly from the Hadow Committee are rather exaggerated. For in the former's frame of reference the technical secondary school was to provide essentially a broad "liberal" education rather similar to that in the normal grammar schools which had science sides. The differentiating feature of this school was that in the later years of the course (13+ to 16+) the teaching of science would be carried out with reference to "the application of science both to the processes of manufacture and to the operation of the devices and plant manufactured."[9]

The Spens Committee also endorsed the principle that there should be different types of secondary schools. It rejected the idea of "multilateral" schools as a general policy, although it conceded that "some measure of experiment with multilateral schools may be desirable." Multilateral schools, in its opinion, would jeopardize "much of what is most valuable in the grammar school tradition"; they would be too big for pedagogical and administrative purposes; and the prestige of the academic "side" would prejudice "the free development of the Modern School form of secondary education." Finally, the Committee felt that it would be too drastic a change.[10]

Implicit in the Committee's rationale were elements not dissimilar to the rationale of the Hadow Report, viz., the role of the grammar school as a selective agency for future leadership in the society, and the view that equality of opportunity signified differentiated types and amounts of education.

Finally, the Spens Committee reaffirmed the Hadow principles that there should be "parity of status" among the different types of schools and that there should be transfers from one type of school to another. Such parity could be attained if there were uniform policies governing methods of recruitment into the schools, costs (this would mean the abolition of fees in the grammar schools), teacher salaries, etc.; if the school leaving age was raised to 16; and if a non-humanistic type of education which enabled one to understand the world and its problems was recognized as liberal.[11]

The Spens Committee devoted a considerable portion of its report to the curriculum of the schools, especially the secondary grammar schools. Like the Hadow Committee, it argued that liberal education should not be construed exclusively in terms of the traditional subjects; that the curriculum should take into consideration the "practical affairs of life"; and that it should aim at the fullest development of the individual. It is significant to observe that the two Committees reached a consensus on certain curriculum principles in spite of the fact that they dealt essentially with different types of schools. In addition to the above, both Committees stressed that the curriculum should "cater for the special needs of adolescence"; that it should take into consideration the physical, the emotional and the aesthetic as well as the intellectual aspects of education;[12] and that for the first two years (ages 11–13) it should be essentially the same.

However, both Committees also assumed that not all students are alike and that the various types of schools performed different functions as well. The Spens Report reinforced the Hadow assumption that there were essentially two typologies of students, those who "are most capable of being taught to think in abstract terms," and those whose competencies lie in more practical pursuits. The former type would best develop their potentialities in a grammar school or technical school, and the latter in a modern school.[13] Thus, whether justifiable or not, the two major institutional typologies and their rationale which were inherent in Hadowism were firmly reaffirmed as guides to educational policy.

What followed the Spens Report has been the subject of several studies and is too well-known to require any detailed treatment.[14] Here we shall merely point to certain crucial ideological principles in order to show the continuity between Hadowism and the reforms of the forties.

THE REFORM MOVEMENT AND THE EDUCATION ACT OF 1944

No sooner had England become embroiled in another major conflict, the Second World War, than educational controversies erupted again and contending parties clamored for a new order in education. The educational ferment of the war years reminds one of what happened during the First World War and to some extent during the period of the Boer War. Indeed, it is interesting to observe that the three major educational Acts of the twentieth century affecting secondary education were passed at times when England was engaged in or was emerging from a state of war.

By 1941 the ferment for educational change had spread, and a plethora of ideas and schemes by individuals and groups (social, political, economic, religious and educational) representing every conceivable segment of British life were presented at public meetings and forums, in the public press, and in books and pamphlets. There were discussions on the role of education in a democratic society, the implementation of the idea of equality of educational opportunity, the extension of adult education, the role of religion in education, etc.[15]

The upshot of this ferment in so far as secondary education was concerned was a White Paper issued by the Government in 1943, a report by the Committee of the Secondary School Examinations Council headed by Sir Cyril Norwood in the same year, the Education Act of 1944, and a pamphlet by the newly established Ministry of Education in 1947.

The White Paper entitled "Educational Reconstruction," was presented by the President of the Board of Education to Parliament in July 1943. In it the Government set forth the reforms it proposed to incorporate within a forthcoming Bill and some general principles upon which the proposals were based. In a quotation from Disraeli affixed at the head of the Paper,[16] education was linked with national survival, and in the introduction the doctrine of secondary education for all had at long last appeared as an expressed official Government policy. In subsequent sections it was proposed that the school-leaving age be raised to 16; that the statutory system of education be organized in three "progressive" stages, primary, secondary and further; and that at the age of 11+ a classification of students be made for purposes of allocation to different types of secondary schools. Selection at that age would be based not on the results of a competitive test, but "on an assessment of their (the students') individual aptitudes largely by such means as school records, supplemented, if necessary, by intelligence tests, due regard being had to their parents wishes and the careers they have in mind."[17] The institutional framework within which the principles of secondary education for all would be organized was the "tripartite" system recommended by the Spens Report, namely, grammar, modern and technical schools. In addition it was proposed that all types of secondary schools be conducted under a single code of regulations "as recommended in the Spens Report."[18]

One cannot fail to observe striking similarities between these recommendations and those of the Hadow and the Spens Committees. Indeed, the Paper specifically referred to both reports to bolster its stance on certain major questions. It endorsed the Hadow principle that at the age of 11 all children should be transferred to separate schools. It also reaffirmed the principle of selection by differentiation, and the psychological and social rationale upon which it was based. And it further reinforced the institutional framework embodied in the two previous documents.

In the same year there also appeared the Report of the

Committee of the Secondary School Examinations Council which had been appointed by the President of the Board of Education in 1941. The Norwood Report, as this report is more commonly known, focused its attention on the curriculum and examinations in the secondary schools, but the first part was devoted to the nature and function of secondary education. In a well-known and frequently quoted section, the Norwood Report, like the Hadow and Spens Reports, justified institutional typologies on the grounds that there were corresponding pupil typologies and that they had been recognized in practice in England and in other countries. The Norwood Committee identified three types of pupils: (a) "The pupil who is interested in learning for its own sake, who can grasp an argument or follow a piece of connected reasoning, who is interested in causes, whether on the level of human volition or in the material world, who cares to know how things came to be as well as how they are, who is sensitive to language as expression of thought, to a proof as a precise demonstration, to a series of experiments justifying a principle"; (b) "the student whose interests and abilities lie markedly in the field of applied science or applied art"; and (c) "the pupil . . . (who) deals more easily with concrete things than with ideas."[19]

According to the Report, these varieties in capacity could best be developed in three separate corresponding types of schools, the grammar, the technical and the modern. In words which but for minor extensions were mere echoes of the previous reports, the Norwood Committee lent further support to the principles of secondary education for all, selection at 11+, a curriculum based on the identified aptitudes and interests of the students, transfer from one school to another during the early years, parity of status, and, in general, secondary education as a stage in a continuous process rather than as a type of program.[20]

In 1944, while the war was still waging, the Coalition Government passed a Bill which was first read in December 1943, and which received the Royal Assent on August 3rd, 1944. The Education Act of 1944 marked a "climax" in the development of secondary education which began in 1902. It made statutory most of the principles and proposals of the Hadow, Spens, and Norwood Committees and the White Paper on education reconstruction.

The law, for the first time in the history of English education, charged the newly appointed Minister of Education, the local education authorities and the parents, with the *duty* of "promoting" and "providing" a national, comprehensive system of education according to the different "ages, abilities, and aptitudes" of the pupils. The local education authorities were required to organize the statutory system of public education into "three progressive stages to be known as primary education, secondary education and further education." The doctrine of secondary education for all children received statutory sanction when local education authorities were instructed to provide opportunities for all pupils during "the different periods for which they may be expected to remain at school."[21]

Beyond the provision that there should be "variety of instruction and training," the Act made no mention of the institutional form that "secondary education for all" would take. But in introducing the second reading of the Bill, R. A. Butler, the President of the Board of Education and a Conservative M.P., intimated that there *would* be different types of schools and not "multilateral" or "comprehensive" schools.

In the new attitude to secondary education we have two main objectives. The first is that, as far as possible, provision of various types of education should be accessible to all, whatever their social or financial circumstances; and secondly, that traditions and standards which have been a feature of our British education should, so far as possible, be preserved.

According to Butler, the Government's aim was not to "level down," but "to bring everybody, ever upward."[22] The position of the Government was quite clear. It wanted the removal of social and economic barriers for access into the secondary schools, and at the same time it endorsed the ideological principle of Hadowism that "equality of opportunity" did not mean "identical" education, but "unequal schooling." In 1952, Butler, expressing the "view of a conservative," stated that "equal educational opportunity," for which he had a desire, "is not identical educational opportunity." Referring to the American experience, he argued that nonselectivity and nondiversity would stunt and retard the growth of the "uncommon child."[23]

The Bill as introduced by Butler was favorably received by Labour as well. Mr. Parker, a Labour front bencher, pledged the support of his Party for the Bill. The only point he criticized was that the Bill allowed for the continued existence of the independent or Public schools, and thereby to him it also allowed for the continuation of a type of privilege. One important point to remember is that the Bill was supported by both parties in the name of social equality and the removal of class barriers.[24] Even after the Act of 1944, the successful establishment of "tripartitism" by the Ministry was, as Banks points out, partly due to "lack of enthusiasm within the leadership of the Labour Party as well as the distrust within official circles of the Ministry" of "multilateral" or "comprehensive"

308 POLITICS, SOCIETY AND SECONDARY EDUCATION

schools.[25] The inevitable conclusion that may therefore be drawn is that, at the time of the Act, the question of selection through differentiation and allocation into different types of schools was not a political issue of any great intensity.[26]

When the Education Bill was introduced to the House it was the first of the Government measures of social reform, which partly attests to the priority that the Government gave to education in its plans for post-war reconstruction. The aim, as stated by Butler, was "to provide a new framework for promoting the national growth and development not only of children but of national policy itself towards education in the years to come."[27] While the purpose was to provide a new "legal" framework, like most of the other Education Acts of the past 100 years, it was not a revolutionary measure in the strict meaning of the term. Rather it sought to provide a synthesis of the best of the old and the new. In Butler's words:

Perhaps the Bill owes its welcome to an appreciation of the synthesis it tries to create between order and liberty, between local initiative and national direction, between the voluntary agencies and the State, between the private life of a school and the public life of the districts which it serves, between manual and intellectual skill and between those better and less well endowed.[28]

The Act, of course, like all Parliamentary Acts, merely provided the legal framework. In its provisions on secondary education it set down some general lines of policy, but did not elaborate on what form the provisions would take or how they would be implemented. This was the responsibility of the newly established Ministry of Education, the local education authorities, the parents, the teachers and the public in general. In order to guide the local education authorities in their plans in accordance with the Act's stipulations, the Ministry of Education issued a pamphlet which provided a blueprint of institutional organization and which, but for minor variations, set the pattern of the current secondary school system in England.

In line with Butler's views, the Ministry interpreted the Act's provision of "variety of instruction" as implying different types of secondary education and recommended the now familiar tripartite pattern of grammar, modern and technical schools. In the main the ideological principles of this institutional framework were a mere regurgitation of Hadowism and the extensions made of it by the Spens and the Norwood Committees. The Ministry acknowledged and reaffirmed the Hadow principle of selection through differentiation in order to provide an education suited to the pupils' different aptitudes and abilities.

Everyone knows that no two children are alike. Schools must be different, too, or the Education Act of 1944 will not achieve success. They must differ in what they teach and how they teach it, just as pupils differ in tastes and abilities. The secondary school system must consequently offer variety in the curriculum and variety in the approach, suited to the differing aptitudes and abilities and stages of development of the children concerned.[29]

In addition, differentiation at 11+ was justified on a psychological and pedagogical rationale which was nothing more than a *melange* of Hadow, Spens and Norwood. The Ministry identified two broad typologies of students. On the one hand, there were the very able few who at 11 have already disclosed "particular interests and aptitudes well enough marked for them to require any other course." The "natural bent" of these few might be either in the direction of studies and activities bearing upon industry, commerce, agriculture, etc., or in the direction of "books" and "ideas" with a view to continuing their intellectual training in the "sixth form." On the other hand, there were the many, the vast majority of boys and girls who had not yet exhibited the marked talents and interests which characterized the few, but who might show "a marked practical bent."[30]

On the basis of this classification, the Ministry averred that the very able few would benefit most from an education given in technical and grammar schools corresponding to the two special "bents," and the rest from a rather "general" education given in modern schools. The difference between the modern and the other types of schools was that the former would be broader "in outlook and objective"; they would provide "a good all-round" education based on the interests of the children; they would seek to stimulate the pupils' ability to learn and pursue "quality in thought, expression and craftsmanship"; they would "interpret the modern world"; and, they would prepare for life.[31]

The Ministry also reaffirmed the principle of selection at the age of 11+ through several evaluative criteria including the "intelligence quotient." However, like the Hadow Committee and the subsequent statements by other committees, it stressed that the criterion for allocation in the several schools should not only be intellectual aptitude but also pupil interests and vocational aspirations. Thus, pupils at the "top-layer" in intelligence need not automatically go to grammar schools if they were not particularly interested in the type of education given in these schools or in the careers associated with them.[32] In order to lend greater force to this rather optimistic and "pious wish," the Ministry called for "parity of esteem" among the different secondary schools. It realized that this might take time; for it depended largely on the confidence local authorities and parents had on the value of "modern" schools, for example, and on what steps they took to equalize the conditions (teaching staff, books, equipment etc.) under which the several schools functioned.

As regards the curriculum, the Ministry recommended that in the first 2 years it should be general in all three types of schools and that it should contain many common elements (English, mathematics, science, history, geography, physical training, art, music), not only because of their value for general education in a democracy, but also because they would render transfer from one school to another easier. However, since each school would perform special functions as well, there would be curriculum differentiation after the general stage in accordance with the students' abilities and their educational and vocational aspirations.[33]

It is significant also to observe that in the case of the "modern school" the Ministry continued, in the same vein as that found in Hadowism, to stress the importance of a close relationship between the school and the affairs of life outside. Furthermore, "practical" studies were justified as ingredients of a "liberal" education on essentially the same grounds as those of the Hadow Report.[34]

THE DEBATE ON SELECTION AND TRIPARTITISM

The 1944 Act was passed by a coalition government in the name of social justice and equality of educational opportunity. However, since that time the policy of selection at 11+ and the tripartite institutional arrangement have been the focus of intense controversy. Although the examination of the post-war educational climate is outside the compass of this study, it would be appropriate to comment briefly on some aspects of it in order to place the period we have discussed into its proper historical perspective.

The Hadow Report, as this study has shown, articulated certain basic principles of educational policy and charted a course which culminated in the 1944 Act and the reforms that followed it. One such principle was the principle of selection through allocation of students to different types of schools on the basis, in theory at least, of demonstrated achievement and aptitude. The theory of "merit," which had its roots even earlier than the Hadow Report, since 1944 has become a catchall, and a different form of "cracy," a meritocracy, has entered the educational vocabulary. Paradoxically, however, with the popularization of merit, which in the past had been felt to be a more equitable basis for educational selection, questions of social classes, educational discrimination, equality of opportunity, etc., have also become more rather than less acute. And in the minds of some, at least, it is not quite clear or self-evident that a meritocracy is less "anti-democratic" or more humane than an aristocracy or any other form of "cracy."

The critics have contended that the policy of selection at 11+ and of tripartitism are anti-pedagogical, anti-psychological, inequalitarian, and downright inhumane. Psychologists have questioned the accuracy and fairness of the tests which purport to measure native intelligence on the grounds that they are culturally biased; hence it is difficult to disentangle heredity and environment and "coaching to pass tests." This naturally discriminates against children who come from culturally disadvantaged homes and favors others who are culturally more privileged.

Educationalists have argued that the 11+ examination puts instruction and the curriculum of the primary schools into a straightjacket: teachers are forced to gear their instruction to the demands of the examinations. Others have criticized the age of 11 as the cutting point; they have maintained that a child of that age is too young to be subjected to the "ordeal" of the 11+, that at that age level it is not possible to detect latent capacities and hence the system discriminates against "late bloomers," and that it is unfair and perhaps socially undesirable to determine a person's future career at such an early age. Parents have complained about the emotional strain and the anxiety that the 11+ engenders in themselves and their children.[35]

Closely associated with the 11+ has been the tripartite system of schools whereby on the basis of the results of several procedures at the age of eleven, children are sorted out and allocated into different types of secondary schools. The critics, who range over a wide spectrum of public opinion, have argued that the tripartite system—actually it has been in the main a "bi-partite" system[36]—is based on certain questionable assumptions about "typologies of students," about the meaning of equality and about the interpretation of "secondary education for all." Futhermore, it has been argued that tripartitism discriminates socially against working class children. According to John Vaizey, for example, "it seems a travesty of the aim of giving equal treatment to all children, to send some at the age of eleven to a well-equipped, well-staffed, old-fashioned school, while others (in effect) stay on at their old elementary schools." Much of the controversy, Vaizey adds, centering around equality—and by implication around tripartitism—is based on three questionable assumptions: (a) that "educational resources" will continue to be scarce

and therefore choices must be made in educational provision—more and better for some and less for others;
(b) that the functioning of society depends on the identi-
fication of the ablest individuals who will ultimately become the leaders, "while the great mass would be doing
routine and humdrum jobs well within the capabilities of
anybody with a minimum of intelligence and training";
and (c) that "ability is a fixed quantum which can be
identified and which to all intents and purposes remains
constant throughout life." Such assumptions, Vaizey argues,
are no longer true in a society which possesses wealth to
afford good education for everybody, which depends upon
a wide range of ability, and where ability is known to vary
depending on socio-economic and cultural factors. Accordingly, Vaizey has suggested a stronger definition of the term
equality:

> It (strong definition of equality) asserts that subject to dif-
> ferences in heredity and infantile experience, every child
> should have the same opportunity for *acquiring* measured
> intelligence, in so far as this can be controlled by social action.

In effect, Vaizey contends that public attention should
shift toward the creation of better living and earning conditions for the underprivileged, that every child should
be sent to a "good school" until he is at least seventeen
years old, and that selection should be postponed until
that age.[37]

The arguments against the existing policies of selection
and tripartitism have been in part buttressed by the findings of social scientists who have scrutinized the patterns
of recruitment into the various types of secondary schools
and the effects of schools upon the society. In this connection the research on the social composition of the student population in the grammar schools is particularly

pertinent. A spate of studies on particular schools or regions has almost invariably reached similar conclusions: that relative to the social composition of the population at large, there is an over-representation of middle-class children in the grammar schools and of working class children in the modern schools; that among grammar school "wastage" (drop-outs), there is a disproportionately higher number from the working classes; that the tests of ability, or the criterion of "measured intelligence," are enmeshed in socio-economic and cultural factors; that very often factors other than ability, e.g., regional variations in the proportion of grammar school places available relative to the population, seem to be important in determining the I.Q. cutting point; that sub-culture pressures influence entrance into grammar schools of children from the lower social strata; and that once admitted into grammar schools, many working-class children find it difficult to adjust to what seems to be a different culture. Concerning what appear to be social disparities in educational opportunity, Jean Floud's conclusion is particularly relevant:

> Although more working class children than ever before are now reaching the Grammar schools, and they form a large group in the population of these schools today, the likelihood, probability or chance that a working class boy will get to a Grammar school is not strikingly different from what it was before 1945 . . . Class differences in the proportion of boys of 11+ awarded Grammar school places are considerable and even with the working class there is a marked difference between the skilled and unskilled groups.[38]

An intensive study by Jackson and Marsden of education, particularly of grammar school education, in an industrial city in the north of England has shed light on several of the aforementioned social aspects of the selective examinations and of segregated education: an over-representation of middle-class children in the grammar schools, especially in "the vital upper reaches of these schools"; an "over performance" of middle-class compared to working-class children and a higher wastage of talent among the latter; anxieties over the 11+; and conflicts between "school" and "neighbourhood," or between "school culture" and "home culture" in the case of working-class education. Interestingly, however, far from turning their working-class recruits into "angry young men," or *déclassés* the grammar schools of "Warburton" manage to create satisfied bourgeois middle-class conservative men and women, self-conscious of what the effects of education had been upon them, pleased with the grammar schools they attended, and in fact eager to make them more selective![39]

It would be relevant in this connection to stress that research into the recruitment patterns of the grammar schools has also shown that today many more working-class children than ever before are able to enter grammar schools. A substantial percentage of the working-class children investigated by Jackson and Marsden come from families for whom a grammar school education had previously been only a dream. Indeed, Jean Floud quickly points out that class differences in opportunity and school achievement could be accounted for by "class differences in ability." According to Floud, there were class differences in the children's scores on the tests which sought to measure "Grammar school intelligence," that is, relative to the social composition of the male population over fifteen years of age, there was a higher proportion of middle-class than working-class children who possessed grammar school level "intelligence." On the basis of this social distribution she concluded that, when "measured intelligence" is taken as the basic criterion of selection into grammar schools, class discrimination is more apparent than real, and a boy's chances are almost entirely independent of his social background.[40]

As has traditionally been the case with English education, the controversies over selection and tripartitism have entered the political arena. After a period of ambivalence and divided loyalties—indeed, as we have shown, of support for segregated education—the Labour Party came out in favor of the comprehensive school arrangement, and criticized the 11+ policy. In 1953, the Labour Party pledged a complete overhaul of the entire system and promised that "Labour will abolish the practice of eleven-plus for different types of schools because it is convinced that all children would benefit if, during the whole of the period of their secondary education, they shared the facilities, both social and educational, of one comprehensive school".[41] Liberal spokesmen took a similar position.[42]

On the other hand, the selective procedures in the secondary schools and the tripartite system have been defended by several individuals and groups, by the Conservatives,[43] and by the influential *Times Educational Supplement*. In a recent editorial on the subject, the *Supplement* frankly stated that selection is unavoidable since, whether people liked it or not, the English society is "a selective society." The *Supplement,* which as we have shown was a pioneer in the clamor for secondary education for all, underscored the basic rationale for selection and tripartitism, viz., that talent "is the all important word here" and that it must be given "full rein"; that no better and more equitable alternative than the 11+ has been found; and that the tripartite system is in accord with "human nature." To some, especially to the advocates of equalitarianism, the *Supplement's* defence of selection may have sounded too much of an apology for conservatism and the maintenance of the *status quo*. But one cannot deny a stark realism in the following statement:

> Criticisms of the eleven-plus would hold more water if the alternatives to it were more clear. Are we really to suppose that if it were abolished our society would cease to be selective? And if that is not to be will not selective processes persist in one way or another with comprehensive schools or any other alternatives? Ought we not rather to take stock of what we have in hand rather than fight for an unsubtantial moon in the pond that is by no means clear? . . . the tripartite system *could* work and we have the physical framework of it. Let us stop assuming that education can alter nature. We might then allow education a chance to give nature a fair and efficient start.[44]

In a similar vein, Mr. Kenneth Thompson, Parliamentary Secretary to the Ministry of Education, is reported to have said in 1962: "We could not afford a nation to neglect the skills and talents which are given perhaps to only a few but upon which the rest of us may come to depend."[45]

And so the debate goes on. What seemed to be relatively unquestioned solutions to the democratizing trend toward secondary education for all have been subjected to microscopic inspection. Previous assumptions about education, society, and individual welfare have been re-evaluated and new solutions and assumptions have been offered. The basic principles of Hadow, Spens, and Norwood provided the ideological justification of secondary educational reorganization and policies; but clearly none of these precursors could have foreseen the post-war conditions and developments so brilliantly analyzed by Crowther, Newsome, and Robbins. English educational thinking is perhaps entering another phase in its development. At this time it is not quite clear what the future pattern is going to be, and whether the new Labour Government will succeed in its plan of radical educational reconstruction. Were one to characterize the climate of the recent years, one would not be overstretching the point by saying that English education has entered another phase in its development, which for lack of a better word might be called the stage of "equalitarianism." Perhaps the necessary consequence of the evolving Welfare State idea and of the increasing complexity of a growing industrial democracy, questions of equity in educational provision, of maximum utilization of manpower and talent, and of an education suited to individual character and abilities have acquired greater prominence and have re-emerged in different forms. It may be of interest, however, to mention that in this "equalitarian" stage of English educational development certain arguments ring a strange sound on this side of the Atlantic. Americans, until recently, have been pointing with pride to the comprehensive school, to the absence of early selective devices, to freedom and elasticity in the curriculum, and so on; but none of these factors has obviated social inequalities or wastage of talent. To be sure, they may have contributed to the blurring of social classes, but they may also have contributed to the blurring of intellectual differences and to a levelling down in terms of accomplishment. Ironically, "equalitarian" America seems to be introducing practices which equalitarians in England have criticized as reinforcing class privileges and discrimination. In their quest for better solutions, English reformers might take stock of what has happened in the United States and the bland belief in the ability of the comprehensive school to solve by itself all social and moral problems.

XIV
General Conclusions

Any undertaking which aims at examining English education over time is a formidable one to say the least. It would entail, as H. G. Wells once said, the disentangling of "all the muddle of impulses and antagonisms, the commercialism, utilitarianism, obstinate conservatism, humanitarian enthusiasm, out of which our (the British) present educational organisation arose." It would further entail the examination of what Dent called "the most powerful and persistent of all forces" that influenced the evolution of English education, namely, the Christian religion.[1] Lastly one should not omit the conditions which may have given rise to "the muddle of impulses etc.," namely, the inexorable advances in knowledge and technology, the changes in the social, economic and political structure, as well as the changes in education itself.

The foregoing historical analysis has not aimed as such completeness, were such a goal ever possible to attain. It has emphasized, rather, two major and indeed persistent aspects of one branch of the English educational system. The first was the social role of secondary education, that is, the relationship of education to the social, political and cultural spheres of English society; the second was the

320

pedagogical aspect of secondary education, that is, the aims, nature and scope of the curriculum. Even within this narrower scope, the prime concern was the changes in educational ideologies which legitimized, so to speak, existing practices, and which provided strategies for educational change.

André Maurois, we noted, cautioned against drawing sharply defined historical periods; for, "overlapping edges are always to be found at both ends of these periods."[2] Thus, strictly speaking, the lines of demarcation of the period encompassed in this study are arbitrary. Yet in terms of our two major foci, the reports of the Bryce Commission of 1895 and the Hadow Committee of 1926, respectively, marked the convergence of a cluster of ideas that had been gradually developing in the decades preceding them. Specifically, the Hadow Report laid down certain ideological principles which, but for certain extensions, persisted in the ensuing years and essentially constituted the core of the conceptual outlook that underlay the changes of the forties.

In a public speech soon after the Hadow Report appeared, Ernest Barker, one of the members of the Consultative Committee, described the Report as "an educational and social revolution."[3] Barker may have been exaggerating, but this depends on how one interprets the term "revolution." Since we do not have a full record of his speech, we might take his terms and see in what sense one could or could not describe Hadowism as a revolutionary ideology. If by "revolution" we mean a *complete* break with the past, then clearly Hadowism cannot be described as revolutionary. For as shown here, certain of its ideological principles, e.g., secondary education for all, selection at 11+, institutional and pedagogical differentiation, etc., had in some form or another been stated prior to 1926. Furthermore, two of the basic elements of its institutional framework, e.g., the grammar school and the modern school, had their roots in the past.

Yet in many respects certain constituent elements of Hadowism were quite novel and in a rather loose interpretation of the term "revolutionary." At the time of the Bryce Commission, secondary education was envisaged as the education of a small rather socially and economically exclusive segment of the population. The transfer from elementary to secondary schools was not automatic, and selection took place through elimination based on social, economic and intellectual criteria. Insofar as official educational opinion was concerned, the Hadow Committee was the first body to promulgate the principle of secondary education for all and the view that elementary and secondary education were two successive stages in a continuous process. Selection in the Hadow conceptual framework would still take place, but now it becomes a question of *allocation* of students to different types of schools which, ideally at least, were to be considered equal in status. In both the Hadow and the Bryce Reports, what has come to be known as the American idea of a comprehensive secondary school was rejected in favor of a differentiated institutional pattern with each type of school performing different functions. Moreover, both reports set school goals with a view to the future occupational destinations of students. However, there were also marked differences between the two reports. The Bryce Commission explicitly "graded" three different types of schools according to function. It also restricted the social base of recruitment and envisaged the three grades as corresponding to social gradations and relative emphasis on a literary-humanistic type of instruction. The Hadow Committee, on the other hand, gave a totally different meaning to the nature and scope of secondary education. Although in one sense the "grades" of schools in the Bryce framework corresponded in some of their functions to the different types of schools in Hadowism, in the latter criteria for selection into these schools, the social base of recruitment and the rationale for differentiation were envisaged to be totally different. In Hadowism, intellectual capacity and interests of pupils, rather than ascriptive criteria, emerge as the significant factors to be taken in the selective process, and one type of education emerges ideally at least as good as another. In this sense, therefore, namely in replacing social and economic criteria of selection by intellectual, and in adhering to the principle that the schools should deliberately select with a view to future occupations, the Hadow Report was an important stage in the gradually evolving system of English meritocracy so brilliantly analyzed by Michael Young.[4]

The reasons for these ideological shifts were found to be many and complex. There was first an increasingly marked re-alignment of political power and shifts in political ideologies. In 1867, Walter Bagehot justified his thesis of the rule of the 10,000 on the grounds that the general populace were narrow-minded, unintelligent, confused, erroneous, and content to be voteless.[5] But by 1918 the franchise was extended to almost all members of society and thus the question of political citizenship of the majority of the population had been solved. It was soon realized that the extension of the franchise meant a new source of potential political strength and in the last quarter of the nineteenth century both Liberals and Conservatives vied with each other to introduce policies which would attract popular support. Even so, and in spite of the formation of the Labour Party in the first decade of the twentieth century, the *actual* political power of Labour was rather limited. There was not as yet a uniform social philosophy that Labour could claim as peculiarly its own, nor was there any sizeable representation in Parliament. Thus labor groups often aligned themselves with the other political groups, mostly the Liberals, and, except for the 1902 Act, they followed in the main the Liberal policies. But by the twenties, Labour emerged as a major force in British politics and indeed for the first time in English history it formed a government. Throughout the period encompassed in this study and increasingly during and after the First World War, organized Labour groups actively and effectively campaigned for the extension of educational opportunities at the "secondary" level and for the elimination of educational inequalities. This campaign reached its climax in the early twenties with the famous Tawney manifesto *Secondary Education for All*. By this time also the Labour Party had developed a more uniform and solid *Labour* social philosophy and programs of action that were essentially its own, distinct from Liberal associations. However, certain caveats must be entered here. In their emphasis upon "equality of advantages" and distributive justice, Labour groups were neither egalitarian in their ideology in the strict meaning of the term, nor militant or revolutionary in their methods. In the last decade of the nineteenth century and the first decade of the twentieth, when the working-class movement was still inchoate in its political organization and when it lacked powerful spokesmen in Parliament, the interests of the working population were advanced through the existing parties by means of the Fabian strategy of "permeation."

Believing further in the doctrine of "inevitability of gradualism," the Labour groups called for the widening of the rungs of the educational ladder so that through scholarships and bursaries more working-class children could gain access into the existing type of secondary schools. Thus, in this respect they operated *within* the existing ideological and institutional framework rather than *without*. Indeed the radical Labour view of equalitarianism in education outside the existing system is a post-World War II phenomenon and in no way can it be traced to the beginning of the LabourParty. Even when after the First World War Labour emerged as a powerful political force and espoused the doctrine of secondary education for all, it did not completely reject the traditional principles associated with its political opponents. It accepted the notion of selection at 11+, and of allocation into separate institutions, as well as the curriculum provisions of the various schools.

At the same time, however, that Labour was consolidating itself, there were significant shifts in the political ideologies of both the Conservatives and the Liberals. By the First World War both groups had abandoned their extreme laissez-faire doctrines, especially in the area of secondary education. The Conservatives, partly because of vested religious interests—in 1902, for example, they supported public "control" and "support" of education to salvage the voluntary schools—partly because of their commitment to a policy of imperial expansion which necessitated national efficiency, and partly because of political pressures from the newly enfranchised laboring classes, were largely responsible for the epoch-making Education Act of 1902 which laid the foundation for a national system of secondary education. This ideological shift can never be exaggerated, especially when one considers that in 1870 the Conservatives were the staunchest adherents of voluntarism and sectarianism. The Liberal Party went through a period which was marked by trials and tribulations. In the Act of 1870 the more radical in their midst were the staunchest supporters of the interests of the less affluent segments of society in sharp contrast to the Tory-Anglican alliance; and in the area of elementary education they stood for a secular, compulsory and free system of education. The Gladstonian Liberals stood in between these extremes and advocated a "pluralistic" system of control including both voluntary agencies and the State. In 1895, however, the Liberal Party was split in two, and the more radical group, now called Liberal Unionists, joined forces with the Conservatives, a coalition made on the issues of Irish Home Rule and Imperialism. Although in the area of education the Liberal Unionists had not abandoned the traditional Liberal pluralistic policy, when the Education Bill of 1902 was introduced, they found themselves in an embarrassing position in that they were forced to be partners to a legislative measure which aimed at placing voluntary schools—largely Anglican—on the local rates and eliminating the School Boards which were largely in the hands of Liberal-Nonconformists. In the end they supported the Conservatives, perhaps because they felt that the educational question was not as significant as other questions. The Liberal Opposition also found themselves in an anomalous and paradoxical position. Traditionally the party represented radical middle- and lower-class interests and had waged many of its campaigns in the name of reform and distributive justice. But now they fought against an Act which aimed at establishing a more national system of education, controlled and supported by "democratically" elected local councils. The Liberal split might well have sealed the fate of the Liberal Party there and then, had it not been for the political acumen and oratorical skill of Lloyd George and other leaders of the Liberal camp. In the midst of the debate over the 1902 Education Bill, Lloyd George, under the banner of freedom from the Conservative-Anglican yoke, grasped the opportunity to rally the Liberals together, and by 1905 the Liberals sprang back to power, having inflicted a devastating blow upon the Conservatives. But the emergent triumphant Liberalism of 1906 was also found to be a reconstructed Liberalism in its political and educational ideologies. It rejected extreme laissez-faire and sought to give more positive meanings to the cardinal Liberal concepts of freedom and equality. Thus, during the ensuing years a series of political and social reforms were undertaken. Specifically, in secondary education the New Liberalism was responsible for the free-place system and the Education Act of 1918.

Both Liberals and Conservatives, throughout the period under study, envisaged a selective system of secondary education with ample provisions for scholarships and/or free places so that a closer link could be made between elementary and secondary education. At best, however, their reforms provided the initial necessary conditions in the evolving concept of secondary education for all. When all the political parties are taken into account and despite the overlap in political ideologies, it was the Labour Party which in the end came out boldly in favor of secondary education for all.

The restructuring of political power and the changing political ideologies, however, could not be understood by themselves without reference to significant changes in the social, economic, intellectual and educational conditions of England during this period. Throughout this study, an attempt was made to show how both external and internal forces, e.g., the Boer War, the First World War, the threat of foreign competition especially that of Germany, the spread of elementary education, the scientific and technical advances, the changes in the economic sphere, and the relative blurring of social class, contributed not only to changes in political ideologies, but also created a general consensus for educational change at the secondary level, and for the breaking down of the class associations of elementary and secondary education. Perhaps the most outstanding single force in this complex was the First World War. The Lloyd George-Asquith rift over the conduct of the war proved irreparable and signaled the demise of the Liberal Party. The working-class movement emerged as a solid, powerful force to challenge old privileges and the Victorian *noblesse oblige* philosophy. Science and modern subjects challenged the supremacy of the classics. The upward thrust of elementary education which started in 1870 had at long last come to maturity in the central school, which, although still under the shadow of the grammar school, was too firmly entrenched to suffer the fate of the higher grade and the higher elementary schools. The war, in addition, created an unprecedented interest in education. The ferment for change spread to all segments of society and for the first time in English educational history the doctrine of secondary education for all was not only vigorously advanced, but was also taking definite shape. It is easy to make hasty generalizations and draw quick conclusions; but it seems quite clear that because of the war the course of secondary education in the twenties was quite different from what it was in the pre-war decades.

It should be borne in mind, however, that, in spite of the ideological shift from a relatively exclusive type of secondary education to the more inclusive one of secondary education for all, Hadowism did not abandon the traditional view that one of the essential functions of secondary education was the selection and training of future leaders in the society. The grammar school in the Hadow framework was envisaged to be the school for future leaders. This indeed has been one of the persistent features of English education and partly accounts for the ambivalent attitude towards comprehensive schools even today.

Turning now to the strictly pedagogical aspect of education, the study has shown that the question first raised by Herbert Spencer in 1859, namely, "What Knowledge is of Most Worth?" and the meaning of "liberal education" were constantly areas of controversy and re-examination. In many respects the developments of the early decades of the twentieth century would have astounded even Spencer himself. Science, a peripheral subject at the time when Spencer wrote, and still highly controversial as an ingredient of a "good liberal education" at the end of the nineteenth century, had by the twenties emerged as an essential and indisputable element of general education. In addition to science, however, Hadowism stands out as an educational landmark in its insistence on the educational value of "practical" and "artistic" studies and its over-all view of "a humane or liberal education" as one which "is not given through books alone."

Yet, in spite of this acceptance of the value of "practical studies," Hadowism still upheld the view that the prime educational function of all types of secondary schools should essentially be "general education" rather than a narrowly vocational preparation. This view, one might further add, has persisted up to the present time.

In the evolving pedagogical and indeed in the previously mentioned social aspects of secondary education, it was found that the post-World War I educational thinkers and psychologists played an important role. For the first time in English educational history, the principles of selection at 11+, curriculum differentiation and types of schools, and generally the whole sphere of secondary education were justified on psychological grounds as well. In its attempts to ground educational theory and practice in psychological theories about human development and attainment, Hadowism pioneered the way for a new dimension in the rationale that has characterized subsequent policies in the sphere of secondary education.

In retrospect, Hadowism, as an over-all ideological pattern woven out of a multiplicity of threads which partook of both the old and the new, cannot but be regarded as a historical landmark. And if in the field of the statutory system of public secondary education, the reforms of the forties represented the climax of a movement dating back to the Act of 1902, Hadowism must be regarded as the ideological forerunner of that revolutionary change.

Notes

INTRODUCTION

1 Royal Commission on Secondary Education, *Report of the Commissioners* (London, 1895), Vol. I., pp. iii–iv. Hereafter cited as Bryce Commission.

2 Sir Charles Petrie, *The Victorians* (London: Eyre and Spottiswoode, 1960), p. 13.

3 Lytton Strachey, *Eminent Victorians* (Garden City, New York: Garden City Publishing Co., Inc., n.d.), p. v.

4 David Thomson, *England in the Nineteenth Century (1815–1914)* (London: Penguin Books, 1953), pp. 33–34.

5 Esmé Wingfield-Stratford, *Those Eminent Victorians* (London: William Morrow and Company, Inc., 1930), p. 59.

6 These developments are treated in greater detail in Chapter IV.

7 R. H. Tawney, *Equality* (New York: Capricorn Books, 1961), pp. 91 ff.

8 Michael Young, *The Rise of the Meritocracy 1870–2033: The New Elite of Our Social Revolution* (New York: Random House, 1959).

9 Tawney, *Equality*, p. 109.

10 Schools Inquiry Commission, *Reports of Assistant Commissioners* (London: Her Majesty's Stationery Office, 1868), Vol. VII, pp. 12–13, 35. Hereafter cited as Schools Inquiry Commission.

11 *Ibid.*, p. 94.

12 *Ibid.*, p. 237.

13 In a recent study, T. W. Bamford showed that in eight "acknowledged Public Schools" there was a marked preponderance of boys from the "gentry" and the "titled aristocracy," although professional and clerical groups were also represented. See T. W. Bamford, "Public Schools and Social Class, 1801–1850," *British Journal of Sociology*, 12:224–35 (September, 1961).

14 *Hansard Parliamentary Debates*, Vol. CLXV, 1862, p. 240.

15 See Frank Smith, *A History of English Elementary Education* (London: University of London Press, 1931), p. 253. Also see Asa Briggs, *Victorian People: A Reassessment of Persons and Themes*, 1851–67 (Chicago, The University of Chicago Press, 1954), p. 258.

16 Walter Bagehot, *The English Constitution* (London: Oxford University Press, 1928), p. 6.

[17] Bryce Commission, I, pp. 183–186.

[18] See for example, Schools Inquiry Commission, Vol. VII, pp. 12–13, 35, 94, 237. Also see *Hansard*, Fourth Series, Vol. CLXV, 1862, p. 240.

[19] Bryce Commission, I, p. 17.

[20] Board of Education, *Report of the Consultative Committee on the Education of the Adolescent* (London: H.M.S.O., 1926). Hereafter cited as Hadow Report.

I

[1] H. A. L. Fisher, *James Bryce* (New York: The Macmillan Company, 1927), Vol. I, p. 38.

[2] This was evident in Bryce's position on the Education Act of 1902 and the policy of the Liberal Government in 1906 which are discussed in chapters IV and VII.

[3] As a student at Glasglow and Oxford he received a "shower of academic honours" in Greek, History and Law. No less than 31 academic degrees were conferred on him by British and foreign universities including 15 American colleges and universities. He held honorary and regular membership in numerous continental and British learned societies, covering all spheres of intellectual activity, and served as President of the British Academy and the Alpine Club and as Honorary Fellow of the Royal Geographical Society. By the time he was appointed chairman of the Royal Commission, Bryce had already published his *The Holy Roman Empire* which won him the Arnold Prize in 1862, and his monumental *The American Commonwealth* which was heralded from the very beginning as a political and historical masterpiece. See Fisher, *James Bryce*, Vol. I, pp. 46–47, 61ff, 222ff, Vol. II, pp. 330–333.

[4] *Ibid.*, Vol. I, pp. 48–49.

[5] *Ibid.*, p. 105.

[6] Sadler's views on the relative emphasis that should be given to this type of education are discussed in chapter V.

[7] Of Sadler's qualities as a reformer, see Lynda Grier, *Achievement in Education: The Work of Michael Ernest Sadler, 1885–1935* (London: Constable and Co., Ltd., 1952), p. 8.

[8] *Ibid.*, pp. 31–32.

[9] *Ibid.*, p. 32.

[10] *The Dictionary of the National Biography*, 1901–1911, 1912–1921, 1922–1930, 1931–1940, 1941–1950, and *Who Was Who*, 1897–1916, 1916–1928. No information was found on Edward Lyttelton who in the roster of the Commissioners is simply referred to as "clerk, Master of Arts."

[11] In 1893 Yoxall was adopted as Liberal candidate for the Northern Division of Nottingham, and in the elections of 1895 he won. He was the first successful candidate sponsored by the National Union of Teachers.

[12] Bryce was educated at Glasgow College and Oxford, Sadler at Rugby and Oxford, Jebb at Charterhouse and Cambridge, Maclure at Manchester Grammar School and Oxford, Smith at Bristol Grammar School

and Oxford, Hobhouse at Eton and Oxford, and Hibbert at Shrewsbury and Cambridge.

13 Report of the Committee of Ten on Secondary School Studies: With the Reports of the Conferences Arranged by the Committee (New York: American Book Company, 1894). Hereafter cited as Committee of Ten.

14 These were: Charles W. Eliot (Harvard University), James B. Angell (University of Michigan), James B. Taylor (Vassar College), James H. Baker (University of Colorado), and Richard H. Jesse (University of Missouri).

15 Bryce Commission, Vol. I, pp. iii–iv.

16 Ibid., Vol. I, p. 140.

17 See, for example, the data collected by Mr. F. E. Kitchener, Assistant Commissioner, Ibid., Vol. VI, p. 206.

18 Ibid., pp. 379–381.

19 Ibid., pp. 115–121.

20 Ibid., Vol. II, p. 196.

21 See the report by Mr. R. E. Mitcheson, an assistant commissioner, who reported on secondary education in the county of Bedford. Ibid., Vol. VI, p. 28.

22 Ibid., Vol. I, p. 140.

23 Ibid., Vol. VI, p. 206.

24 Ibid., Vol. II, pp. 199–200.

25 Ibid., Vol. IX, p. 256.

26 Ibid., p. 228.

27 Ibid., pp. 381–383.

28 See evidence given by Miss Cooper and Mr. Vardy, Ibid., Vol. II, p. 182.

29 Ibid., Vol. VI, p. 57.

30 Ibid., p. 297.

31 See for example the list of schools compiled by Mr. Kitchener. Ibid., p. 207.

32 Ibid., Vol. III, p. 221.

33 Ibid., Vol. VII, pp. 159–162.

34 Ibid., Vol. VI, p. 186.

35 Ibid., Vol. II, pp. 33–34.

36 Ibid., Vol. VI, pp. 207, 211. Scientific and mathematic subjects included arithmetic, Euclid algebra, trigonometry, chemistry, mechanics, heat, sound, light, electricity and magnetism, physiology, practical plane and solid geometry, machine construction and mechanical drawing; technical subjects included bookkeeping, shorthand, needlework, and manual instruction in wood and iron; artistic subjects included freehand and model drawing and music; and literary subjects included English literature and composition, French, Latin, history and geography.

37 Ibid., p. 15.

38 Ibid., Vol. VII, pp. 172–183, pp. 183–185.

39 Computed from the statistics gathered by the Commission. Ibid., Vol. IX, pp. 385–401.

40 *Ibid.*, Vol. II, p. 284. Also see the reports by A. P. Laurie for Yorkshire, *Ibid.*, Vol. VII, pp. 184–185, and by F. E. Kitchener for Lancashire, *Ibid.*, Vol. VI, p. 210, and the memorandum by J. G. Fitch, *Ibid.*, Vol. V, p. 93.

41 *Ibid.*, Vol. VII, p. 189.

42 See specifically Kitchener's report on such schools in Lancashire. *Ibid.*, Vol. VI, p. 210.

43 See, for example, the evidence given by Sir George Young, one of the Charity Commissioners. *Ibid.*, Vol. II, p. 29.

44 On this point specifically see the evidence of the Rev. T. W. Sharpe, Her Majesty's Chief Inspector of Schools, and that of Sidney Webb. *Ibid.*, Vol. II, p. 160, 259. Also see the evidence by Mr. Vardy and Miss Cooper. *Ibid.*, p. 180.

45 *Ibid.*, Vol. VI, pp. 87–88.

46 *Ibid.*, p. 310.

47 See evidence given by Miss Cooper. *Ibid.*, Vol. II, p. 196.

48 *Ibid.*, Vol. V, p. 92.

49 *Ibid.*, Vol. III, p. 192.

50 *Ibid.*, Vol. V, p. 399.

51 *Ibid.*, p. 451.

52 *Ibid.*, Vol. II, p. 43.

53 See for example the report submitted by Mr. Sidney Webb and Dr. W. Garrett on behalf of the London Technical Education Board. *Ibid.*, p. 557.

54 *Ibid.*, Vol. V, p. 491.

55 *Ibid.*, p. 451.

56 *Ibid.*, pp. 40–44.

57 *Ibid.*, Vol. I, pp. 48, 424. Enrollments in private schools were not included as the great diversity in such schools rendered any reliable estimates impossible.

58 *Ibid.*, Vol. V, p. 45.

59 *Ibid.*, Vol. VII, p. 52.

60 *Ibid.*, Vol. VI, pp. 234–235.

61 *Ibid.*, p. 71.

62 *Ibid.*, p. 235. Also see Mr. Mitcheson's report for Bedfordshire and Mr. Gerrans' report for Devonshire, *Ibid.*, pp. 19–20, 69–72.

63 See for example, Ministry of Education, *15 to 18. A Report of the Central Advisory Council for Education (England)* (London: Her Majesty's Stationery Office, 1959), p. 11. Hereafter cited as the Crowther Report.

64 Bryce Commission, Vol. I, pp. 431–433.

65 *Ibid.*, Vol. II, p. 196.

66 Vardy testified that he "remembered" one son of an artisan whose weekly wage was not more than 40 shillings who climbed the ladder from the elementary school to Oxford, and took a first in "Moderations" and a second in "Classical Greats," *Ibid.*

67 *Ibid.*, Vol. V, p. 119.

68 *Ibid.*, Vol. IX, pp. 226–373.

II

[1] See for example, H. C. Dent, *Change in English Education: A Historical Survey* (London: University of London Press, 1952), p. 89. David Glass refrains from making such judgments, but he calls the Commission's view "revolutionary." See A. H. Halsey, J. Floud and C. A. Anderson, editors, *Education, Economy, and Society. A Reader in the Sociology of Education* (Glencoe, Illinois: The Free Press, 1961), p. 399.

[2] Bryce Commission, Vol. I, p. 130.

[3] *Ibid.*, Vol. II, p. 155.

[4] *Ibid.*, Vol. V, pp. 89–90.

[5] *Ibid.*, Vol. II, pp. 110–111.

[6] *Ibid.*, Vol. III, p. 488.

[7] *Ibid.*, Vol. II, p. 369.

[8] *Ibid.*, Vol. III, p. 404.

[9] *Ibid.*, Vol. V, pp. 494–498.

[10] *Ibid.*, Vol. II, p. 291. For similar views also see the evidence by J. Bidgood of the Higher Grade Board School Newcastle on Tyne. *Ibid.*, p. 393.

[11] *Ibid.*, Vol. V, pp. 389ff, 456.

[12] *Ibid.*, p. 491.

[13] *Ibid.*, p. 442.

[14] *Ibid.*, Vol. I, p. 130.

[15] *Ibid.*, pp. 132–135.

[16] *Ibid.*, p. 135.

[17] *Ibid.*, pp. 135–136.

[18] *Ibid.*, p. 136.

[19] H. C. Dent, *Secondary Education for All: Origins and Development in England* (London: Routledge and Kegan Paul, 1949), pp. 31–32.

[20] John Graves, *Policy and Progress in Secondary Education, 1902–1942* (London: Thomas Nelson and Sons, 1943), p. 21.

[21] Halsey, Floud and Anderson, *Education, Economy and Society*, p. 399.

[22] Bryce Commission, I, p. 80.

[23] *Ibid.*, Vol. II, p. 557.

[24] Quoted in Gerrans' report on Devonshire. *Ibid.*, Vol. VI, p. 71.

[25] R. L. Archer, *Secondary Education in the Nineteenth Century* (London: Cambridge University Press, 1921), p. 354.

[26] Bryce Commission, I, pp. 48, 61–63.

[27] *Ibid.*, pp. 299–303.

[28] *Ibid.*, pp. 183–186.

[29] *Ibid.*, p. 74.

[30] *Ibid.*, p. 273.

[31] *Ibid.*, pp. 257, 268–270.

[32] *Ibid.*, p. 326.

[33] *Ibid.*, pp. 272–273.

III

¹ For a summary of comments in the press, see "The Press and the Royal Commission on Secondary Education Report," *The Journal of Education* 17:753–4 (December, 1895). Also see Joseph Whitaker, *An Almanack for the Year of our Lord 1896* (London: Paternoster Row, 1896), pp. 636–641.

² "The Secondary Education," *The Athenaeum*, No. 3549:609 (November 2, 1895). For other comments in non-professional journals, see H. E. Armstrong, "The Royal Commission on Secondary Education," *Nature*, 53:79–82 (November 28, 1895); and "Secondary Education," *The Liberal Magazine*, 4:39,44–47.

³ "Editorial Comment," *The Educational Times*, :455 (November 1, 1895). Also see C. L. Pulliam, "Current Educational Literature," *The School Review*, 4:641–5 (October, 1896).

⁴ See, for example, "First Impressions of the Report," *The Journal of Education*, 17:645 (November, 1895); "Editorial," *The Educational Review* 4:514 (December, 1895); and "Foreign Notes," *Education*, 16:514 (December, 1895).

⁵ "Foreign Notes," *Education*, 16:374–5 (February, 1896). Also see "The Headmasters' Conference," *The Journal of Education*, 18:69 (January, 1896).

⁶ Great Britain, Secondary Education Commission, *Copy of the Joint Memorandum from the Incorporated Association of Head Masters and Mr. Laurie on Matters of Public Interest Connected with the Report of the Royal Commission on Secondary Education*, (London: H.M.S.O., 1897), p. 4. Also see *The Times* (London), January 17, 1896, p. 55. For other reports on the proceedings and comments at professional conferences, see "Foreign Notes," *The School Review*, 4:58 (January, 1896) ; "Colonial and Foreign Notes," *The Journal of Education*, 18:47 (January 1896); "Colonial and Foreign Notes," *The Journal of Education*, 18:117 (February, 1896); *The Record of Technical and Secondary Education*, 5:154, 277 (April, 1896); *The Journal of Education*, 18:106, 139–140 (February, 1896).

⁷ "The Cambridge Conference," *The Educational Times*, 49:245 (May, 1896). Also see "The Cambridge Conference on Secondary Education," *The Journal of Education*, 18:319–321 (May, 1896).

⁸ See *The Journal of Education*, 17:753–4 (December, 1895).

⁹ See, for example, "First Impressions of the Report," *The Journal of Education* 17:646 (November, 1895), and "Foreign Notes," *Education*, (January, 1896).

¹⁰ H. E. Armstrong, for example, deplored the fact that the Commissioners did not tackle adequately the problem of the curriculum and especially scientific and technical education, *Nature*, 53:80–81 (November 28, 1895). T. J. Macnamara felt that the Report failed to press its recommendations to their logical conclusion and thus achieve "the finest social and educational stroke of the century." T. J. Macnamara, "The Report

of the Secondary Education Commission," *The Fortnightly Review*, 58:893–901 (December, 1895).

11 "Occasional Notes," *The Journal of Education*, 18:236 (April, 1896).

12 *Hansard*, Fourth Series, Vol. XLI, 1896, p. 1268.

13 *Hansard*, Fourth Series, Vol. XXXIX, 1896, p. 554. For other similar statements by supporters of the Bill, see the speeches by W. Hart Dyke and Ernest Grey. *Ibid.*, pp. 556–561.

14 *Hansard*, Fourth Series, Vol. XL, 1896, p. 568.

15 *Ibid.*, p. 595.

16 *Ibid.*, pp. 689–690.

17 *Hansard*, Fourth Series, Vol. XXXIX, 1896, p. 538.

18 By this Act, money known as "whisky money" was allocated for the support of technical instruction by the county councils. See *Local Taxation (Customs and Excise) Act*, 1890 (53 & 54 Vict., c.60).

19 By the Education Act of 1870, public rate-supported schools could be set up in places where the existing provision of elementary education was found not to be "sufficient, efficient, and suitable," under the supervision of *ad hoc* bodies called School Boards, elected by a ballot of rate-payers. See *Elementary Education Act, 1870* (33 & 34 Vict. Ch. 75). Hereafter cited *Elementary Education Act, 1870.*

20 "A Bill to Make Further Provision for Education in England and Wales," *Bills, Public*, Vol. I, 1896, I(1), 3(1), 12(1)(3), 13(2).

21 See, for example, the speeches by J. H. Yoxall, a member of the Commission, and by Bryce. *Ibid.*, pp. 565, 572.

22 *Hansard*, Fourth Series, Vol. 39, 1896, p. 565.

23 See Bryce's statement. *Ibid.*, p. 573.

24 *The Journal of Education*, 18:320 (May, 1896).

25 "The Teachers Guild of Great Britain and Ireland," *The Journal of Education*, 18:387 (June, 1896).

26 *Hansard*, Fourth Series, Vol. 39, 1896, pp. 569–570.

27 *Ibid.*, pp. 573–575. The Cowper-Temple Clause, named after Cowper-Temple, a Conservative M.P. at the time of the passing of the Education Act of 1870, and in effect since then, read as follows: "No religious catechism or . . . formulary which is distinctive of any particular denomination shall be taught in the (Board) school." *Elementary Education Act, 1870*, 14, (2).

28 *Ibid*, p. 575.

29 Reported in *The Times* (London), April 15, 1896, p. 10. For the views of the Congregationalists and the Unitarians in England see *The Times* (London), April 15, 1896, p. 10 and April 17, 1896, p. 11; for the position of the Wesleyans, see *The Times* (London), April 24, 1896, p. 12. For the stance of the Nonconformists in Wales and Monmouthshire, see *The Times* (London), April 10, 1896, p. 8. Also see the report on the meeting of the National Education League of Free Churches at Rochdale on April 15, 1896 in *The Times*, (London), April 16, 1896, p. 12, and that of the London Nonconformist, in *The Times* (London), April 18, p. 10.

30 Reported in *The Times* (London), April 8, 1896, p. 5. Also see *The*

Annual Register: A Review of Public Events at Home and Abroad For the Year 1896 (London: Longmans, Green, and Co., 1897), Hereafter cited as *The Annual Register for 1896.*

31 The position of these groups and individuals was similar to that of the Liberals in Parliament. See for example, what *The Times* called the manifesto of the Birmingham Liberal Association, *The Times* (London), April 15, 1896, p. 10, and the report on the meeting of the General Committee of the National Liberal Federation in *The Times* (London), April 30, 1896), p. 11.

32 Reported in *The Times* (London), April 3, 1896, p. 8.

33 Reported in *The Times* (London), April 29, 1896, p. 12. Also see the reports of the Conferences of the Norwich and Exeter Dioceses in *The Times* (London), April 10, 1896, p. 8 and April 11, 1896, p. 8.

34 See report on the conference held at the Sanctuary in Westminster, *The Times* (London), April 16, 1896, p. 12.

35 See, for example, the views of the Bishop of Hereford as reported in *The Annual Register for 1896,* p. 107.

36 Reported in *The Times* (London), April 24, 1896, p. 12.

37 Reported in *The Times* (London), April 8, 1896, p. 5.

38 For a fuller analysis of the position of the radicals on the 1870 Act, see C. E. Bidwell and A. M. Kazamias, "Religion, Politics, and Popular Education: An Historical Comparison of England and America." *The Comparative Education Review,* 6:99–100 (October, 1962). On this point also see Frank Smith, *A History of English Elementary Education 1760–1902* (London: University of London Press, 1931), pp. 284, 292–4, and M. Cruickshank, *Church and State in English Education, 1870 to the Present Day* (London: St. Martins Press, 1963), pp. 15–16.

39 *Ibid.,* pp. 41, 44, 56. Also see *The Annual Register for 1896,* p. 107.

40 *Ibid.,* p. 107.

41 See *The Times* (London), April 25, 1896, p. 9.

42 *The Times* (London), April 11, 1896, p. 11.

43 *The Times* (London), April 16, 1896, p. 9.

44 See, for example, "The Education Bill," *The Educational Times,* 49:199 (April 1, 1896).

45 *Hansard,* Fourth Series, Vol. 40, 1896, pp. 556–558.

46 *Ibid.,* pp. 558–564.

47 The reference here was to the "time-table conscience clause" of the 1870 Act and still in effect, which provided for the withdrawal of children from all schools when religious instruction was given. *Elementary Education Act, 1870.*

48 *Hansard,* Fourth Series, Vol. 40, 1896, pp. 564–566.

49 See *The Annual Register* for 1896, p. 104.

50 *Hansard,* Fourth Series, Vol. 40, 1896, pp. 567–595.

51 See for example, the speeches by Viscount Cranbone and Arthur Balfour on behalf of the Conservatives. *Ibid.,* pp. 629–30 and 1241–1252, Channing, Yoxall and Bryce on behalf of the Liberals, *Ibid.,* pp. 595–603, 657–667, 687–705; and the speech by George Dixon on behalf of the Liberal Unionists. *Ibid.,* 637–646.

52 *Ibid.*, pp. 603–606.

53 See the speech by John Dillon. *Ibid.*, pp. 1216–1224.

54 *The Annual Register for 1896*, p. 125.

55 *Ibid.*, p. 130. For an excellent resume of the political climate inside and outside Parliament, see *Ibid.*, pp. 128–133.

56 *Hansard*, Fourth Series, Vol. 41, 1896, p.

57 "Abortive Bill," *The Educational Times*, 49:398–9 (July 1, 1896).

58 "The Education Bill," *The Educational Times*, 49:199 (April 1, 1896).

59 "Notes on Elementary School," *The Journal of Education*, 17:405 (July, 1895).

60 *The Educational Times*, 49:308 (July 1, 1896).

61 See "Mr. Balfour and Professor Jebb on Technical and Secondary Education," *Nature*, LIX (February 9, 1899), p. 352; E. Lyulph Stanley, "The Government Education Bill," *The Contemporary Review*, 81:610 (May 1902), "Secondary and Technical," *The Educational Times*, 51:305–6 (April 1, 1898).

62 On this point, also see "An Eirenicon," *Education*, 4:19 (January 22, 1898), and R. R. Scott, editor, *What is Secondary Education? and Other Short Essays* (London: Rivingston, 1899), p. v.

63 Particularly see Education Department, *Special Reports on Educational Subjects, 1896–1897* (London: H.M.S.O., 1897), Vol. I, pp. 333–335, 387, 453. Hereafter cited as Special Reports.

64 See for example, the "Draft Scheme for a Secondary Education Bill," adopted by the Headmasters' Association. *The Educational Times*, 50:280 (July, 1897).

65 Scott, *What is Secondary Education*, p. 168. Also see pp. v, 211.

66 Quoted by F. Campbell, *Eleven Plus and All That: The Grammar School in a Changing Society* (London: C. A. Watts and Co., Ltd., 1956), p. 145.

67 See Cloudesley Brereton, "The Return of Secondary Education in the Light of Proposed Legislation," *The Fortnightly Review*, 64:766 (November, 1898).

IV

1 *The Educational Times*, 49:308 (July 1, 1896).

2 "Occasional Notes," *The Journal of Education*, 19:18 (January 1897). For other evidence of the influence of the Report in discussions and proposals, see *Ibid.*, pp. 33–4, 97; "Secondary Education in 1897," *The Journal of Education*, 20:18 (January 1898); "A Promise and a Programme," *Education*, 4:52 (February 12, 1898). Also see "Draft Scheme for a Secondary Education Bill," reported in *The Educational Times*, 50:28 (July, 1897), and "The Teachers' Guild of Great Britain and Ireland," *The Journal of Education*, 19:202 (March 1897).

3 *Hansard*, Fourth Series, Vol. 49, 1897, pp. 1018–1019; Vol. 54, 1898, p. 1185; Vol. 62, 1898, pp. 255–256.

4 *Hansard*, Fourth Series, Vol. 61, 1899, pp. 328–329.

5 *Hansard*, Fourth Series, Vol. 54, 1898, p. 1186.

6 By this Act the Endowed Schools Commission was set up whose function was merely the better application of endowments. *The Endowed Schools Act, 1869* (32 & 33 Vict., C. 56).

7 André Maurois, *The Edwardian Era* (New York: D. Appleton-Century Company, 1935), p. 286.

8 See M. Arnold, *Arnold's Works* (New York: Macmillan and Co., 1883), Vol. II, pp. 18, 38, 53–67. Also see Arnold, "A French Eton: or Middle Class Education and the State," in *The Works of Matthew Arnold* (London: Macmillan and Co., Ltd., 1904), Vol. XII, pp. 42–3.

9 John Ruskin, *The Works of John Ruskin*, edited by Cook, E. T. and A. Wedderburn (London: George Allen, 1904), Vol. X, p. 96.

10 Thomas Carlyle, *Critical and Miscellaneous Essays* (New York: Charles Scribner's Sons, 1901), Vol. IV, p. 155.

11 Green served as an assistant commissioner to the Schools Inquiry Commission, as a member of the Oxford School Board, and as a member of the Oxford City Council. He founded the City of Oxford School for Boys, and he took an active part in the agitation for temperance reform.

12 R. N. Nettleship, editor, *Works of T. H. Green* (London: Longmans and Co., 1906), Vol. III, p. 371.

13 T. H. Huxley, "Natural Rights and Political Rights," in M. Goodwin, editor, *Nineteenth Century Opinion* (Penguin Books, 1951), pp. 179–181. Also see Huxley's "The Struggle for Existence," "On the Natural Inequality of Men," and "Government." *Ibid.*, pp. 204–206, 224, 230.

14 J. S. Mill, *Principles of Political Economy With Some of their Applications to Social Philosophy* (London: Longmans, Green, and Co., 1920), pp. 953–6.

15 Mill, *Utilitarianism* (New York: The Liberal Arts Press, 1953), pp. 17–18.

16 Mill, *Autobiography* (London: Oxford University Press, 1924), p. 196.

17 See R. H. Tawney, *The Attack and Other Essays* (New York: Harcourt Brace and Co., 1953), p. 117, and Ernest Parker, *Political Thought in England 1848–1914* (London: Oxford University Press, 1915), p. 192.

18 Labour Representation Committee, *Report of the First Annual Conference of the Labour Representation Committee* (London: Labour Representations Committee, 1901), p. 1.

19 R. C. K. Ensor, *England, 1870–1914* (Oxford: At the Clarendon Press, 1936), p. 88.

20 *Ibid.*, pp. 203, 213.

21 On the collectivist implications of company ownership, see A. V. Dicey, *Lectures on the Relations Between Law and Public Opinion in England During the Nineteenth Century* (London: Macmillan and Co., Ltd., 1948), pp. 246–7.

22 For evidence of this, particularly see Royal Commission on Technical Instruction, "Second Report, Vol. I," *Reports from Commissioners*, 1884, Vol. XXIX, p. 506. Hereafter cited as Royal Commission on Technical Instruction.

23 L. C. A. Knowles, *The Industrial and Commercial Revolutions in*

Great Britain During the Nineteenth Century (London: Routledge, 1921), p. 139.

24 See Ensor, *England*, pp. 269–281. Also see British and Foreigh Trade and Industry, *Memoranda, Statistical Tables, and Charts prepared in the Board of Trade with reference to various matters on British and Foreigh Trade and Industrial Conditions* (London: H. M. S. O., 1903), p. 32.

25 On the connection between English and German idealism, see B. Pfannenstill, *Bernard Bosanquet's Philosophy of the State: A Historical and Systematic Study* (Lund: Hakan Ohlsson, 1936), pp. 66–90.

26 See B. Bosanquet, *The Philosophical Theory of the State* (London: Macmillan and Co., 1910), pp. viii, 77–78.

27 R. B. Haldane, "Hegel," *Contemporary Review*, 67:232 (February, 1895).

28 Haldane, *An Autobiography* (New York: Doubleday, Doran and Co., 1929), pp. 97–98.

29 Royal Commission on Scientific Instruction, *First, Supplementary, and Second Reports, with Minutes of Evidence and Appendices*, 1872, Vol. I, pp. xv–xvi, 382–3. Also see "Sixth Report," *Reports from Commissioners*, 1874, Vol. XXII, pp. xii–xiii, liv, 1–2, 10.

30 Royal Commission on Technical Instruction, "Second Report," Vol. I, *Reports from Commissioners*, 1884, Vol. XXIV, pp. 506, 515–7, 538.

31 Quoted from H. Hobhouse, "Secondary Education in England," *Edinburgh Review*, 189:164 (January, 1899).

32 Specifically see Michael Sadler, "The Oberrealschulen of Prussia, with Special Reference to the Oberrealschule at Charlottenburg," *Special Reports*, Vol. I, p. 453.

33 *Ibid.*, p. 438.

34 Michael Sadler, "Problems in Prussian Secondary Education for Boys, With Special Reference to Similar Questions in England," *Special Reports*, 1898, Vol. III, p. 89.

35 *Ibid.*, p. 95.

36 *Ibid.*, p. 145.

37 See, for example, the report presented to the Technical Instruction Committee of the City of Manchester by the deputation appointed to visit technical schools, institutions, and museums in Germany and Austria, in July and August 1897. *Ibid.*, p. 145.

38 G. F. Abbott, "Educational Ideals," *Edinburgh Review*, 195:67–69 (January, 1902).

39 *Ibid.*, p. 69. Also see Lord Rosebery's inaugural address to the University of Glasgow, on November 16, 1900. *Ibid.*, pp. 70–2, and R. Haldane, *Education and Empire* (London: John Murray, 1902), p. ix.

40 On the Board of Education Bill, 1899, see Lord Reay's comments on the First Reading of the Board of Education Bill (1899) in *Hansard*, Fourth Series, Vol. 70, 1899, p. 324, and Jebb's speech on the Second Reading of the Board of Education Bill (1899) in *Ibid.*, Vol. 73, 1899, p. 626. On the Education Bill, 1902, see speeches by A. J. Balfour in *Hansard*, Fourth Series, Vol. 105, 1902, pp. 850, 854, Sir H. Campbell-Bannerman

(Leader of the Opposition) in *Ibid.*, p. 870, and by Sir Albert Rollitt, *Ibid.*, p. 914.

41 The South African War lasted from 1899 to 1902. Parliamentary debate on the Education Bill of 1902 had started when the war was in its final stage. The war ended in March and the Bill received royal sanction in December.

42 D. W. Brogan, *The English People: Impressions and Observations* (New York: Alfred A. Knopf, 1943), p. 8.

43 See "The War and Its Lessons," *The Quarterly Review*, 195:320–321 (January–April, 1902).

44 *Hansard*, Fourth Series, Vol. 107. pp. 753–754. See also the views of the Committee on Military Education in "Efficiency in the Service," *The Quarterly Review*, 196:292 (July, 1902).

45 *Hansard*, Fourth Series, Vol. 105, 1902, pp. 850–854. See also the speeches by Sir H. Campbell-Bannerman, (Leader of the Opposition), *Ibid.*, p. 870, and Haldane, *Ibid.*, pp. 904–905.

46 Lord Salisbury complained to a deputation of clergy of the heavy expenditure of the School Boards and thought that some check on them was necessary. See *Annual Register for 1895*, p. 196. In introducing the 1902 Bill, Balfour expressed similar concern over the expenditures of School Boards, and added . . . "I do not believe that this system of *ad hoc* authority with unlimited rating is one which really has any important experimental endorsement behind it at all." *Hansard*, Fourth Series, Vol. 105, 1902, p. 851.

47 For further information on the press revolution of the eighties and nineties see Ensor, *England,* pp. 310–316.

48 See the speech by Mr. Peel, Member of Parliament from Manchester South. *Hansard*, Fourth Series, Vol. 107, 1902, pp. 881. Also see G. A. N. Lowndes, *The Silent Social Revolution* (London: Oxford University Press, 1937), p. 87.

49 These were The Charity Commission, the Education Department, and the Science and Art Department. All three authorities had a statutory connexion with education. Bryce Commission, Vol. I, pp. 17–31.

50 *Ibid.*, pp. 85–86.

51 *Ibid.*, pp. 256–7.

52 *Ibid.*, p. 324.

53 *Hansard*, Fourth Series, Vol. 70, 1899, pp. 322 ff.

54 *Board of Education Act, 1899* (62 and 63 Vict., C. 33), Section I (2).

55 *Ibid.*, Section 3 (1).

56 Grier, *Achievement in Education*, pp. 66–8.

57 The Bishop of Winchester agreed with the Primate that inspection should be voluntary. See *Hansard*, Fourth Series, Vol. 70, p. 345.

58 *Ibid.*, Vol. 73, p. 635.

59 *Ibid.*, p. 632.

60 *Ibid.*, Vol. 70, pp. 335–6, 338; Vol. 73, p. 641.

61 *Ibid.*, Vol. 73, p. 617.

62 By the Local Government Act of 1888, the county councils were set up for purposes of local administration. This Act was followed by the

Technical Instruction Act, 1889, and the Local Taxation (Customs and Excise) Act, 1890. From the educational point of view these three acts had established for each county, and large county borough, a local authority with powers and money for educational developments (mostly technical education).

63 Bryce Commission, Vol. 1, pp. 256–297.

64 "In 1895, 2,446,000 children attended the voluntary schools, only 1,848,000 attended the board schools and the vast majority of the voluntary schools were Anglican." Elie Halévy, *Imperialism and the Rise of Labour: A History of the English People in the Nineteenth Century* (London: Ernest Benn Ltd., 1926), p. 165.

65 It should be noted that both Anglicans and Nonconformists had grievances that were more religious than educational in nature. The Anglicans distrusted the School Boards for fear of secularization, and the Nonconformists were in favor of extension of the scope of the School Boards, for, as things were, many children of Noncomformists were forced to send their children to Church schools, which, according to Lloyd George, "are mission rooms to educate the children of the poor in the principles of the church." *Hansard*, Fourth Series, Vol. 107, 1902, p. 1102; Halévy, *Imperialism and the Rise of Labour,* pp. 164–5.

66 "The higher grade school set up by the minute . . . was to be a higher primary school, not a lower elementary school and so its course was planned to end at 15 . . . Primary education aimed at training the mind as well as giving useful knowledge; but on account of the limited time, it was more practical and gave a larger place to immediate utility than secondary education did, where the foremost object was a liberal training of the mind." Mr. Webb, in *The Times* (London), May 4, 1900, p. 10. See also the comments of approval by Hobhouse, a member of the Liberal Opposition, and Sir John Gorst, in *Ibid.*, p. 11.

67 See, for example, Balfour's views in *The Times* (London), June 17, 1899, p. 9 and Gorst's in *Hansard*, Fourth Series, Vol. 90, 1901, p. 613.

68 Edward R. Pease, *The History of the Fabian Society* (New York: E. P. Dutton and Co., 1916), pp. 142–3.

69 The Fabian Society, *The Education Muddle and the Way Out,* Fabian Tract 106 (London: The Fabian Society, 1901), pp. 7, 11–12.

70 *Ibid.*, pp. 15–18.

71 Pease, *History of the Fabian Society*, p. 144.

72 Mary A. Hamilton, *Sidney and Beatrice Webb: A Study in Contemporary Biography* (Boston: Houghton Mifflin Co., 1933), pp. 127–8.

73 Beatrice Webb, *Our Partnership*, edited by Barbara Drake and Margaret Cole (London: Longmans, Green and Co., 1948), pp. 239–241, pp. 244–7. See also Hamilton, *Sidney and Beatrice Webb,* p. 128.

74 See *Education Act, 1902* (2 Edw. 7, ch. 42), Part I.

75 *Ibid.*, Part II, Section 2 (1) (a).

76 *Ibid.*, Part I, Section 1.

77 *Ibid.*, Part IV, Section 17 (1).

78 "Religious instruction given in a public elementary school not provided by the L. E. A. shall as regards its character be in accordance with

the provisions (if any) of the trust deed relating thereto, and shall be under the control of the managers."

79 The clause read as follows: "In a school or college receiving a grant from, or maintained by a council under this Part of this Act (a) A scholar attending as a day or evening scholar shall not be required, as a condition of being admitted into or remaining in the school or college, to attend or abstain from attending any Sunday School, place of religious worship, religious observance, or instruction in religious subjects in the school or college or elsewhere, and (b) The times for religious worship or for any lesson on a religious subject shall be conveniently arranged for the purpose of allowing the withdrawal of any such scholar therefrom." *Ibid.*, Part II, Section 4 (1) (2).

80 *Hansard*, Fourth Series, Vol. 107, 1902, pp. 1102–1103.

81 *Ibid.*, pp. 1108–9.

82 *The Times* (London), April 24, 1902, p. 12. See also *Hansard*, Fourth Series, Vol. 107, pp. 728–9.

83 *Ibid.*, Vol. 107, pp. 650, 654.

84 *The Times* (London), April 16, 1902, p. 5. On the opposition of the Protestant Dissenters also see *The Times* (London), April 9, 1902, p. 6.

85 *Hansard*, Fourth Series, Vol. 107, pp. 706–7.

86 *Ibid.*, p. 712.

87 ". . . the idea of the voluntary schools being swept away by an Act of Parliament or by any other method, is absurd." *Hansard*, Fourth Series, Vol. 105, 1902, pp. 854–5.

88 See Edmund Talbot's remarks in *Hansard*, Fourth Series, Vol. 107, pp. 717–8.

89 *Education Act, 1902*, Part III, 7 (6).

90 See Chapter III and the beginning of this Chapter.

91 *Board of Education Act, 1899*, Section 1 (1).

92 *Education Act, 1902*, Part II, Section 2 (1) (a).

93 *Education Act, 1944* (7 & 8 Geo. 6 Ch. 31), Part I, Section I (1).

94 Bryce Commission, Vol. I, pp. 256–7, 324.

95 On this point, see Sidney Webb's assessment. The Fabian Society, *The Education Muddle*, p. 14.

V

1 Board of Education, *Regulations for Secondary Day Schools* (London: H. M. S. O., 1902), pp. 7, 18.

2 *Ibid.*, p. 8. The "obligatory subjects," which were offered in elementary and advanced courses, were entirely "subjects of Science." The "general elementary course" which "may extend over two years" included Mathematics, Physics, including the fundamental principles of Mechanics (theoretical and practical), Chemistry (theoretical and practical), Drawing and Practical Geometry. The "advanced courses" were divided into 3 special areas: (1) Physical Course (Mathematics, Geometry, Physics, Inorganic Chemistry), (2) Mechanical Course (Mathematics, Geometry,

Physics, Mechanics), and (3) Biological Course (Geometry, Physiology, Botany, Inorganic Chemistry). *Ibid.*, pp. 9–12.

3 See Board of Education, Schools of Science, *Return of the Statistics of Schools of Science Conducted Under the Regulations of the Board of Education* (London: H. M. S. O., 1902).

4 In order to qualify for grants, a "Division B" secondary school had to provide "not less than nine hours per week of Science instruction, including not more than five hours of Mathematics." See Board of Education, *Regulations for Secondary Day Schools,* 1902, p. 18. Also see Board of Education, *Regulations for Secondary Schools* (London: H. M. S. O., 1903), p. 14.

5 Board of Education, *Report of the Board of Education for the Year 1902–1903,* (London: H. M. S. O., 1903) , p. 55.

6 *Hansard,* Vol. 125, 1903, p. 173. See also Board of Education, *Report of the Board of Education for the Year 1903–1904* (London: H. M. S. O., 1904), p. 54.

7 Board of Education, *Report for 1902–1903,* pp. 55–7.

8 The evidence for this is legion. See, for example, the report of T. King, Senior Chief Inspector, in T. King, *General Report for the Year 1899* (London: H. M. S. O., 1900), p. 23; M. Sadler, *Special Reports on Educational Subjects,* 1898, Vol. III, p. 145; H. Hobhouse, "Secondary Education in England," *Edinburgh Review,* 189:152 (January, 1899); *Hansard,* Fourth Series, Vol. 70, 1899, p. 323, Vol. 73, p. 626, Vol. 105, 1902, pp. 850, 870, 912, 914, Vol. 107, p. 664.

9 "Occasional Notes," *The Journal of Education,* 21:684 (November 1, 1899) . Also see the speech by Professor Richard Jebb who referred to the example of Germany where, according to him, the basis of commercial and technical education was "Liberal." *Hansard,* Fourth Series, Vol. 73, 1899, p. 626.

10 C. A. Buckmaster, Board of Education, "General Report for the year 1902," in *General Reports of Higher Education with Appendices for the Year 1902* (London: H. M. S. O., 1903), p. 11.

11 J. W. Headlam, "Report on the Teaching of Literary Subjects in Some Secondary Schools for Boys," *Ibid.,* pp. 62–63.

12 *Ibid.,* pp. 62–65.

13 *Ibid.,* p. 65.

14 *Ibid.,* p. 66.

15 *Hansard,* Vol. 125, 1903, pp. 179–180.

16 See reprinted letter in United States Bureau of Education, *Education in Great Britian and Ireland* (Washington: Government Printing Office, 1904), pp. 256–258.

17 *Hansard,* Vol. 125, 1903, p. 181.

18 *Ibid.,* pp. 231–232.

19 *Ibid.,* pp. 232–3.

20 *Ibid.,* p. 233.

21 Board of Education, *Regulations for Secondary Schools* (London: H. M. S. O., 1904), p. 5.

22 *Ibid.,* pp. 7, 17.

23 *Ibid.*, p. 7.

24 *Ibid.*, pp. 7–8. The Regulations stated the average age as follows: "the average age of the scholars in any class commencing the Course must be not less than 12 years, and the Inspector must be satisfied that the class as a whole is qualified to commence the Course." *Ibid.*, p. 17.

25 *Ibid.*, p. 8.

26 *Ibid.*, p. 18.

27 *Ibid.*, p. 24.

28 *Ibid.*, p. 20.

29 See Board of Education, *Regulations for the Instruction and Training of Pupil-Teachers and Students in Training Colleges* (London: H. M. S. O., 1903). Also see statements in the House of Commons. *Hansard*, Vol. 125, pp. 183–4, 190, 202, 208.

30 See Board of Education, *Regulations for the Training of Teachers and for the Examination of Students in Training Colleges* (London: H. M. S. O., 1904), pp. vii–viii, xii. See also Board of Education, *Regulations for the Instruction and Training of Pupil-Teachers* (London: H. M. S. O., 1904); Board of Education, *Report of the Board of Education for the Year 1903–1904*, p. 49.

31 See Board of Education, *Regulations for Secondary Schools* (London: H. M. S. O., 1905), pp. v–viii, and *Regulations for Secondary Schools* (London: H. M. S. O., 1906), pp. vi–viii, 1–2.

32 Board of Education, *Report of the Consultative Committee on Secondary Education with Special Reference to Grammar Schools and Technical High Schools* (London: H. M. S. O., 1938), pp. 66–72. Hereafter cited as Spens Report.

33 H. C. Dent, *Secondary Education for All*, p. 34. Also see Dent, *Change in English Education: A Historical Survey* (London: University of London Press, 1952), pp. 67–8.

34 John Graves, *Policy and Progress*, p. 44.

35 S. J. Curtis, *History of Education in Great Britain* (London: University Tutorial Press, 1945), p. 323. Also see his *Education in Britain Since 1900* (London: Andrew Dakers, 1950), pp. 51, 53.

36 H. C. Barnard, *A Short History of English Education From 1760 to 1944* (London: University of London Press, 1947), pp. 255–6.

37 Dent, *Change in English Education*, p. 33; Graves, *Policy and Progress*, p. 63.

38 Olive Banks, *Parity and Prestige in English Secondary Education: A Study in Educational Sociology* (London: Routledge and Kegan Paul, 1955), p. 42.

39 *Ibid.*, pp. 39–50.

40 County Borough of Huddersfield Education Committee, *Report on Secondary & Technical Education in Huddersfield*, by Michael E. Sadler (London: Eyre and Spottiswoode, 1904), pp. 26–7.

41 City of Liverpool Education Committee, *Report on Secondary Education in Liverpool including the Training of Teachers for Public Elementary Schools*, by Michael E. Sadler (London: Eyre and Spottiswoode, 1904), pp. 4, 8, 17–18, 133–135.

42 Also see Administrative County of Essex Education Committee, *Report on Secondary and Higher Education in Essex,* by Michael E. Sadler (Chelmsford: J. M. Nichols, Secretary, Essex Education Committee, 1906), pp. 24–33.

43 "Local Inquiries Respecting Secondary Schools in English Counties, Lancashire," *The Record of Technical and Secondary Education,* 13:448–449 (December, 1904).

44 *Ibid.,* pp. 425–439.

45 *Ibid.,* p. 473.

46 Incorporated Association of Assistant Masters in Secondary Schools, "Conference at Liverpool," *The Educational Times,* 8:437–8 (October 2, 1905).

47 See "Local Inquiries Respecting Secondary Schools in English Counties," *The Record of Technical and Secondary Education,* Vol. 21:62–66 (January–March, 1904); *Hansard,* Fifth Series, Vol. 19, 1910, p. 414; H. Bompas Smith, "The New Regulations for Secondary Schools," *The School World,* No. 68:288 (August, 1904).

48 Incorporated Association of Assistant Masters in Secondary Schools, *The Educational Times,* 8:437 (October 2, 1905).

49 County Borough of Birkenhead Education Committee, *Report on Secondary Education in Birkenhead* by M. E. Sadler (London: George Philip and Son, Ltd., 1904), pp. 41–52.

50 Bryce Commission, Vol. I, pp. 299–300.

51 *Ibid.,* p. 108.

52 Board of Education, *Report of the Board of Education for the year 1908–9* (London: His Majesty's Stationery Office, 19), pp. 31–2.

53 See Report of *Proceedings at the Thirty-Sixth Annual Trades Union Congress* (London: Co-operative Printing Society, 1903), pp. 86–87; *Report of the Proceedings at the Thirty-Seventh Annual Trades Union Congress* (London: Co-operative Printing Society, 1904), p. 119. Also see *Report of the Sixth Annual Conference of the Labour Party* (London: The Labour Party, 1906), p. 52. The claims made by H. C. Dent and Olive Banks who traced the demands for such a notion to 1905 and the Trade Union Movement in the 1890's seem to be rather exaggerated. Banks, *Parity and Prestige,* p. 116.

54 See F. Bealey and Henry Pelling, *Labour and Politics* (London: Macmillan and Co., 1958), p. 175.

55 *Ibid.,* p. 203.

56 C. F. G. Masterman, *The Condition of England* (London: Methuen & Co., 1909), p. 116.

57 See Board of Education, *Regulations for the Instruction and Training of Pupil-Teachers and Students in Training Colleges,* 1904, p. 13.

58 Board of Education, *General Report on the Instruction and Training of Pupil-Teachers, 1903–1907* (London: His Majesty's Stationery Office, 1907), p. 14. Also see Board of Education, "Hints on the Organization of the Instruction of Pupil-Teachers," *Enclosure to Circular 494,* 18th December, 1903, p. 1, and *Hansard,* Vol. 125, p. 190.

59 Board of Education, *Report of the Board of Education for the Year 1905–1906* (London: His Majesty's Stationary Office, 1906), p. 47.

VI

1 Board of Education, *Minute of the Board of Education, April 6, 1900, Establishing Higher Elementary Schools* (London: H. M. S. O., 1900), pp. 3–5. Also see Board of Education, *Report of the Board of Education, 1899–1900*, Vol. I (London: H. M. S. O., 1900), p. 11, and Board of Education, *Report of the Board of Education for the year 1901–1902* (London: H. M. S. O., 1902), p. 41.

2 Compiled from Board of Education, *Report of the Board of Education for the Year 1900–1* (London: H. M. S. O., 1901), p. 9; *Report for the Year 1901–2*, p. 41; *Report for the Year 1902–3*, pp. 46–7; *Report for the Year 1903–4*, p. 33.

3 Board of Education, *Report of the Board of Education for the Year 1904–5* (London: H. M. S. O., 1905), p. 26.

4 *Hansard*, Vol. 150, 1905, p. 1199.

5 Board of Education, *Report of the Board of Education for the Year 1904–5*, p. 26.

6 Board of Education, *Code of Regulations for Public Elementary Schools With Schedules* (London: H. M. S. O., 1905), pp. iii–iv.

7 *Ibid.*, pp. iv–v.

8 *Ibid.*, pp. v–vii.

9 On this point, see the statement by the Parliamentary Secretary to the Board of Education. *Hansard*, Vol. 150, 1905, p. 1199.

10 "Report of the Consultative Committee Upon Questions Affecting Higher Elementary School," Reprinted in *The Record of Technical and Secondary Education*, 15:267 (July–September, 1906).

11 *Ibid.*, pp. 268–9.

12 *Ibid.*, pp. 271–283.

13 *Ibid.*, pp. 283–4.

14 *Ibid.*, p. 284.

15 *Ibid.*, p. 791.

16 "The total number of children in Secondary Schools which receive grant under the Secondary School Regulations is larger than the number of children in respect of whom this grant is paid, and by removing those children who do not complete the full four years' course from the Secondary Schools, local funds will be released and the amount remaining will then be all available for aiding secondary education proper. At the same time the aim of the Secondary School will emerge with greater clearness." *Ibid.*, p. 308.

17 Administrative County of Essex Education Committee, *Report on Secondary and Higher Education*, p. 65.

18 Compiled from Board of Education *Statistics of Public Education in England and Wales, 1905–6–7* (London: H. M. S. O., 1908), p. 71; *Statistics of Public Education in England and Wales, 1907–8*, Part I, pp. 83, 87; *Statistics of Public Education in England and Wales, 1908–9*, Part I,

pp. 85, 89; *Statistics of Public Education in England and Wales, 1909-10,* Part I, pp. 89, 93; *Statistics of Public Education in England and Wales, 1910– 1,* Part I, p. 89; *Statistics of Public Education in England and Wales, 1911–12,* Part I, p. 91; *Statistics of Public Education in England and Wales, 1913–14,* Part I, p. 83; *Report of the Board of Education for the Year, 1917–18,* p. 10; *Report of the Board of Education for the Year, 1918–19,* p. 22.

[19] *Report on Secondary and Higher Education,* p. 66.

[20] *Ibid.,* p. 67. Note also his cautious statement that "in the last year of the course (14–15) a certain degree of limited specialization should be allowed in view of the future employment of the different children." *Ibid.,* p. 66.

[21] *Ibid.,* p. 67.

[22] "For administrative reasons, I propose in this report to call one of the branches of secondary education (namely, that which is planned in choice of subjects and activities to meet the needs of boys and girls who will enter practical life at fifteen) 'higher elementary.' The branch which meets the needs of those who will continue their day school life up to sixteen or seventeen I shall refer to as 'secondary.' To that which provides a day-school course up to eighteen or nineteen, I shall give the name 'Higher secondary.' But it is essential that there should be the same spirit in all three. Where they will differ, so far as differ they must, will be in the degree of attention which it is possible to give, at any particular stage of the school course, to certain subjects or to certain parts of subjects, partly in view of the different life-needs of the children concerned, but much more in view of the different length of the school life still to come." *Ibid.,* p. 28.

[23] Lynda Grier records that Sadler's general views on higher elementary education and its relation to secondary may also be construed from the remarks that Sadler inscribed in his copy of the Report of the Consultative Committee. Specifically she refers to several indignant "whys" that are to be found in the margin beside the passages which state the difference between a higher elementary and a secondary school. See Grier, *Achievement in Education,* pp. 142–144.

[24] "Whitehall and Secondary Education: Criticisms from the Oxford Conference," *The Educational Times,* 60:207–8 (May 1, 1907).

[25] *The Times* (London), Thursday, April 4, 1907, p. 8.

[26] "The Teachers' Guild," *The Educational Times,* 60:69 (February 1, 1907).

[27] "The Report of the Consultative Committee on Higher Elementary Schools," *The Journal of Education,* 38:599–600 (September 1, 1906).

[28] "Occasional Notes," *The Journal of Education,* 38:310 (May 1, 1907).

[29] See "Incorporated Association of Headmasters," *The Journal of Education,* 37:155 (February 1, 1906). See, for example, Gilson's statement: "Scholars ought to acquire the manual dexterity they required in the last two years of their elementary school life . . . They did not want the new schools, but they did want the tops of the ordinary schools improved,"

and W. A. Knight's: ". . . the establishment of the higher elementary school would lead to overlapping with secondary school."

30 "Conference of Headmistresses," *The Journal of Education*, 38:462 (July 1, 1907).

31 "The Teachers' Guild," *The Educational Times*, 60:69 (February 1, 1957).

32 J. L. Paton, "The National Union of Teachers: The President's Address," *The School World*, IX:171 (May, 1907).

33 "Practice and Precept," *School: A Monthly Record of Educational Thought and Progress*, 7:117–8 (May, 1907).

34 See "National Union of Teachers," *The Schoolmasters Yearbook and Directory*, 1908 (London: Swan Sonnenschein & Co., Ltd., 1908), p. 196.

35 "Occasional Notes," *The Journal of Education*, 38:104–5 (February 1, 1907).

36 *Ibid.*, p. 107.

37 See, for example, "Higher Education in Rural Counties: The New Scheme in Gloucestershire," *The Record of Technical and Secondary Education*, 13:263–6 (April–June, 1904), and "Higher Education in a Rural County," *The Record of Technical and Secondary Education*, 15:354–5 (July–September, 1906); "Higher Education in Country Areas (a) Middlesex (b) Shropshire," *The Record of Technical and Secondary Education*, 15:461–4 (October–December, 1906); "Local Authorities: Kent," *The Journal of Education*, 37:250 (April 2, 1906); "Local Authorities: Secondary Schools in Somerset," *The Journal of Education*, 37:386 (June, 1906).

38 "Local Authorities: Secondary Education in Cheshire," *The Journal of Education*, 37:182 (March 1, 1906).

39 *Final Report of the School Board for London, 1870–1904* (London: P. S. King & Son, 1904), pp. 133–134.

40 London County Council Education Committee, *Annual Report of the Education Officer: Part I—Elementary Education*, 1909–10, July, 1911, p. 12.

VII

1 Elie Halévy, *The Rule of Democracy, 1905–1915*, Bk. I (London: Ernest Benn, Ltd., 1932), p. 11. For accounts on the importance of the emergence of Labour, see *The Times* (London), January 30, 1906, p. 4, February 3, 1906, p. 10. Also see R. B. Haldane, *An Autobiography* (New York: Doubleday, Doran and Co., Inc., 1929), p. 224 and J. A. Spender, *The Life of the Right Hon. Sir Henry Campbell-Bannerman, G. C. B.* (London: Hodder and Stoughton, Ltd., 1923), Vol. II, pp. 224–226. For a breakdown of the House in terms of religious affiliation and social class background, see *The Times* (London), February 1, 1906, p. 8, Halévy, *The Rule of Democracy*, p. 11, and Spender, *The Life of Campbell-Bannerman*, p. 224.

2 See Herbert Samuel, *Liberalism: An Attempt to State the Principles and Proposals of Contemporary Liberalism in England* (London: Grant Richards, 1902), p. 154.

3 L. T. Hobhouse, *Liberalism* (New York: Henry Holt and Company, 1911), p. 32. For an excellent analysis of the reconstructed Liberalism see Howard J. Thompson, "The New Liberalism in Great Britain: The Liberal Mind and Party Politics in a Time of Crisis and Reconstruction (1890–1914)." Unpublished Ph.D. thesis, Harvard University, Cambridge, Mass., April 5, 1954.

4 In the area of social and economic reform, one may cite the Trades Disputes Act of 1906, the Workmen's Compensation Act, the Old Age Pensions Act, the Labour Exchanges Act, the Budget of 1909, the Wages Boards Act, the Insurance Act, and the Education (Provision of Meals) Act. In political reform there was the Parliamentary Act of 1911. On the significance of these measures, see Halévy, *The Rule of Democracy*, pp. 93–98, Haldane, *An Autobiography*, pp. 226–7, and Ensor, *England*, p. 430.

5 See J. Hugh Edwards, *David Lloyd George: The Man and the States-man* (New York: J. H. Sears & Company, Inc., 1929), Vol. I, pp. 237 et seq.

6 "A Bill to make further provisions with respect to Education in England and Wales," [Education (England and Wales) Bill] 6 Edw. 7. in *Bills; Public*, Vol. I, 1906.

7 *Hansard*, Fourth Series, Vol. 155, 1906, p. 1017.

8 *Ibid.*, p. 1022.

9 "Education (England and Wales) Bill," 1906, pp. 1–2.

10 *Hansard*, Fourth series, Vol. 156, 1906, p. 1052.

11 See, for example, Mr. Asquith's support during the debates on the second reading of the Bill in *Hansard*, Fourth Series, Vol. 156, p. 1518 ff. Also see, Bryce's comments in *Ibid.*, pp. 1317 ff., and Birrell's introductory speech, *Hansard*, Vol. 155, 1906, p. 1023.

12 *Hansard*, Vol. 156, 1906, pp. 1075–77.

13 See for example the speeches made by Sir William Anson (Oxford University) in *Hansard*, Vol. 155, 1906, pp. 1041–46; Mr. Wyndman (Dover), *Hansard*, Vol. 156, 1906, pp. 1015–16; Mr. A. J. Balfour (City of London), in *Ibid.*, pp. 1589–91; Mr. Middlemore (Birmingham N.), in *Ibid.*, p. 1582.

14 *Ibid.*, p. 1042.

15 Specifically see the speeches by Mr. J. R. MacDonald, *Hansard*, Vol. 155, 1906, pp. 1051–57, and Vol. 156, 1906, pp. 1075–86.

16 *Ibid.*, p. 1075.

17 See Mr. Birrell's speech on Dec. 10, 1906, *Hansard*, Vol. 166, 1906, pp. 1580–99.

18 See Haldane, *An Autobiography*, p. 234.

19 "A Bill to make provision for relieving the local education authority of the cost of giving Special Religious Instruction in schools not provided by the authority," 7. Edw. 7, in *Bills; Public*, Vol. I, 1907.

20 *Hansard*, Fourth Series, Vol. 169, 1907, p. 1453.

21 "A Bill to regulate the conditions on which public money may be applied in aid of Elementary Education in England and Wales, and for other purposes incidental thereto." 8. Edw. 7. in *Bills; Public*, Vol. II, 1908.

22 For a fuller discussion of the reasons for the defeat of these Bills, see Halévy, *The Rule of Democracy*, pp. 69–76.

23 "A Bill (as Amended by the Select Committee and in Committee) to make provision for Meals for Children attending Public Elementary Schools in England, Wales, and Scotland," 6 Edw. 7, in *Bills: Public*, Vol. I, 1906.

24 *Hansard*, Fourth Series, Vol. 152, 1906, p. 1390.

25 *Ibid.*, p. 1392.

26 *Ibid.*, p. 1391.

27 *Ibid.*, pp. 1440–1441.

28 *Ibid.*, p. 1442. See also the speech by Dr. Macnamara (Camberwell, N), *Ibid.*, p. 1423.

29 See the speeches by Harold Cox (Preston), *Ibid.*, pp. 1412 ff., and Sir William Anson (Oxford University), *Ibid.*, pp. 1436 ff.

30 *Ibid.*, p. 1391. Also see statements by Sir W. J. Collins (St. Pancras, W.), a medical man and Chairman of the Education Committee of the London County Council. *Ibid.*, p. 1405.

31 *Ibid.*, p. 1440. See also J. W. Taylor's speech in *Ibid.*, p. 1428.

32 The Board of Education hailed it as "an event of the first educational importance." See Board of Education, *Report of the Board of Education for the Year 1906–1907* (London: H. M. S. O., 1907), p. 8.

33 "A Bill (as amended by Standing Committee B) to make Provision for the Better Administration by the Central and Local Authorities in England and Wales of the Enactments relating to Education," 7 Edw. 7, p. 5, in *Bills; Public*, Vol. I, 1907.

34 See *Hansard*, Fourth Series, Vol. 179, 1907, pp. 1097, and specifically Sir William Anson's remarks. *Ibid.*, p. 1100. Also see Board of Education, *Memorandum on Medical Inspection of Children in Public Elementary Schools under Section 13 of the Education (Administrative Provisions) Act, 1907*, (Circular 576), p. 4.

35 It should not be forgotten that elementary education often extended up to the age of 14 and 15.

36 See Board of Education, *Report of the Board of Education for the year 1906–1907*, p. 9.

37 See Board of Education, *Annual Report for 1910 of the Chief Medical Officer of the Board of Education* (London: H. M. S. O., 1911), pp. 22–23.

38 Education (Administrative Provisions) Bill, 1906, pp. 4–5.

39 Board of Education, *Report of the Board of Education for the Year 1905–1906* (London: H. M. S. O., 1906), p. 44.

40 *Ibid.*, pp. 60–61.

41 *Ibid.*, p. 61.

42 *Ibid.*, p. 62.

43 *Ibid.*, pp. 46, 62.

44 *Hansard*, Fourth Series, Vol. 171, 1907, pp. 91–92.

45 *Ibid.*, pp. 94–95.

46 *Ibid.*, p. 114. Also see Atkins' remarks: *Ibid.*, pp. 121–122.

47 *Ibid.*, pp. 106–107.

48 *Hansard*, Fourth Series, Vol. 174, 1907, p. 1037.

49 *Ibid.*, p. 1038.

50 See, for example, Atkins' and Shackleton's speeches. *Ibid.*, pp. 1040–1041, 1037.

51 *Ibid.*, pp. 1047–1049, 1050–1052.

52 *Hansard*, Fourth Series, Vol. 174, 1907, p. 1056.

53 Board of Education, *Regulations for Secondary Schools* (In force from 1st August, 1907) (London: H. M. S. O., 1907), p. xiv.

54 *Ibid.*, pp. 5–6.

55 *Ibid.*, p. 6.

56 *Hansard*, Fourth Series, Vol. 174, 1907, p. 1054.

57 Board of Education, *Regulations for Secondary Schools*, 1907, p. xiv.

58 *Ibid.*, p. 5.

59 *Hansard*, Fourth Series, Vol. 174, 1907, p. 1054.

60 ". . . where (a) by the spontaneous action of school authorities themselves free places have been given in excess of the Board's requirements; or (b) the school life of fee paying pupils falls considerably short of that of holders of free places." Board of Education, *Report of the Board of Education for the Year 1909–10* (London: H. M. S. O., 1911), p. 69.

61 *Ibid.*, p. 69.

62 Board of Education, Regulations for Secondary Schools (London: H. M. S. O., 1909), p. ix.

63 Board of Education, *Report of the Board of Education for the Year 1909–10*, p. 70. Also see Board of Education, *Report of the Board of Education for the Year 1911–1912* (London: H. M. S. O., 1913), p. 5.

64 See also Sir William Anson's speech in *Hansard*, Fourth Series, Vol. 178, 1907, pp. 75–82.

65 "Review of the Year," *The Schoolmasters' Yearbook and Directory, 1908* (London: Swan Sonnenschein & Co., Ltd., 1908), p. viii.

66 "Occasional Notes," *The Journal of Education*, 29:521 (August 1, 1907).

67 "New Regulations for Secondary Schools," *The Journal of Education*, 29:534 (August 1, 1907).

68 "Headmasters' Association," *The Journal of Education*, 30:147 (February 1, 1908).

69 "The New Regulations for Secondary Schools," *The School World*, 9:282 (August 1907).

70 "Incorporated Association of Headmasters," *The Journal of Education*, 31:144 (February 1, 1909).

71 *The Journal of Education*, especially, continued its criticisms. See, for example, "Scholar of Free-Placer," *The Journal of Education*, 31:453 (July 1, 1909); "25 per cent of Free Places," *The Journal of Education*, 31: 531 (August 2, 1909); "The Education Estimates," *Ibid.* See also P. Shaw-Jeffrey, "Free Places," *The Journal of Education*, 31:104–5 (February 1, 1909).

72 See, for example, the opinion of H. M. Inspectors. Board of Education, *Report of the Board of Education for the Year 1911–1912* (London: H. M. S. O., 1913) , pp. 31–33.

73 "The New Secondary Education," *The Times Educational Supplement*, September 6, 1910, p. 19.

74 *Ibid.*

75 Board of Education, *Report of the Board of Education for the Year 1911–1912*, p. 12.

76 *Ibid.*, p. 15.

77 See D. V. Class, editor, *Social Mobility in Britain* (London: Routledge and Kegan Paul, Ltd., 1954), p. 106.

78 Mastermann, *The Constitution of England*, p. 116.

79 See M. D. Young and P. Willmott, *Family Kinship in East London* (London: Routledge and Kegan Paul, 1957), pp. 146–149.

VIII

1 Board of Education, *Regulations for Secondary Schools*, 1907, pp. vi–ix, 2. See article 7 which urges the provision of Singing "in some portion at least of the school." *Ibid.*, p. 3. Also see Board of Education, *Report of the Year 1906–1907*, pp. 67–69.

2 Board of Education, *Regulations for Secondary Schools* (London: H. M. S. O., 1908), pp. vii, 3. Also see Board of Education, *Report of the Board of Education for the Year 1907–1908* (London: H. M. S. O., 1909), p. 55. It should be emphasized here that in no instance did the Board deviate from the position that the primary function of the secondary school was a good liberal education.

3 Board of Education, *Regulations for Secondary Schools* (London: H. M. S. O., 1909), pp. vi–vii.

4 Board of Education, *Report of the Board of Education for the Year 1908–1909* (London: H. M. S. O., 1910), pp. 133–137.

5 Board of Education, *Report of the Board of Education for the Year 1909–1910* (London: H. M. S. O., 1911), pp. 72–73.

6 Board of Education, *Memoranda on Teaching and Organization in Secondary Schools: Modern Languages* (London: H. M. S. O., 1912), pp. 7–8, 16, 27 ff. Also see Board of Education, *The Teaching of English in Secondary Schools*, Circular 753 (London: H. M. S. O., 1910), and *Memorandum on Physical Training in Secondary Schools*, Circular 779 (London: H. M. S. O., 1911).

7 Board of Education, *Report of the Board of Education for the Year 1911–1912*, pp. 73–74.

8 Board of Education, *Memoranda on Teaching and Organization in Secondary Schools: Curricula of Secondary Schools* (London: H. M. S. O., 1913), pp. 5–6.

9 *Ibid.*, p. 8.

10 *Ibid.*, p. 9.

11 *Ibid.*, p. 6.

12 *Hansard*, Fifth Series, Vol. 28, 1911, p. 501. See also Sir William

Anson's speech in *Ibid.*, p. 558. Also see statement by J. A. Pease, Runciman's successor, in *Hansard*, Fifth Series, Vol. 39, 1912, p. 318.

13 Board of Education, *Report of the Consultative Committee on Practical Work in Secondary Schools* (London: H. M. S. O., 1913).

14 *Ibid.*, p. 1.

15 "We propose . . . for the sake of convenience, to use . . . the term 'Handwork' or 'Educational Handwork' or 'Handcraft,' in a wider meaning as including, besides the subjects just mentioned, Gardening and the various Domestic Subjects for girls. These last we shall take to include Needlework, Cookery, Laundry and Housewifery." *Ibid.*, pp. 3–4.

16 *Ibid.*, pp. 5–8.

17 *Ibid.*, p. 12.

18 *Ibid.*, pp. 13–14.

19 *Ibid.*, pp. 36–39.

20 *Ibid.*, p. 65.

21 Board of Education, *Report of the Consultative Committee on Attendance, Compulsory or Otherwise, at Continuation Schools* (London: H. M. S. O., 1909), p. 36.

22 *Ibid.*, pp. 300–308.

23 *Ibid.*, p. 37.

24 *Ibid.*, p. 39.

25 *Ibid.*, pp. 39–40. See also the answers given by 95 persons on "secondary day schools" on pp. 260–262.

26 *Census of England and Wales, 1901: Summary Tables, Area, Houses and Population; also Population Classified by Ages, Condition as to Marriage, Occupations, Birthplaces, and Infirmities,* 63 Vict. c. 4 (London: H. M. S. O., 1903), p. 188.

27 *Census of England and Wales, 1911: Occupations and Industries,* Vol. X, Part I (London: H. M. S. O., 1914), p. 14.

28 Board of Education, *Report of the Consultative Committee on Attendance, Compulsory or Otherwise, at Continuation Schools: Summaries of Evidence,* Vol. II (London: H. M. S. O., 1909), pp. 333–334.

29 See comparative tables given in *Census of England and Wales, 1911,* pp. lxxviii ff.

30 *Census of England and Wales, 1901,* pp. 186–187.

31 *Census of England and Wales, 1911,* pp. xiii–xvi.

32 See Halévy. *The Rule of Democracy,* pp. 262–265.

33 J. A. Hobson, *The Crisis of Liberalism: New Issues of Democracy* (London: P. S. King and Son, 1909), pp. 109–111.

34 Hobhouse, *Liberalism,* p. 32. See also his remarks on p. 40.

35 See, for example, the statements by Campbell-Bannerman. The Liberal Publication Department, *Pamphlets and Leaflets for 1905* (London: The Liberal Publication Department, 1906). Pamphlet No. 13, p. 16. Also see Sir H. Campbell-Bannerman, "Liberal Policy, A Speech Delivered by the Right Hon. Sir Henry Campbell-Bannerman at the Albert-Hall on December 21, 1905," *Pamphlets and Leaflets for 1906* (London: The Liberal Publication Department, 1907), Pamphlet No. 7, pp. 7–10.

36 S. A. Burstall, "Variant Types of Curricula in Secondary Schools," *The School World,* 12:323–4 (September 1910).

[37] "Commercial Education in Secondary Schools," *The School World,* 16:16–7 (January 1914).

[38] *Ibid.,* p. 19.

[39] *Ibid.,* pp. 22–24.

[40] *Ibid.,* pp. 17–19.

[41] "Review of the Year," *The Schoolmasters Yearbook and Directory, 1909* (London: The Year Book Press, 1909), p. xlix.

[42] "Review of the Year," *The Schoolmasters Yearbook and Directory, 1910,* pp. lix–lxi.

[43] "Review of the Year," *The Schoolmasters Yearbook and Directory, 1911,* p. lxxx.

[44] "Review of the Year," *The Schoolmasters Yearbook and Directory, 1913,* pp. lxxi–xxii. Also see "Review of the Year," *The Schoolmasters Yearbook and Educational Directory, 1914,* p. lxxxviii.

[45] "Colonial and Foreign Notes," *The Journal of Education,* 31:329 (May 1, 1909).

[46] *Ibid.,* p. 329.

[47] "The Education Estimates," *The Journal of Education,* 31:540 (August 2, 1909).

[48] See "Colonial and Foreign Notes," *The Journal of Education,* 33:243 (April 1, 1911); "Colonial and Foreign News," *The Journal of Education,* 33:470 (July 1, 1911); and "Colonial and Foreign News," *The Journal of Education,* 33:776 (November 1, 1911).

[49] "Colonial and Foreign Notes," *The Journal of Education,* 34:550 (August 1, 1912).

[50] "Occasional Notes," *Ibid.,* p. 522.

[51] "Occasional Notes," *The Journal of Education,* 35:463 (July 1, 1913).

[52] "Equality of Opportunity," *The Educational Times,* 64:364 (September 1, 1911).

[53] "Circular 826," *The Educational Times,* 66:443 (November 1, 1913).

[54] "National Union of Teachers: Educational Ideals," Recorded in *The Educational Times,* 64:204 (May 1, 1911).

[55] *Ibid.,* p. 205.

[56] This association consisted of (a) bodies of governors, trustees, or other governing bodies of secondary schools, (b) "members, being persons who are governors, or duly appointed representatives of a secondary school," and (c) "Associates, being persons who are interested in secondary education." *The Schoolmasters Yearbook and Directory, 1911,* p. 100.

[57] "Secondary Schools Association," *The Educational Times,* 64:206 (May 1, 1911).

[58] "Headmistresses in Conference," *The Journal of Education,* 33:456 (July 1, 1911).

[59] Also see F. Stoor, "Domestic Science in Secondary School," *The School World,* 12:405–8 (November, 1910).

[60] James Oliphant, "Secretarial Training for Girls", *The School World,* 15:242 (July, 1913).

[61] Cloudesley Brereton, "The Character-forming Influence of Vocational Education," *The Journal of Education,* 34:779–80 (November 1, 1912).

[62] A. H. Angus, "The Place of Handiwork in the Secondary School," *The School World*, 13:245–6 (July 1911).

[63] Frank J. Atkins, "A Counterblast Against Vocationism," *The School World*, 16:9–12 (January 1914).

[64] Board of Education, *Report of the Board of Education for the Year 1909–1910*, p. 71.

[65] Board of Education, *Report of the Board of Education for the Year 1911–1912*, p 76.

[66] Board of Education, *Report of the Board of Education for the Year 1912–1913*, p. 111.

[67] Board of Education, *Report of the Consultative Committee on Practical Work in Secondary Schools*, pp. 244–5.

[68] Board of Education, *Report of the Board of Education for the Year 1911–1912*, p. 74.

[69] Board of Education, *Report of the Board of Education for the Year 1912–1913*, p. 110.

[70] Compiled from Board of Education, *Statistics of Public Education in England and Wales, Part I, 1911–1912* (London: H. M. S. O., 1913), p. 112.

[71] Compiled from Board of Education, *Statistics of Public Education in England and Wales, Part I, 1909–1910* (London: H. M. S. O., 1911), p. 122.

[72] Compiled from Board of Education, *Statistics of Public Education in England and Wales, Part I, 1911*–12, p. 124.

[73] Compiled from Board of Education, *Statistics of Public Education in England and Wales, Part I, 1912–13* (London: H. M. S. O., 1914), p. 114.

[74] Board of Education, *Report of the Consultative Committee on Examinations in Secondary Schools* (London: H. M. S. O., 1911).

[75] *Ibid.*, pp. 67–68.

[76] *Ibid.*, pp. 73–74.

[77] On the persistence of this psychological doctrine see the memorandum submitted to the London County Council by Dr. F. H. Hayward, an assistant inspector in London County Council Education Committee, *Annual Report of the Education Officer, 1909–10*, p. 4.

[78] *Ibid.*, p. 73.

[79] This point will be discussed more fully in Chapter X.

[80] London County Council Education Committee, *Annual Report of Education Office, 1909–10*, pp. 12–13.

[81] *The Times* (London), March 3, 1910, p. 7.

[82] *The Times* (London), August 23, 1910, p. 9.

[83] "Central Schools: A London and Manchester Experiment," *The Times Educational Supplement*, No. 1 (September 6, 1910), p. 5.

[84] Board of Education, *Report of the Board of Education for the Year 1911–1912* (London: H. M. S. O., 1913), p. 43.

[85] *Ibid.*, pp. 42–43.

[86] Board of Education, *Report of the Board of Education for the Year 1913–1914* (London: H. M. S. O., 1915), p. 60.

87 Quoted from L. Haden Guest, ed., *The New Education: A Critical Presentation of the Education Scheme of the London Education Authority, October, 1920* (London: Hodder and Stoughton Ltd., 1920), pp. 99–100. See also Board of Education, *Report of the Board of Education for the Year 1911–12*, pp. 42–43.

88 For more details on the curriculum of the elementary schools see Board of Education, *Code of Regulations For Public Elementary Schools in England* (London: H. M. S. O., 1912), pp. 1–4. In the case of London, see London County Council, *Report of the Education Committee Submitting the Report of the Education Officer for the Educational Year 1908–9, Part I—Elementary Education* (London: Alexander and Shepheard Ltd., 1910), pp. 2–15.

89 *Code of Regulations for Public Elementary Schools, 1905*, introduction. On the purpose of the public elementary school also see Board of Education, *Suggestions for the Consideration of Teachers and Others Concerned in the Work of Public Elementary Schools* (London: H. M. S. O., 1905), pp. 7–9.

IX

1 See Board of Education, *Emergency Measures With Regard to Public Elementary Schools*, Circular 855 (Whitehall, 8th August, 1914); Board of Education, *Occupation of School Buildings for Military Hospitals and Other Military Purposes*, Circular 859 (Whitehall, 17th August, 1914); Board of Education, *Occupation of Public Educational Buildings for Hospital Purposes*, Circular 864 (Whitehall, 25th August, 1914).

2 "Schools and the War," *The Educational Times*, 67:451 (October 1, 1914). On the shortage of teachers see "Occasional Notes," *The Journal of Education*, 36:745 (November 2, 1914).

3 See Board of Education, *Report of the Board of Education for the Year 1914–1915* (London: H. M. S. O., 1916), p. 37, and Board of Education, *Report of the Board of Education for the Year 1916–1917* (London: H. M. S. O., 1918), p. 1.

4 See Board of Education, Circular 859, p. 1.

5 Board of Education, *Report of the Board of Education for the Year 1914–1915*, pp. 37–38. Also see Board of Education, *Report of the Board of Education for the Year 1915–1916* (London: H. M. S. O., 1917), p. 26; *Report of the Board of Education for the Year 1916–1917*, pp. 26–28.

6 Board of Education, *Report of the Board of Education for the Year 1914–1915*, pp. 38–39.

7 Board of Education, *Report of the Board of Education for the Year 1915–1916*, p. 27.

8 Board of Education, *Report of the Board of Education for the Year 1916–1917*, p. 27.

9 Compiled from *Reports of the Board of Education for the Years* 1913–1914, 1914–1915, 1915–1916, 1916–1917, 1917–1918.

10 On this point see the speech on "Educational Estimates," delivered

by H. A. L. Fisher on April 19, 1917, in H. A. L. Fisher, *Educational Reform Speeches* (Oxford: At the Clarendon Press, 1918), p. 4.

[11] According to the statistics given by Cole, from July 1914 to June 1915 there occurred a net increase of 30 per cent on food. See G. D. H. Cole, *Labour in War Time* (London: G. Bell and Sons Ltd., 1915), p. 119.

[12] A. L. Bowley, *Prices and Wages in the United Kingdom, 1914–1920* (Oxford: At the Clarendon Press, 1921), pp. 90–95. On this point also see Cole, *Labour in War Time, op. cit.,* pp. 117–120.

[13] See Frank W. Hirst, *The Consequences of the War in Great Britain* (London: Humphrey Milford, 1934), p. 70.

[14] *Ibid.,* p. 75.

[15] *Ibid.,* pp. 75–77. Also see J. R. M. Butler, *A History of England, 1815–1918* (London: Oxford University Press, 1928), p. 254.

[16] H. A. L. Fisher, *An Unfinished Autobiography* (London: Oxford University Press, 1940), p. 94. On the increased interest in education, also see Board of Education, *Report of the Board of Education for the Year 1914–1915,* p. 43; Board of Education, *Report of the Board of Education for the Year 1916–1917,* p. 32.

[17] "The Outlook for 1914," *The Times Educational Supplement,* January 6, 1914, p. 11.

[18] "Tradition and Reform," *The Times Educational Supplement,* January 4, 1917, p. 1.

[19] Labour Party, *Fourteenth Annual Conference, Glasgow, 1914; Annual Report, Statement of Accounts, List of Affiliated Societies Delegates, etc.* (London: Victoria Street, 1914), p. 41. This was the plan suggested by the Committee of the Party set up after the Birmingham Conference of January 24, 1912, at which a resolution was passed to the effect that the school leaving age should be raised to 16 years. See The Labour Party, *Report of the Twelfth Annual Conference of the Labour Party* (London: The Labour Party, 1912), p. 104.

[20] The Labour Party, *Report of the Sixteenth Annual Conference of the Labour Party* (London: The Labour Party, 1917), p. 136.

[21] The Labour Party, *Report of the Seventeenth Annual Conference of the Labour Party* (London: The Labour Party, 1918), p. 122.

[22] *Ibid.,* p. 135.

[23] "The Constitution of the British Labour Party, as Adopted by the Party Conference held in London on February 21, 1918," Reprinted in full in P. U. Kellogg and A. Gleason, *British Labour and the War: Reconstructors for a New World* (New York: Boni and Liveright, 1919), Appendix III.

[24] "Resolutions on Reconstruction Adopted by the Conference of the British Labour Party, London, June 26, 1918," reprinted in full in *Ibid.,* Appendix V, p. 405.

[25] "W. E. A. Memorandum to Board of Education Departmental Committee on Employment of Children during the War," *The Highway,* 8:167, No. 94 (July 1916).

[26] *Ibid.,* pp. 168–169.

27 J. M. Mactavish, "The W. E. A. Campaign in Education," *The Highway*, 8:199 (September 1916).

28 *Ibid.*

29 "Educational Recommendations," *The Highway*, 9:50–1 (December 1916).

30 *Ibid.*, p. 52.

31 "W. E. A. National Conference," *The Highway*, 9:148–9 (June 1917).

32 "Council Meeting Resolutions," *The Highway*, 10:7–8 (October 1917).

33 The Education Reform Council, "A Programme of Education Reform," reprinted in *The School World*, 19:21–4 (January 1917).

34 *Ibid.*, pp. 21–22.

35 "British Association," *Journal of Education*, 38:640 (November 1, 1916).

36 "Reconstruction in Education," *The School World*, 19:315 (September 1917).

37 "The War and Education," *The Athenaeum*, No. 4609 (September 1916), Supplement, p. vii.

38 See, for example, "A Footnote on Educational Reconstruction," *The Athenaeum*, No. 4621:431–4 (September 1917).

39 J. E. G. DeMontmorency, "Secondary Education for All: A Plan for a National System," *The Times Educational Supplement*, May 6, 1913, p. 81.

40 "Mr. Fisher and Reform," *The Times Educational Supplement*, January 4, 1917, p. 7.

41 "After Fourteen," *The Times Educational Supplement*, March 8, 1917, p. 85.

42 "Education Schemes," *The Times Educational Supplement*, March 20, 1919, p. 139.

43 Board of Education, *Interim Report of the Consultative Committee on Scholarships for Higher Education* (London: H. M. S. O., 1916), pp. 8–9.

44 Departmental Committee on Juvenile Education in Relation to Employment After the War, *Final Report of the Departmental Committee on Juvenile Education in Relation to Employment After the War*, Vol. I (London: H. M. S. O., 1917), pp. 3–4.

45 *Ibid.*, p. 2.

46 *Ibid.*, pp. 8, 10, 12. The local education authorities would be responsible for the provision of such classes, and all "young persons" would be obligated to attend, except in the case of those who were receiving part-time or full-time education elsewhere, or had attended a secondary school. *Ibid.*, p. 27.

47 H. A. L. Fisher, *Education Reform Speeches* (Oxford: At the Clarendon Press, 1918), pp. xii–xiii.

48 *Ibid.*, p. xiv.

49 *Ibid.*, pp. xv–xvi.

50 *Hansard*, Fifth Series, Vol. XCII, 1917, pp. 1904–1908.

51 *Ibid.*, pp. 1887–1888. This amount represented a £3,829,548 increase over that of the previous year (1916–1917). *Ibid.*, p. 1889.

52 *Hansard*, Fifth Series, Vol. XCVII, 1917, p. 795.

53 *Hansard*, Fifth Series, Vol. XCVII, 1917, p. 795.

54 *Ibid.*, pp. 799–800. Elsewhere, Fisher commended highly the efforts of Labour leaders in enlightening public opinion on education. In the Preface to his *Educational Reform Speeches* he said: "The Leaders of the Labour World having discovered Education some time since are now communicating the message to those below." Fisher, *Educational Reform Speeches*, p. ix.

55 *Hansard*, Fifth Series, Vol. XCVII, pp. 799–806.

56 *Ibid.*, pp. 809–810. Also see Fisher's answer to John McConnell, Vice-Chairman of the Fine Cotton Spinners' Association, in his Manchester speech in September 25, 1917, in Fisher, *Educational Reform Speeches*, pp. 53–55.

57 *Ibid.*, p. 82.

58 "A Bill to Make Further Provision with Respect to Education in England and Wales and for Purposes Connected Therewith," 8. Geo. 5. *Bills; Public*, Vol. I, 1918.

59 See, for example, Peto's critique of Clauses 10, 11, 12. *Hansard*, Fifth Series, Vol. 104, 1918, pp. 342–353, and Acland's and Fisher's defense, *Ibid.*, pp. 335–342, 386–399.

60 *Ibid.*, pp. 336–338.

61 *Ibid.*, p. 386.

62 "Education Bill, 1918," pp. 1–2, 22. Also see *Hansard*, Fifth Series, Vol. 104, 1918, p. 388.

63 *Education Act*, 1918 (8 & 9 Geo. 5, Ch. 39), Section 4–(4).

X

1 See A. C. Benson, editor, *Cambridge Essays on Education* (Cambridge: At the University Press, 1918), pp. 4–5. Also see "Review of the Year," *The Schoolmaster's Yearbook and Educational Directory, 1918* (London: H. F. W. Deane and Sons, The Yearbook Press, Ltd., 1918), pp. lxvi–lxvii.

2 "Review of the Year," *The Schoolmasters' Yearbook and Educational Directory, 1917*, p. lxiii.

3 *Ibid.*, lxiii–lxiv.

4 "Labour and Education," *The Times Educational Supplement*, March 27, 1919, p. 145.

5 Ministry of Reconstruction, *Interim Report of the Committee on Adult Education: Industrial and Social Conditions in Relation to Adult Education* (London: H. M. S. O., 1918), p. 3.

6 "Capitalism and Education," *The Athenaeum*, No. 4627:131 (March 1918).

7 *Ibid.*, p. 133. This notion *The Athenaeum* had maintained even earlier. In another leader of August 1917, it had asserted that "education is a prime human need, and not an accomplishment to adorn the highborn or the wealthy." "Education and the Social Idea," *The Athenaeum*, No. 4620:375 (August 1917).

8 Ministry of Reconstruction, *Adult Education*, 1918, p. 3. Board of Education, *Report of the Board of Education for the Year 1915–1916*, p. 3.

9 R. W. Livingstone, *A Defence of Classical Education* (London: Macmillan and Co., Ltd., 1916), pp. 30–34.

10 *Ibid.*, pp. 34–35.

11 *Ibid.*, pp. 40–54.

12 *Ibid.*, pp. 154–159.

13 H. G. Wells, "The Case Against the Classical Languages," *The Fortnightly Review*, 107:571 (April 1917).

14 *Ibid.*, p. 573.

15 *Ibid.*, p. 574.

16 See, for example, W. R. Roberts, *Greek Civilization as a Study for the People* (London: British Academy, 1916), pp. 1–13, reprinted from *Proceedings of the British Academy*, Vol. VII; Sir William Osler, *The Old Humanities and the New Science* (London: John Murray, 1919).

17 Committee to Inquire into the Position of Classics in the Educational System of the United Kingdom, *Report of the Committee Appointed by the Prime Minister to Inquire into the Position of Classics in the Educational System of the United Kingdom* (London: H. M. S. O., 1921), pp. 42–43.

18 *Modern Studies: Being the Report of the Committee on the Position of Modern Languages in the Educational System of Great Britain* (London: H. M. S. O., 1918), pp. 46–47. Hereafter cited as the Leathes Committee.

19 *Ibid.*, pp. 47–51.

20 *Ibid.*, pp. 17–32.

21 "Neglect of Science: A Cause of Failures in War," *The Times* (London), February 2, 1916, p. 10.

22 "Science and Greek: The Claim of Modern Subjects," *The Times* (London), May 4, 1916, p. 6.

23 Committee to Enquire into the Position of Natural Science in the Educational System of Great Britain, *Report of the Committee appointed by the Prime Minister to Enquire into the position of Natural Science in The Educational System of Great Britain* (London: H. M. S. O., 1918), p. 7. Hereafter cited as Thomson Report.

24 *Ibid.*, pp. 8–10.

25 *Ibid.*, p. 17.

26 *Ibid.*, pp. 18, 21–23.

27 "Limitations of Science: A Plea for Tradition," *The Times* (London), May 4, 1916, p. 6.

28 "The School Curriculum," *The Journal of Education*, 38:558 (September 1, 1916).

29 "Occasional Notes," *The Journal of Education*, 38:633 (November 1, 1916).

30 "Mathematical Education," *The School World*, 18:480 (December 1916).

31 On the organization of these groups and the various steps taken, see Frederick G. Kenyon, editor, *Education: Scientific and Humane, A Report of the Proceedings of the Council for Humanistic Studies* (London: John Murray, 1917), pp.12–13.

32 *Ibid.*, p. 14.

33 *Ibid.*, p. 20, 23.

34 Board of Education, *Regulations for Secondary Schools in England, Excluding Wales and Monmouthshire* (London: H. M. S. O., 1917), pp. 12–13.

35 *Ibid.*, pp. 7–9, 20–21.

36 J. S. Mill, *Inaugural Address Delivered to the University of St. Andrews, February 1, 1867* (Boston: Littell and Gay, 1867), p. 5.

37 See *Thomson Report*, p. 7; *Leathes Committee*, pp. 46–47; Livingstone, *op. cit.*, pp. 235–236. For an analysis of the controversies of the 1860's, see A. M. Kazamias, "What Knowledge is of Most Worth? An Historical Conception and a Modern Sequel," *Harvard Educational Review*, 30:309–314 (Fall, 1960).

38 *Value of the Classics*, Conference on Classical Studies in Liberal Education (Princeton: Princeton University Press, 1917), p. 4. On the controversies in America, also see Paul Shorey, *The Assault on Humanism* (Boston: Atlantic Monthly Company, 1917); F. W. Kelsey, *Latin and Greek in American Education, With Symposia on the Value of Humanistic Studies* (New York: The Macmillan Co., 1911); C. W. Eliot, *The Tendency to the Concrete and Practical in Modern Education* (Boston: Houghton Mifflin Co., 1913); University of Pennsylvania, *Symposium on the Value of the Classics* (Philadelphia: University of Pennsylvania Press, 1919).

XI

1 These are the election results as analyzed by *The Times*, and as recorded in *The Annual Register for 1918*, p. 164. D. C. Somervell gives the following figures: Coalition 526; Labour 63; Asquithian Liberals 33; Irish Republicans 73. D. C. Somervell, *British Politics Since 1900* (London: Andrew Dakers Limited, 1950), p. 121.

2 The reference here is to the so-called "Black Friday" event (April 15, 1921) which ended the "Triple Alliance" of the Labour movement and "brought an epoch in the Labour movement's history to an end." For further elaboration of this, see G. D. H. Cole, *A History of the Labour Party From 1914* (London: Routledge & Kegan Paul, Ltd., 1948), pp. 114–120.

3 On the question of unemployment in the post-war years, see F. W. Hirst, *The Consequences of the War to Great Britain* (London: Humphrey Milford, 1934), pp. 281–283.

4 On the policy of "decontrol," see Charles L. Mowat, *Britain Between the Wars, 1918–1940* (Chicago: The University of Chicago Press, 1955), pp. 28–30.

5 J. Hugh Edwards, *David Lloyd George: The Man and the Statesman* (New York: J. H. Sears & Co., Inc., 1929), Vol. II, pp. 644–645.

6 Mowat, *Britain Between the Wars*, p. 133.

7 For an analysis of the electoral results, see *The Annual Register for 1922*, p. 120.

8 K. Hutchison, *The Decline and Fall of British Capitalism* (New York: Charles Scribners Sons, 1950), p. 187.

9 See Mowat, *Britain Between the Wars*, pp. 156–162; Somervell, *British Politics*, pp. 142–147.

10 *The Annual Register for 1923*, p. 140.

11 Kellogg and Gleason, *British Labour and the War*, Appendix III.

12 The authorship of this manifesto has been ascribed to Sidney Webb. It was submitted at the 17th Annual Conference (January 23–25, 1918) and adopted as the Labour doctrine on reconstruction. *Ibid.*, Appendix IV.

13 Somervell, *British Politics*, p. 156.

14 *The Annual Register for 1924*, pp. 9–10.

15 *Ibid.*, p. 9.

16 Committee on National Expenditure, *First Interim Report of Committee on National Expenditure* (London: H. M. S. O., 1922), p. 2.

17 *Ibid.*, pp. 114, 123.

18 *Ibid.*, p. 122.

19 For statistical evidence on the expenditure of the Board of Education from 1913–14 to 1924–25, see Board of Education, *Memorandum on the Board of Education Estimates, 1923–1924* (London: H. M. S. O., 1923); and Board of Education, *Memorandum on the Board of Education Estimates, 1925–1926* (London: H. M. S. O., 1925), p. 4.

20 *Education Act, 1918*, Section 4.—(4).

21 Board of Education, *Report of the Board of Education for the Year 1918–1919* (London: H. M. S. O., 1920), pp. 40–41.

22 Board of Education, *Report of the Board of Education for the Year 1923–1924* (London: H. M. S. O., 1925), p. 67.

23 *Education in England and Wales: Being the Report of the Board of Education And the Statistics of Public Education for the Year 1926–1927* (London: H. M. S. O., 1928), p. 22.

24 *Ibid.*, p. 25.

25 *Hansard*, Fifth Series, Vol. 119, 1919, p. 1234.

26 Departmental Committee on Scholarships and Free Places, *Report of the Departmental Committee on Scholarships and Free Places* (London: H. M. S. O., 1920), p. 60.

27 *Ibid.*, p. 9.

28 Compiled from *Ibid.*, Table B, pp. 62–63.

29 *Education Act, 1918*, Section 1.

30 Departmental Committee on Scholarships and Free Places, *Report of 1920*, pp. 8–9. This conclusion was reached after an examination of the evidence presented by many witnesses including the famous psychologist Cyril Burt.

31 *Ibid.*, p. 34.

32 *Ibid.*, pp. 11–13.

33 *Ibid.*, p. 24.

34 *Ibid.*, pp. 37–38.

35 The Labour Party, *Report of the Eighteenth Annual Conference of the Labour Party* (London: The Labour Party, 1918), p. 22.

36 *Ibid.*, p. 72.

37 The Labour Party, *Report of the Nineteenth Annual Conference of the Labour Party* (London: The Labour Party, 1919), p. 164.

38 See The Labour Party, *Report of the Twenty-First Annual Conference of the Labour Party* (London: The Labour Party, 1921), p. 208; also see The Labour Party, *Report of the Twenty-Second Annual Conference of the Labour Party* (London: The Labour Party, 1922), pp. 201, 229–230; and The Labour Party, *Report of the Twenty-Third Annual Conference of the Labour Party* (London: The Labour Party, 1923), p. 235.

39 *Ibid.*, p. 236.

40 R. H. Tawney, editor, *Secondary Education For All: A Policy for Labour* (London: The Labour Party, 1922), p. 7.

41 *Ibid.*, p. 8–9. Tawney drew heavily from this committee's report as is shown by the frequent references and the appendices.

42 *Ibid.*, p. 11.

43 *Ibid.*, pp. 17, 26.

44 *Ibid.*, p. 29. He further accepts the Board's "catholic definition of a secondary school," as well as the "comprehensiveness" and "variation" of the curriculum.

45 *Draft Statutory Rules and Orders: Regulations for Secondary Schools, England, 1921*, pp. 7–8.

46 Tawney, *Secondary Education for All*, pp. 29–30.

47 References were made to two well-known educational thinkers, viz., John Adams and Percy Nunn. *Ibid.*, p. 65.

48 See the resolution moved by C. P. Trevelyan and passed, in The Labour Party, *Report of the Twenty-Seventh Annual Conference of the Labour Party* (London: The Labour Party, 1927), pp. 213–214.

49 The Labour Party, *Report of the Twenty-Fifth Annual Conference of the Labour Party* (London: The Labour Party, 1925), p. 102.

50 R. H. Tawney, *Education: The Socialist Policy* (London: Independent Labour Party Publication Department, 1924), p. 26.

51 A. M. Carr-Saunders and D. Caradog Jones, *A Survey of the Social Structure of England and Wales As Illustrated by Statistics* (London: Oxford University Press, 1927), pp. 125–126.

52 For more detailed information on this, see Kenneth Lindsay, *Social Progress and Educational Waste: Being a Study of the "Free-Place" and Scholarship System* (London: George Routledge and Sons, Ltd., 1926).

53 The Fisher Act stipulated that a child under the age of twelve could not be employed in any capacity, and, from twelve to fourteen, a child was not to be employed on Sunday for more than two hours, nor normally on school days before the close of school, nor on any day before six o'clock in the morning or after eight o'clock at night. See *Education Act, 1918*, Section 13 (I).

54 See Carr-Saunders and Jones, *Social Structure of England and Wales*, p. 134.

55 *Ibid.*, pp. 134–135.

56 See *Report of the Ministry of Labour for the Year 1925* (London: H. M. S. O., 1926), pp. 42–43.

[57] Labour policy had this object in mind. See also Lindsay, *Social Progress and Educational Waste*, p. 30.

[58] *Ibid.*, p. 33.

[59] Carr-Saunders and Jones, *Social Structure of England and Wales*, pp. 70–72. The only group of people, according to these writers, that came close to being described a cohesive, self-conscious "class" was the wage-earning group.

[60] Mowat, *England Between the Wars*, p. 203. On the decline of old aristocratic families see C. F. G. Masterman, *England After the War: A Study* (London: Hodder and Stoughton, 1922), pp. 46–47.

[61] For more detailed information on this, see K. B. Smellie, *A Hundred Years of English Government* (London: Duckworth, 1937), pp. 335–341.

[62] *Ibid.*, p. 336. Also see Carr-Saunders and Jones, *Social Structure of England and Wales*, pp. 161–3, 186.

[63] Lindsay, *Social Progress and Educational Waste*, p. 28. On this point, see also Tawney, *Secondary Education for All*, p. 33.

[64] For the growth of the Civil Service, see the statistics given by Smellie, *A Hundred Years of English Government*, p. 455. For the increase in professions and other occupations, see Carr-Saunders and Jones, *Social Structure of England and Wales*, pp. 48–73.

[65] Of this book, Sir Cyril Burt, another famous British psychologist, wrote: "This . . . must certainly rank as the best seller in the whole realm of psychology . . . During the next twenty years over a hundred thousand copies were sold, and at the author's death (1939) it had reached the twenty-fourth edition." See Sir Cyril Burt's introductory essay to William McDougall, *Psychology: The Study of Behaviour* (London: Oxford University Press, 1952), pp. xii–xiii.

[66] William McDougall, *An Introduction to Social Psychology* (London: Methuen & Co., 1908), p. 16.

[67] For the most orthodox exposition of associationism, see James Mill, *Analysis of the Phenomena of the Human Mind* (London: Baldwin and Cradock, 1829), Vol. I, Ch. III. For other attacks on it, beside McDougall's, see James Ward, *Psychological Principles* (Cambridge: at the University Press, 1918), Chs. III, IV, V, and G. F. Stout, *A Manual of Psychology* (London: University Correspondence College Press, 1899), Ch. III.

[68] *Ibid.*, p. 15.

[69] *Ibid.*, pp. 26–29. Also see J. C. Flugel, *A Hundred Years of Psychology, 1833–1933: With Additional Part on Developments 1933–1947* (London: Gerald Duckworth & Co., Ltd., 1951), pp. 274–275.

[70] McDougall, *An Introduction to Social Psychology*, p. 159.

[71] See, for example, J. Welton, *The Psychology of Education* (London: Macmillan and Co., Ltd., 1911); James Drever, *Instinct in Man: A Contribution to the Psychology of Education* (Cambridge: At the University Press, 1917) and *An Introduction to the Psychology of Education* (New York: Longmans, Green & Co., 1923). Also see G. H. Thomson, *Instinct, Intelligence and Character: An Educational Psychology* (London: George Allen and Unwin, Ltd., 1924).

72 As early as 1909, Nunn, at the time Vice-Principal of the London University Day Training College, was invited by the Consultative Committee of the Board of Education to give evidence on the college and thus help in the preparation of the report on "Practical Work in Secondary Schools." By the time he wrote *Education: Its Data and First Principles,* he had published various other books on education and had become principal of the aforementioned college.

73 "The word 'hormic' is from the Greek 'horme' which means a vital impulse or urge to action. Schopenhauer's 'will-to-live,' Professor Bergson's 'elan vital,' and Doctor C. G. Jung's 'libido,' are alternative expressions for the purposive or hormic energy that is manifested in human and animal behavior. In adopting this word I am following the suggestion of Professor T. P. Nunn in his very excellent little book, 'Education, Its Data and First Principles.' " McDougall, *Outline to Psychology* (New York: Charles Scribner's Sons, 1923), p. 72.

74 T. Percy Nunn, *Education: Its Data and First Principles* (London: Edward Arnold, 1921), pp. 12–17.

75 *Ibid.,* pp. 18–19.

76 *Ibid.,* p. 3. In another instance, Nunn said: "Individuality develops only in a social atmosphere where it can feed on common interests and common activities." *Ibid.,* p. 8.

77 *Ibid.,* pp. 18–19.

78 See, for example, Chapter XII on "the growth of the self." *Ibid.,* p. 140.

79 *Ibid.,* p. 198.

80 *Ibid.,* p. 202.

81 The term "play-way in education" was later substituted by "freedom in education." See the revised copy of the third edition reprinted in 1956, Chapter VIII.

82 *Ibid.,* pp. 198–200, 210–211.

83 *Ibid.,* p. 211.

84 *Ibid.,* pp. 205–206. For the psychological foundations of this position see *Ibid.,* pp. 148–151.

85 See Nunn's interpretation of "play." *Ibid.,* pp. 71–72. Also see J. J. Findlay, *The Foundations of Education: A Survey of Principles and Projects, Vol I. The Aims and Organization of Education* (New York: Henry Holt and Company, 1925), and *The Foundations of Education: A Survey of Principles and Projects, Vol. II. The Practise of Education* (New York: Henry Holt and Company, 1927); H. Bompas Smith, *The Nation's Schools: Their Task and Their Importance* (London: Longmans, Green and Co., Ltd., 1927).

86 Board of Education, *Report of the Consultative Committee on Differentiation of the Curriculum for Boys and Girls Respectively in Secondary Schools* (London: H. M. S. O., 1923), pp. 80ff.

87 *Ibid.,* pp. 62–63.

88 *Ibid.,* p. 121.

89 *Ibid.,* p. 134.

90 For a good analysis of this educational theory, see H. R. Hamley,

"Memorandum on the Cognitive Aspect of Transfer of Training," *Report of the Consultative Committee on Secondary Education*, Appendix V, p. 439.

91 See John Adams, *The Herbartian Psychology Applied to Education* (Boston: D. C. Heath & Co., 1898), pp. 107–134.

92 Stout, *Manual of Psychology*, p. 103.

93 E. L. Thorndike and R. S. Woodworth, "The Influence of Improvement in One Mental Function Upon the Efficiency of Other Functions," *The Psychological Review*, 8:249–250 (May, 1901).

94 P. B. Ballard, *The Changing School* (London: Hodder and Stoughton, 1925), pp. 152–153.

95 McDougall's biological interpretations of the human mind cost him his job at Oxford, thereby "forcing" him to go to Harvard!

96 See Herbert Ward, "The Training of Teachers," in J. Dover Wilson, editor, *The Schools of England: A Study in Renaissance* (London: Sidgwick & Jackson, Ltd., 1928), p. 217.

97 See H. C. Ballard, *The Changing School*, pp. 167–168, and Hamley, "Memorandum," p. 440.

XII

1 See, for example, H. C. Dent, *Secondary Education for All*, p. 60.

2 *The Dictionary of National Biography, 1931–1940* (London: Oxford University Press, 1949), pp. 386–387.

3 Hadow Report, p. xvii.

4 *Ibid.*, p. iv.

5 *Ibid.*, p. xix.

6 *Ibid.*, p. 95.

7 *Ibid.*, p. 78. Also see Kenneth Lindsay, *Social Progress and Educational Waste*, p. 28.

8 References to this pedagogical principle are numerous. See, for example, *Ibid.*, pp. xix, 77, 139.

9 See, for example, F. Clarke, *Essays in the Politics of Education* (London: Oxford University Press, 1923), especially Chapter II, "Education and Society," pp. 23–47. Also see E. T. Campagnac, *Education in its Relation to the Common Purposes of Humanity* (London: Sir Isaac Pitman and Sons, 1925).

10 T. H. Marshall, "Social Selection in the Welfare State," in Halsey, Floud and Anderson, *Education, Economy and Society*, pp. 148–149.

11 *Hadow Report*, p. 101.

12 *Ibid.*, p. 71.

13 See, for example, Board of Education, *Curriculum and Examinations in Secondary Schools: Report of the Committee of the Secondary School Examinations Council Appointed by the President of the Board of Education in 1941* (His Majesty's Stationery Office, 1943), pp. 16–17. Hereafter cited as the Norwood Report. For a more recent statement on this question, see "Selective Society," *The Times Educational Supplement*, February 16, 1962, p. 305.

14 *The Times Educational Supplement,* December 15, 1961.
For more information on this, see A. H. Passow, *Secondary Education for All: The English Approach* (Columbus: Ohio State University Press, 1961), pp. 52–76.

15 Bryce Commission, Vol. V, pp. 456–457.

16 *Ibid.,* p. 91.

17 *Ibid.,* Vol. I, pp. 299–300.

18 See Campbell, *Eleven-Plus and All That,* p. 97.

19 Board of Education, *Circular 1350* (London, 1925).

20 Departmental Committee on Scholarships and Free Places, p. 37.

21 Nunn, *Education,* pp. 205–206.

22 Tawney, *Secondary Education for All,* p. 11.

23 Hadow Report, p. 71.

24 S. J. Curtis and M. E. A. Boultwood, *A Short History of Educational Ideas* (London: University Tutorial Press, 1953), p. 525.

25 See Board of Education, *Report of the Consultative Committee on the Primary School* (London: H. M. S. O., 1931).

26 Hadow Report, pp. 74–75.

27 *Ibid.,* pp. 78–79.

28 *Ibid.,* p. 80.

29 On this point also see Banks, *Parity and Prestige,* p. 124.

30 Hadow Report, pp. 79–80, 95–96.

31 *Ibid.,* p. 93.

32 See, for example, Dent, *Secondary Education for All,* p. 68.

33 Hadow Report, p. 121.

34 *Ibid.,* pp. 115–116, 120.

35 Crowther Report, *15 to 18,* pp. 21–22.

36 Hadow Report, p. 84.

37 *Ibid.,* pp. 109, 175.

38 *Ibid.,* p. 41.

39 *Ibid.,* p. 101.

40 *Ibid.,* p. 115.

41 *Ibid.,* pp. 223–224.

42 *Ibid.,* pp. 188–203.

43 *Ibid.,* pp. 230–238.

44 *Ibid.,* pp. 230–238.

45 *The Times Educational Supplement,* January 1, 1927, p. 7.

46 *The Times Educational Supplement,* January 8, 1927, p. 19.

47 *The Times Educational Supplement,* January 15, 1927, p. 34.

48 "The Education of the Adolescent," *The Journal of Education and School World,* 59:85–6 (February, 1927).

49 See Graves, *Policy and Progress,* pp. 127–128. For other comments on the Report, see J. H. Garrett, *Mass Education in England: A Critical Examination of Problem and Possibility* (London: Ed. J. Burrow & Co., 1928), pp. 93ff.

50 *Education in England and Wales: Being the Report of the Board of Education and the Statistics of Public Education for the Year 1926–1927* (London: H. M. S. O., 1928), p. 8.

[51] Board of Education, *The New Prospect in Education*, Educational Pamphlets, No. 60 (London: H. M. S. O., 1928), p. 16.

[52] See Graves, *Policy and Progress*, pp. 131–133.

[53] Banks, *Parity and Prestige*, p. 122.

[54] W. Kenneth Richmond, *Education in England* (Penguin Books, 1945), p. 117.

XIII

[1] Spens Report, p. iv.

[2] *Ibid.*, pp. xviii–xix, 140.

[3] *Ibid.*, pp. xxiii, 168.

[4] *Ibid.*, p. 311.

[5] *Ibid.*, pp. 311–313.

[6] *Ibid.*, p. 274.

[7] *Ibid.*

[8] *Ibid.*, p. 287.

[9] *Ibid.*, p. 276.

[10] *Ibid.*, pp. xx–xxi, 291–292.

[11] *Ibid.*, pp. xxxi, 275, 279, 293, 297–8, 301, 309, 311.

[12] *Ibid.*, pp. 169–171, 182.

[13] *Ibid.*, pp. xxx–xxxi.

[14] Especially see H. C. Dent, *Education in Transition. A Sociological Study of the Impact of War on English Education, 1939–1943* (New York: Oxford University Press, 1944).

[15] For an excellent discussion of the various viewpoints and the plans for reform, see *Ibid.*, pp. 163–222.

[16] The quotation read: "Upon the education of the people of this county the fate of this county depends." Board of Education, *Educational Reconstruction* (London: H. M. S. O., 1943), p. 3. Hereafter cited as White Paper.

[17] *Ibid.*, p. 9.

[18] *Ibid.*, p. 11.

[19] Norwood Report, pp. 2–3.

[20] *Ibid.*, pp. 6–15.

[21] *Education Act, 1944* (7 & 8 Geo. 6. Ch. 31), Part II, 8.–(1)b.

[22] *Hansard*, Fifth Series, Vol. 396, 1943–1944, p. 222.

[23] R. A. Butler, "Education: The View of a Conservative," *The Year Book of Education* (London: Evans Brothers, 1952). pp. 35–36.

[24] *Ibid.*, pp. 231ff.

[25] Banks, *Parity and Prestige*, pp. 142–143.

[26] Also see J. P. M. Millar, *Post-War Education. A Labour View* (National Council of Labour Colleges, 1943).

[27] *Hansard*, Fifth Series, Vol. 396, 1943–1944, pp. 208–209.

[28] *Ibid.*, p. 231.

[29] Ministry of Education, *The New Secondary Education*, Pamphlet No. 9 (London: H. M. S. O., 1947), p. 22.

[30] *Ibid.*, p. 23.

[31] *Ibid.*, p. 29.

32 *Ibid.*, pp. 54–55.

33 *Ibid.*, pp. 25–28, 34–42, 58–61.

34 *Ibid.*, p. 41.

35 For a review of some of these arguments, see Jöel B. Montague, "English Secondary Education and the Social Class Structure," in *Education in England. Studies in Comparative Education*, U. S. Department of Health, Education, and Welfare, 1961, pp. 20–27. Also see Robin Pedley, *The Comprehensive School* (Penguin Books, Ltd., 1963), pp. 11–20; A. Harry Passow, *Secondary Education for All: The English Approach* (Columbia, Ohio: Ohio State University Press, 1961), pp. 52ff; P. E. Vernon, *Secondary School Selection: A British Psychological Society Inquiry* (London: Methnen and Co., Ltd., 1957); G. B. Jeffrey, editor, *External Examination in Secondary Schools: Their Place and Function* (London: George G. Harrap and Co., Ltd., 1958).

36 In 1959 the Crowther Report stated ". . . we do not now have, and never have had, a tripartite system." According to this report, there are four grammar schools to every technical school, six grammar school pupils to every technical school pupil, and "over 40 per cent of the local education authorities do not provide technical schools." Ministry of Education, *15 to 18. A Report of the Central Advisory Council for Education* (England). London (Her Majesty's Stationery Office, 1959), Vol. I, pp. 21–22.

37 John Vaizey, *Britain in the Sixties: Education for Tomorrow* (Penguin Books, Ltd., 1962), pp. 14–16, 42ff.

38 Jean Floud, "Education and Social Class in the Welfare State," in A. V. Judges, editor, *Looking Forward in Education* (London: Faber and Faber, 1955), p. 43. The material on the social aspects of secondary education, particularly the grammar school, is legion. See, for example, Jean Floud, A. H. Halsey and F. M. Martin, *Social Class and Educational Opportunity* (London: Heinemann, 1957); Jean Floud, "Social Class Factors in Educational Achievement," in A. H. Halsey, editor, *Ability and Educational Opportunity* (Organisation for Economic Co-operation and Development, 1961), pp. 91–113; Jean Floud and A. H. Halsey, "Social Class, Intelligence Tests, and Selection for Secondary Schools," in A. H. Halsey, et. al. *Education, Economy, and Society: A Reader in the Sociology of Education* (The Free Press of Glencoe, Inc., 1961), pp. 209–216.

39 Brian Jackson and Dennis Marsden, *Education and the Working Class* (London: Routledge and Kegan Paul, 1962).

40 Floud, "Education and Social Class in the Welfare State," *op. cit.*, p. 44. Also see Floud, Halsey and Martin, *op. cit.*, p. 58.

41 *Challenge to Britain*, Labour Party publication, 1953.

42 Reported in the *Times Educational Supplement*, December 15, 1961.

43 See *Secondary Education for All: A New Drive* (London: Her Majesty's Stationery Office, 1958), pp. 5–6.

44 "Selective Society," *The Times Educational Supplement* (London), February 16, 1962, pp. 305, 355.

45 Reported in *The Times Educational Supplement* (London), March 30, 1962, p. 631. For a similar argument, see the report of a speech by R. A. Butler in the same issue of the *Supplement*.

XIV

1 H. C. Dent, *Change in English Education* (London: University of London Press, 1952), pp. 19–20.

2 André Maurois, *The Edwardian Era* (New York: D. Appleton-Century Company, 1933), p. 286.

3 "Occasional Notes," *Journal of Education and School World*, 59:87 (February 1, 1927).

4 Michael Young, *The Rise of the Meritocracy, 1870–2033. The New Elite of our Social Revolution* (New York: Random House, 1959).

5 W. Bagehot, *The English Constitution*, p. 6.

Index

Acland, A. H. D., 96, 134–135, 228

Acland Report, 187–189

Adams, J., 269

Adamson, Professor, 156–157

Adkins, F. J., 200–201

Anglican Church, 83, 117–119, 123, 126, 165; *see also* Religion and Politics

Anson, Sir William, 132, 134–135, 149

Apprenticeship, 190, 259

Archer, R. L., 66

Armitage, Mrs., 45

Arnold, Matthew, 17, 102–103, 113

Asquith, H. H., 88–89, 163

Assistant Masters' Association, 75, 142–143

Association of Headmasters, 35, 75, 97–98, 156, 178

Association of Public School Science Masters, 240

Atkins, 173

Balfour, A. J., 90, 112–113, 119, 126

Bagehot, W., 17, 20, 113, 323

Ballard, P., 269

Banks, O., 139–140, 307–308

Barker, E., 272, 321

Barnard, H. C., 139

Bedford Grammar School, 37

Bedford Modern School, 37

Bedfordshire, schools of 42–43, 51

Bentham, J., 17, 103

Birrell, A., 164, 167–168

Board of Education: establishment of, 115

central schools, 207

criticisms of 1904 Regulations, 138–139

curriculum policy of, 183–186, 241

free-place system, 175–176

higher elementary schools, 148–150

policies after 1902 Act, 131–132

reaction to policy on higher elementary schools, 153–160

Regulations for Secondary School (1904), 135–138

special grants for practical subjects, 184–185

Bosanquet, B., 108

Bothamley, C. H., 58

Bradley, F. H., 108

Brereton, C., 200

British Association, 221

Broadhurst, H., 17
Brogan, D., 112
Bryce, J., 15, 27–28, 78, 116, 124–125, 235, 243
Bryce Commission, 16, 21, 29
  and Education Bill, 1896, 77, 91–93
  and Hadow Report, 1926, 278, 280, 281–282, 291, 322–323
  comparison of three grades of schools, 44–46
  concept of secondary education, 60–65
  educational opinion on, 94–96
  educational opportunities, 46–53
  first grade schools, 36–37
  higher grade elementary schools, 42–44
  members of, 27–32
  organization and administration of education, 69–72
  public reaction to report of, 74–77
  second grade schools, 38–41
  secondary and technical education, 62
  secondary education for all, 67–68
  selection into schools, 280
  scholarships, 66–67
  terms of reference, 34–36
  voluntarism, 69
  witnesses giving evidence before, 35–36
Buckmaster, C. A., 133
Burstall, S. A., 194–195
Buss, Miss, 46
Butler, R. A., 306–308
Butterfield, H. C., 24

Caird, E., 108

Cambridge Conference on Secondary Education (1896), 75–76
Campagnac, E. T., 277
Campbell-Bannerman, Sir Henry, 163
Carlyle, T., 17, 103
Carr-Saunders, A. M., 258, 260
Catholic church, 18, 84, 89, 117, 165; see also Religion and Politics
Central schools, 205–209, 229
Chamberlain, J., 125
Channing, F. A., 78, 81
Charles, F., 195–196
Charity Commission, 35, 41–42
Cheshire Education Committee, 159
Clarke, F., 277
Cleghorn, I., 198–199
Clifford, Dr., 82–83, 125
Clifton College, 47
Clover, J. A., 124
Cobden, R., 17
Cockerton Judgment, 119, 129
Code of Regulations (1905), 149, 157
College of Preceptors, 35, 41
Committee of Council on Education, 86
Cooperative and Industrial Societies, 57
Committee of Ten (USA), 33–34
Committee of Humanistic Studies (1916), 240
Committee of Secondary School Examinations Council; report of (1943), 305–307
Committee on Classics (1921), 236
Committee on Modern Languages (Leathes Committee, 1918), report of, 236, 242

Committee on National Expenditure (Geddes Committee), report of, 249–250

Committee on Natural Science (Thomson Committee, 1918), report of, 237–238, 242

Committee on Scholarships and Free Places (Young Committee, 1920), report of, 251–253, 281

Conservatives and Conservative Party, 78–80, 94, 113, 117–118, 126–127, 165, 177, 245–247, 317, 324–326

Consultative Committee: establishment of, 115

Report on Differentiation of the Curriculum for Boys and Girls (1923), 267–268

Report on the Education of the Adolescent (1926), 258

Report on Examinations in Secondary Schools (1911), 204–205

Report on Practical Work in Secondary Schools (1913), 187–189

Report on Secondary Education (1938), 298–350

Report on Scholarships for Higher Education (1916), 223

Report Upon Questions Affecting Higher Elementary Schools (1906), 150–152

Convocation of Canterbury, 83

Cooper, Miss, 38–39

Courtney, L. H., 90

Curriculum:

Board's policy on practical studies (1907), 183–185, 194

Classics in, 234–236, 242–243

differentiation for boys and girls, 267–268

grammar schools, 36–38, 131–132

Hadow Committee on, 291–295

in central schools, 206–208

literary studies in, 63, 134–135, 137–138, 234–235

Ministry of Education on, 311

modern studies in, 236

Norwood Report on, 305–306

practicalism and vocationalism in, 194–201, 203, 230–233

psychological theory, 267–270

scientific studies in, 63, 131–132, 137–138, 237–238

Spens Committee on, 301–302

synthesis of scientific and humane in, 239–240

Cowper-Temple Clause, 81, 83, 87–89, 165

Creak, E. E. M., 59

Curtis, S. J., 139

Darwin, C., 104

DeMontmorency, J. E. G., 222

Dent, H. C., 62, 139, 320

Departmental Committee on Juvenile Education in Relation to Employment After the War (Lewis Committee), report of, 224

Devonshire, Duke of, 101, 115–116

Devonshire, schools of, 39–40, 51, 101

Dickens, Charles, 17

Disraeli, B., 18

Dixon, G., 84
Dunstable Crew's Foundation, 39

Edgbaston High School for Girls, 38
Education Acts, 1870, 1891, p. 21
Education Act, 1899, 115–116
Education Act, 1902, 121, 123–128
Education (Provision of Meals) Act, 1906, 166–168
Education (Administrative Provisions) Act, 1907, 168–170
Education Act, 1918, 227–229
Education Act, 1944, 23, 55, 127–128, 306–309
Education Bill, 1896:
    and Bryce Commission, 77, 91–93
    Anglican church on, 83
    assessment of, 90–98
    Catholics on, 84, 89
    Liberal opposition on, 78–82
    Liberal Unionists on, 84–85
    National Union of Teachers on, 82–83
    Nonconformists on, 82
    press on, 85
    provisions of, 77–79
    School Boards, 80–81, 87
    withdrawal of, 90
Education (England and Wales) Bill, 1906, 164–166
Education Reform Council, 220–221
Educational Reconstruction (White Paper, 1943), 303–304
Educational Committee of the Cooperative Union, 35
Education Department, 22, 35, 79

Elementary Schools, 20, 22, 39, 45, 48, 56–57, 92, 121–122, 138, 151, 174, 179, 255–256
Emmot, Mr., 112
Employment, children, 258–259
Ensor, R. C. K., 106
Equality and Equalitarianism, 19, 163, 192–193, 223, 259–260, 276–277, 283–285, 307, 319, 324–325

Fabians and Fabianism, 105, 120–121, 127, 144, 324
Faculty psychology, 61, 63, 138, 142, 242, 268–270, 281–282
Fearon, R. D., 19
Federation of British Industries, 232
First World War, 210–214, 242–243
Fisher Act, see Education Act, 1918
Fisher, H. A. L., 27–28, 214–215, 225–227, 250–251
Fitch, J. G., 46, 56, 280
Floud, J., 315–317
Forsyth, D., 40
Free-place system, 175–176, 228, 250–252; see also Secondary Education, Secondary Schools

Garnett, W., 119
Germany, 107–110
Gerrans, H. T., 39–40
Giffard, H. A., 19
Gladstone, W. E., 17, 29
Glass, D. V., 62–63
Glazebrook, M. G., 47, 279–280
Gorst, Sir John, 77–78, 86–88, 116–118, 121
Grammar schools, 19, 21–22, 31, 36–38, 48, 130, 285, 294, 299,

315; *see also* Secondary Edu-
tion, Secondary schools,
Bryce Commission, Hadow
Committee, Spens Report
Graves, J., 62, 139
Green, T. H., 17, 103–104, 108
Grier, L., 29

Hadow Committee:
and Bryce Commission, 23,
278, 280, 291, 322–323
and Education Act, 1944, 309
and Norwood Report, 305
and Spens Committee, 298–302
and White Paper on Educa-
tional Reconstruction, 304
equality of opportunity, 276–
277, 283–285
liberal education, 291
members of, 272–273
reaction to, 295
secondary education for all,
274–275
selection at 11+, 278–279,
282–283
selection, concept of, 275–276
technical and vocational education, 288–290
terms of reference, 274
types of schools recommended
by, 285–288
witnesses before, 273–274
Hadowism, 269–297, 302, 307,
311, 321–323, 329–330
Hadow, Sir Henry W., 272–273
Haldane, R. B., 109, 296
Hall, G. S., 267
Harris, W. T., 33
Headlam, J. W., 134
Headmistresses, conference of,
156, 199–200
Henderson, A., 224
Higher elementary schools:

curriculum in, 40, 148–149
definition of, 149
failure of, 160–161
function of, 150
growth of, 149, 152
reaction to, 153–160
relationship with secondary
schools, 15
Higher grade schools, 98; *see
also* Bryce Commission, third
grade schools
Hindley and Abram School, 39
Hobhouse, L. T., 163
Hobson, J. A., 193
Hulme Grammar School, Manchester, 38
Hunt, W. B., 196
Huxley, T. H., 104, 242

Independent Labour Party, 144

Jackman, M., 155
Jackson, B., 315–316
Jebb, R. C., 31, 77, 80, 96

Kekewich, G. W., 56–57, 126
Kenyon Staley Clause, 126
King Edward's School, Birming-
ham, 37
Kitchener, F. E., 37, 41, 52
Kitchener, (Mrs.), 37, 39, 50
Knowles, L. C. A., 107

Labour Party:
child welfare, 167–168
compulsory attendance, 216–
217
Education Act, 1906, pp. 166–
168
Education Act, 1944, 307
equality of opportunity, 284–
285

first Labour Government,
247–248
function of secondary school,
220
nationalization of education,
217, 263–264
secondary education for all,
220, 253–257, 324–325
secondary education in 1900's,
144–146
selection at 11+, 281, 317
specialization in secondary
schools, 216
Labour Representation Committee, 106
Laissez-faire, 16–17, 102–107
Lancashire Local Trades Council, 35
Lancashire, schools of, 40, 42, 51,
53, 141
Laurie, A. P., 40–41
Leeds, higher grade schools in,
40
Leigh Grammar School, 39
Liberals, Liberalism, and Liberal
Party:
and First World War, 214
and social equality, 193
and voluntarism, 167
decline of, 246
Education Act, 1902, 118–119,
125–126
Education Bill, 1896, 78–82
Education Bill, 1906, 1907,
164–166
New Liberalism, 162–163, 168,
192–193
Liberal Unionists, 84–85, 124
Lindsay, K., 260–261
Liverpool, children at school, 50
Livingstone, R. W., 234–235, 242
Lloyd George, 123–124, 164,
244–246

Local education authorities:
Bryce Commission on, 70–71
Education Act, 1902, 121–122,
127–129
Education Acts, 1906, 1907,
168–169
Education Act, 1944, 306
Education Bill, 1896, 82–83,
121–122
free-place system, 170, 174–
176
Hadow committee, 296
higher elementary schools,
159–160
practicalism in the curriculum, 184, 205
selection at 11+, 281
technical schools, 289
Local Government Acts, 1894,
1899, 106
Local Taxation (Customs and
Excise) Act, 1890, 78, 82–83,
102
London Baptist Association, 82
London County Council, 43,
160, 199, 206–208, 280–281
Lowe, R., 20

Mactavish, J. A., 218
Magnus, Sir Philip, 109, 174, 199
Manchester Education Author-
ity, central schools by, 207
Manchester Grammar School,
37, 52
Mann, H., 227
Marshall, T. H., 277
Massie, J., 49–50
Masterman, C. F. G., 145
Maurois, André, 102, 321
McDonald, J. R., 247
McDougall, W., 261–263
McKenna, R., 166, 174–176
McTaggart, J. M. E., 108

Mill, J. S., 104, 241–242
Millington, 142
Mitcheson, Mr., 42–43
Modern schools, 285–288, 310–311
Morant, Sir Robert, 25, 96–97, 118–120, 126, 136–138, 144
Mowat, C. L., 245, 260
Mundella, Mr., 83
Municipal Corporations Association, 35

National Society, 83–84, 94
National Union of Catholic Teachers, 84
National Union of Teachers (N.U.T.):
and Bryce Commission, 35
Education Act, 1902, 120, 127
Education Bill, 1896, 82–83
higher elementary schools, 154–155, 157–158
practicalism in curriculum, 198–199
Newman, Dr. George, 169
Nonconformists, 18, 82, 117–118, 124–125, 164; see also Religion and Politics
North London Collegiate School for Girls, 46
Norton, Lord, 101
Norwood Report, 305–306
Nunn, Sir Percy, 263–267, 273–274, 277–278, 281–283

O'Connor, T. P., 165
Office of Special Inquiries and Reports, 96, 110–111
Pall Mall Gazette, 76
Parker, Mr. (M.P.), 307
Paton, J. L., 157
Pease, E., 120–121
Peterson, A. D. C., 279

Pickles, A. R., 154–155
Piggersgill, 172
Population Census (1901, 1911), 191–192
Prescott Grammar School (Lancashire), 41
Princeton Conference on Classical Studies (USA), 243
Private School Association, 35
Public schools, 20–21, 25, 31, 36–37, 67, 116
Pupil-Teacher Centres, 146

Rayleigh, Lord, 237
Reform Act, 1867, 17
Regulations for Secondary Schools (1904), 135–140
Reigate Grammar School, 19
Religion and Politics, 83–84, 87–89, 90–91, 117, 122, 125, 164–165
Report of Central Advisory Committee (Crowther Report), 289
Richmond, K., 296–297
Royal Commission on Scientific Instruction, 109
Royal Commission on Technical Instruction, 109
Runciman, W., 186–187
Ruskin, J., 17, 103

Sadler, Sir Michael, 28–29, 96–97, 110–111, 116, 140–141, 153–154
Salisbury, Lord, 93–94
School, 157
School Boards, 22, 80–81, 92–93, 117–121
School Guardian, 76
Schools Inquiry Commission (Taunton Commission), 21, 60, 64, 69, 102

Science and Art Department, 22, 35, 56, 119

Secondary education, Secondary schools
access to by poor, 179–181
aims of, 232–233
and English society, 143–146
and social mobility, 146
effects of external examinations on, 204–205
definitions of, 55–60, 131–137, 141–142, 256
democratization of, 255–256
expansion of curriculum in, 184–187
German, 110–111
increase in, 147, 250
increases in State aid for, 170–171
opportunities for, 224–225, 228, 233, 251–252, 258–259
relationship with central schools, 201–208
relationship with higher elementary schools, 151
relationship with primary schools, 255
relationship with social classes, 21–22, 143–144, 171–172, 177–181, 315–317
relationship with technical education, 58–59, 140–141, 231–232
responses to practical courses in, 202–204
scholarships and free places, 174–176, 228, 250–251
selection for, 97–98, 252–253, 256
social factors affecting, 258–261
social functions of, 97
state grants for 131–132, 137, 172, 184
voctional training in, 188–189, 288–289; see also Bryce Commission, Curriculum, Hadow Committee, Grammar schools, Modern schools

Secondary education for all, 24, 67–68, 172, 198–199, 220–253–257, 303–304, 306, 324–325

Selection at 11+, 252–253, 256, 278–280, 304, 309–310, 312–313

Secondary Schools Association, 199

Seth, J., 108

Sharpe, T. W., 56

Shaw, G. B., 105

Sheffield, higher grade schools in, 43

Sidgwick, Henry (Mrs.), 48–49

Silcock, 173–174

Smith, Adam, 17

Smith, C. J. (Rev.), 178

Snow, C. P., 61

South African War (Boer War), 107, 112–114

Spencer, H., 17, 104, 182, 242, 329

Spens Committee, 298–302, 304

Spens, Sir Will, 297

Stanley, E. L., 96

Stanton, C. H., 19

Strachey, Lytton, 15

Tawney, R. H., 18, 187, 189–190, 253–258, 281

Teachers' Guild of Great Britain and Ireland, 80, 156

Teachers' Registration Council, 221
Technical education, Technical schools, 58–59, 62, 231–232, 288–290, 299–300
The Athenæum, 74, 221–222, 232
The Daily News, 73, 76
The Educational Times, 73, 92, 198, 210
The Highway, 218–219
The Journal of Education, 101, 158–159, 177, 197–198, 239–240, 295–296
The Schoolmasters' Yearbook and Directory, 177, 196–197, 231
The School World, 157, 177, 195
The Star, 74
The Times (London), 74, 85, 154, 239
The Times Educational Supplement, 178–179, 207, 215, 221–223, 231–232, 295, 317–318
Thomson, D., 16
Thompson, W., 318
Thorndike, E. L., 269
Titterington, F., 216
Trades and Labour Councils, 57
Trade Unions, 144
Trevelyan, C. P., 248, 257–258
Tripartitism, 64, 311–319

Vaizey, J., 314
Vardy, A. W. (Rev.) 35, 52
Vaughan, Herbert (Cardinal Archbishop), 84
Victoria, Queen, 16
Victorian Age, 16–22

Vocational education, Vocational schools, see Curriculum, Secdary Education, Secondary Schools
Voluntary Schools, Voluntarism, 69, 80–81, 83–84, 86–87, 116–117, 122–123, 126, 128, 164, 167

Walker, M., 195
Wallas, G., 105
Warwickshire, 50–51
Webb, B. (Mrs.), 105, 121
Webb, Sidney, 43, 58, 65, 118, 120–121
Wells, H. G., 121, 235, 320
West Riding (Yorkshire) schools in, 40–41, 51, 134–135
West Riding County Council, 141
Whitaker's Almanack, 74
Whitehead, A. N., 240
Wilson, W. T., 166–167
Workers' Educational Association (W.E.A.), 217–219
Working classes:
    educational opportunities for, 50–53, 58–59, 65–68, 98, 145–146, 173, 180, 213–214
    education of, 231–232
Yorkshire, schools in, 43, 51
    Yorkshire Ladies' Council on Education, 48, 58–59
Young, M., 18, 323
Young, R. F., 138
Young, Sir George, 41–42, 47
Yoxall, J. H., 30, 80–81, 154–155, 173